ANGRY PLANET

ANGRY

Decolonial Fiction and

PLANET

the American Third World

ANNE STEWART

University of Minnesota Press | Minneapolis | London

A portion of chapter 2 was previously published as "Unruly Documentary Objects in John Edgar Wideman's *Philadelphia Fire*," *MELUS* 44, no. 1 (Spring 2019): 22–42; reprinted by permission of Oxford University Press, https://global.oup.com/. A portion of chapter 3 was previously published in "Neoliberal Earthworks," *Studies in American Indian Literatures* 30, no. 2 (2018): 56–78; copyright 2018 University of Nebraska Press.

Published by the University of Minnesota Press
111 Third Avenue South, Suite 290
Minneapolis, MN 55401-2520
http://www.upress.umn.edu

ISBN 978-1-5179-1410-3 (hc)
ISBN 978-1-5179-1411-0 (pb)

A Cataloging-in-Publication record for this book is available from the Library of Congress.

Printed in the United States of America on acid-free paper

The University of Minnesota is an equal-opportunity educator and employer.

For Aidan

CONTENTS

INTRODUCTION
MESSAGES FROM THE
ANGRY PLANET

At the climax of Thomas King's 1993 novel *Green Grass, Running Water,* the Grand Baleen hydroelectric dam bursts. Unusually high rainfall and a series of earthquakes crack the dam in half, "a tremor rolled in out of the west, tipping the lake on its end . . . beneath the power and the motion there was a more ominous sound of things giving way, of things falling apart."[1] This reference to "things falling apart" evokes the global colonial legacy within which King situates the construction of the hydroelectric dam on Blackfoot territory already partitioned by the U.S.-Canada border. In the last decades of the twentieth century, former colonies around the world struggled to define what a decolonized future looked like within and against the intensifying developmentalist mandate of post–World War and then, post–Cold War global capitalism. At the same time, settler-occupied Indigenous communities in North America experienced the persistent impact on traditional ancestral territories of renewed waves of expropriation for massive national infrastructure projects like hydroelectric dams, oil and gas pipelines, highways, and strip mines.[2] While the world spoke the language of decolonization in the latter half of the century, infrastructure continued a conversation with the earth in which colonial development driven by its capitalist economy defined the terms of subterranean and terrestrial grammar.

But in King's novel, the earth also expresses an agenda of its own. The dam's run-of-the-river construction emerges as an imposition on the continental surface that extends the forced displacement of an already expropriated Indigenous population, in service to a more centralized, monied, settler population.[3] Duplessis, the multinational corporation in charge of the dam, conceives of the project as an improvement to undeveloped, underused reservation land. But Duplessis's plans are stymied by a successful injunction made by Eli Stands Alone, a Blackfoot man who identifies something fundamentally precarious about the way the structure relates to the land. "The earth is moving under the dam," he points out to Clifford Sifton, the dam foreman.[4] Eli watches stress fractures form in the dam's concrete base as regolith—the loose mineral aggregate between the dam's base and the bedrock below—begins to flow down the sloped surface of the river's former floodplain, a process known as *slumping*.[5] Eli bluntly asks Sifton, "What happens when it breaks? You can't hold water back forever."[6] Sifton's reply is that of the good company man, "It's not going to break, Eli. Oh, it'll crack and it'll leak. But it won't break. Just think of the dam as part of the natural landscape."[7] Sifton deliberately distorts Eli's point. It is not that the dam is unnatural; it is *too* natural. Like a cliffside or riverbank, it cracks and oozes, its concrete body slumps back toward the earth from which its materials were mined, and when it finally bursts with "a sudden shifting, a sideways turning, a flexing, the snapping of concrete and steel," it demonstrates a clear capacity to move, like the earth, in ways not authorized by or in service to the settler state, corporate power, or any other human agency.[8]

Angry Planet: Decolonial Fiction and the American Third World tracks an undercurrent in literary production that focuses on how the earth *moves* through the cultural imagination. The reading practice that this project develops is guided by Indigenous land-based intelligence and contributes to understandings of literary ecologies by thinking with and through how planetary motion shapes the conditions of possibility for human being-in-the-world. *Angry Planet* develops this practice through U.S. literary and cultural production in the last decades of the twentieth century because of this literature's attention to how planetary motion clashes with the material forces of settler colonialism, capitalist development, racial subjugation, and environmental ruin.[9] In the late

1980s, Gloria Anzaldúa writes in her development of *mestiza*/borderlands consciousness that "the skin of the earth is seamless. / The sea cannot be fenced, / *el mar* does not stop at borders. / To show the white man what she thought of his / arrogance, / *Yemanyá* blew that wire fence down."[10] Like the shifting, trembling earth at King's Canada-U.S. border, the planet is not inert, base matter at Anzaldúa's Mexico-U.S. border; neither the backdrop to capitalist modernity, as it is in much twentieth century literary realism, nor a hapless conduit for anthropogenic force, as it is in the twenty-first century under the sign of the Anthropocene. Instead, the earth moves in and through this literary undercurrent as a furious and rebellious entity, surging and retreating in ways demonstrative of its rejection of the structural conditions shaping its terrestrial surface.

In the years following the end of the Cold War and before the World Trade Center attacks on September 11, 2001, make the celebration of acts of revolutionary destruction taboo, angry planet fiction takes its lead from the angry earth.[11] During these decades of global environmental crisis, the planet expresses a controversial but uncompromising approach to the violent material legacy represented by colonial-capitalist infrastructure: tear it to the ground. The revolutionaries in Leslie Marmon Silko's 1992 *Almanac of the Dead* work toward a day when "all the walls fall down," planning coordinated attacks on prisons, dams, power plants, and computer networks as a convergence of antiracist and anticapitalist energy sweeps the planet clean.[12] The protagonist of Héctor Tobar's 1997 novel, *The Tattooed Soldier,* walks through Los Angeles in the aftermath of the 1992 L.A. riots and laments their conclusion: "He was nostalgic for the running crowds, for the sense of power, for the world turned upside down and the supermarkets where everything was free. An insurrection had taken place on these streets, a beautiful disorder."[13] "They will have to raze the city and cart off the rubble to less populous boroughs and start anew," thinks Lila Mae Watson, the protagonist of Colson Whitehead's 1999 novel, *The Intuitionist,* as she imagines New York City demolished and rebuilt as an Afrofuturist utopia.[14] Riots, wreckage, and city skylines on fire are beautiful in these novels because the everyday organization of American life, which naturalizes Indigenous dispossession, antiblackness, racial violence, xenophobia, gendered inequality, and toxic environments, is intolerable. The potential of complete societal collapse under these conditions points to the possibility of a different world, and takes its lead in this decolonial, anticapitalist mandate from the motion of the planet.

Angry Planet's exploration of planetary motion as a shaping narrative force tracks the rebellious earth occurring across scales and media. This agentic motion is legible when the earth makes its difference from colonial orders of spatial organization known in a seismic tremor, a crumbling coastline, or a catastrophic storm; and when its resistance to capitalist development is felt as the slow and microscopic motion of decay and erosion, which eats away at riverbanks and sidewalks alike, conveying information about being-with the world's impermanence and transformative motion.[15] The angry planet moves across terrestrial media; its motion is present in soil and stone as well as in the materials extracted from the earth's surface to build cities and freeways.[16] The moment we pull stone out of the earth, banking on its promise of stability, it begins to change: "Because rocks were formed at different temperatures and pressures within the earth," geomorphologist Luna Leopold explains, "when they are exposed at the surface they are no longer in equilibrium with their environment and thus begin to decompose."[17] The presence of out-of-equilibrium terrestrial materials—gravel, cement, wood, steel—destabilizes human environments and lends the planetary-material characteristic of *contingency* or what Louis Althusser calls "the aleatory"—to the most seemingly stable bastions of colonial modernity.[18] Although it is not an obviously geological quality—a crashing elevator in *The Intuitionist* and a faulty bulletproof vest in *Almanac of the Dead* make for obscure messengers from the angry planet—these novels present contingency as a force that cannot be synthesized out of the objects and spaces of colonial-capitalist development. The agentic motion of tectonic plates and waterways are translated into the presence of the contingent in our power grids and parking lots.[19] Angry planet fiction recognizes planetary motion and material contingency as forms of nonhuman agency because they generate difference in the relationship between land and infrastructure, demonstrating that this relationship is nonidentical with the developmentalist agenda of settler-colonial land use and its capitalist logic.

The literary undercurrent gathered together in the coming pages tells stories about terrestrial surfaces and planetary tectonics that move against colonial-capitalist modernity and its global infrastructural developmentalism. In other words, the angry people in these stories model their thinking about decolonial destruction and futurity from the angry planet. The authors of these stories are scattered across the 1990s and the settler-colonial North American continent, working from very different geolocations and subject positions marked by distinct histories of racialization and its attendant violence. But these thinkers narrativize a common ground: a decolonial mandate focused on land use and the transformation of material conditions in a historical moment better remembered for its focus on the politics of representation than on materialist analysis. Not all authors of angry planet fiction speak for or from Indigenous experience, but they all embrace variations of a relationship to land that has strong precedents in Indigenous knowledge traditions and practices that, as the authors of a recent Land Back report assert, "embody critical knowledge that can relink society to a healthy balance within the natural world."[20] Importantly, this does not mean that settler societies should be turning an idealizing gaze toward Indigenous peoples to save the world. Rather, *Angry Planet* takes up the challenges to settler land use modeled by Indigenous ontologies to both reimagine the human relationship with the earth and to demonstrate that the force of terrestrial agency has a much longer intellectual history than the recent turn in Western scholarship toward "new" materialist analyses of the human relationship to the physical universe.[21] The Indigenous and non-Indigenous voices in this project call to account the antihuman and environmentally devastating violence of colonialism and its capitalist mode of production as these flourish in the form of neoliberal globalization and its neocolonial structures and practices at the end of the twentieth century.

Part of what this project historicizes is a sense of how decolonization emerges as such an important mandate for both Indigenous and non-Indigenous U.S. cultural producers during these decades. In my thinking, this emergence coalesces around the repeated evocations of an angry planet in multiethnic U.S. literature of this period that makes connections between environmental destruction and social uprising. The angry planet is, in one sense, an angry global population waking up to the persistence of racialized dispossession in the shadow of post–Cold War First World democratic triumphalism. In another sense, the angry planet is a strategic figuration of the earth's reaction to environmental destruction in the form of climate change and environmental disasters as reflecting and amplifying the rage of dispossessed populations. In an era when what Ursula Heise calls "the imagination of the global" vacillated between defining planetarity in primarily economic and idealist terms—as a vast capitalist network, on the one hand, and as the Lovelockian Gaia, "united, limited, and delicately beautiful," on the other—the angry planet is an imaginary invested instead in an at-times furious, at-times brutally indifferent terrestrial entity.[22] The angry planet is not a loving mother or a source of spiritual strength, but it is a model for the absolute rejection of the order of things at millennium's end. Thinking through the conditions of possibility generated by planetary motion, angry planet fiction runs up against the ways that motion is subjugated and rendered invisible by colonial-capitalist modernity and the logic that supports and justifies its developmentalist violence. In other words, thinking with planetary motion guides these authors to think about decolonization, and to focus this thinking on the profoundly material, earthly and earthy, dimensions of a fully realized decolonial future.

"Two Ideas of Land"

That planetary motion is a prompt to decolonial thought is demonstrated by the standoff that King sets up in his novel between Sifton and Eli. This standoff represents a rift between settler colonial and Indigenous land use and knowledge production that is perhaps the most significant barrier to decolonial futurity both at the end of the twentieth century and today. In 1974, George Manuel and Michael Posluns's *The Fourth World: An Indian Reality* describes this barrier through a story that Manuel tells about visiting with the Maori people of Aotearoa/New Zealand in his capacity as a leader within the North American Indian movement. "Wherever I have travelled in the Aboriginal World, there has been a common attachment to the land," Manuel explains: "This is not the land that can be speculated, bought, sold, mortgaged, claimed by one state, surrendered or counter-claimed by another. . . . The land from which our culture springs is like the water and the air, one and indivisible. . . . The struggle of the past four centuries has been between these two ideas of land. Lurking behind this struggle for land was a conflict over the nature of Man himself."[23] "These two ideas of land" define the history of settler colonialism as one of struggle rather than mutuality because the two are irreconcilable. One idea of land is a colonial-capitalist fantasy of destructive power without limit, what Leanne Betasamosake Simpson describes as "a negation" of Indigenous life, of plant and animal life, and of consent-based relationships between settler society and the Indigenous human and nonhuman nations devastated by colonial and capitalist infrastructure.[24] The other idea of land is drawn from Indigenous intelligence based on what Glen Sean Coulthard calls "grounded normativity."[25] Coulthard's description of grounded normativity builds on Vine Deloria Jr.'s work in *God Is Red* (1972) to "explicate the position that land occupies as an ontological framework for understanding *relationships*."[26] This idea of land's priority in knowledge production is not only the affirmative obverse to the colonial-capitalist fantasy; it is also a description of the material conditions that precede colonial settlement on Turtle Island and that delineate the conditions of possibility for the decolonial future that Manuel calls the Fourth World.[27]

In thinking through the conditions of possibility for decolonization—its ontological grounds—this passage from Manuel ties together three core assertions that guide the following project: first, the priority of land as the basis or "spring" for human knowledge about being-in-the-world; second, that land, as this source of knowledge, determines understandings of being human ("the nature of Man"); and third, that this knowledge, although emerging out of Manuel's specific experience growing up on his people's traditional, ancestral, occupied territory in British Columbia, Canada, is nonetheless applicable when transferred to the context of global Indigenous experience and anticolonial struggle. What unites these three assertions is their ontological precision—they remain true regardless of which idea of land is in operation—as well as their political force: they have global geopolitical implications in terms of the world(s) being built under the rubric of First and Second World development races, Third World decolonial struggle, and the Fourth World alternative articulated by Manuel.

The potential for global solidarities in decolonial struggle was no less fraught fifty years ago than it is today, but Manuel's proposal suggests one possible site for such solidarity in the idea of land shared by Indigenous populations around the world. "Our customs and practices vary as the different landscapes of the continent," Manuel writes, "but underlying this forest of legitimate differences is a common soil of social and spiritual experience."[28] By this he means that a shared idea of land as the source for knowledge of being-in-the-world produces cultural difference because the land in which a people develop varies bioregionally; simultaneously, however, the ability to share grounded normativity as an ontological foundation is global in its application.[29] Resonating with this insight from a Caribbean context, another key interlocutor for angry planet fiction, Sylvia Wynter, makes a similar point in the early 1970s, describing what she calls "the plantation-plot dichotomy."[30] "The plantation was the superstructure of civilization," Wynter writes, an idea of land based in the colonial developer's belief in the right to property, to exploitation of the natural world, and to the universal correctness and transportability of this belief.[31] Wynter describes the plantation idea of land as severing humans from their relationship to "Nature," whereby "a process of dehumanization and alienation was set in train."[32] The affirmative obverse to this idea of land in the Caribbean context is, Wynter argues, "the plot system, the indigenous, autochthonous system."[33] The plot system produced not only different cultural forms but an oppositional way of being human, drawing its intelligence from a deep connection to land maintained by slaves ripped from traditional African societies.[34] Like Manuel, Wynter stresses that these two ideas of land are not only dichotomous but in conflict. The plot system was, she writes, "a source of cultural guerilla resistance to the plantation system."[35] The striking similarities between Deloria, Manuel, and Wynter, asserting in this early 1970s moment that ideas of land generate the conditions of possibility for knowledge of what it means to be human, demonstrate a critical decolonial theory that is being articulated in response to the limitations of postcolonial discourse during this period.[36]

   The conflict that these critical decolonial thinkers describe in the early 1970s is extended into the 1990s by U.S. cultural producers committed to a materialist analysis of ongoing conditions of coloniality in the post–Cold War First World. But to think the impasse between these ideas of land—one that instrumentalizes the earth as exploitable property, and one that respects the earth as a sovereign and agential being in its own right—is to gaze out over an abyss that continues to spread between the material conditions of our own present and the threshold of a decolonized future. The settler state is not interested in building a relationship that accedes to land the ontological priority Manuel describes as definitional in shaping what it means to be human. But it is just this priority that contemporary decolonial thinkers like Eve Tuck and K. Wayne Yang evoke when they assert that "the most important concern" when it comes to decolonization in a settler-colonial context "is land/water/air/subterranean earth."[37] Their argument indicts the weakness of any decolonial discourse invested in the "front-loading of critical consciousness building" that does not change (and can even consolidate) practices and structures of colonial violence against land, humans, and nonhuman bodies.[38] Simpson returns to this decolonial mandate again and again in her work on Indigenous resurgence: "By far the largest attack on Indigenous Knowledge systems right now is land dispossession," she writes, emphasizing that when the relationship between knowledge production and land is severed and policed by the idea of land built into the earth's surface by settler colonialism, we lose access to essential information about being-in-the-world.[39] The history of coloniality imposes on the continent what Simpson calls "shattered grounded normativity," a damaged land and land relation that many scholars today compare to an apocalyptic event.[40] From within the ontological framework of shattered grounded normativity, another apocalypse—the bursting of the dam of the world—would be required to access those "nondominating and nonexploitative" relations among humans and their environment that are the best promise of decolonization.[41] As Frantz Fanon warns in the opening to *The Wretched of the Earth*, "Whatever the name used, whatever the latest expression, decolonization is always a violent event."[42] To break the relationship between the settler-colonial idea of land as exploitable property and the antecedent inhumanisms produced thereby may require a restructuring of social order that generates its own set of untenable conditions and modes of precarity for human and nonhuman life. As the novels in the following chapters suggest through their focus on these material conditions—the disasters of racial violence and their normalization through racial capitalist exploitation and inequality—shattered grounded normativity will produce the lessons of an angry planet.

The potentially violent implications of fully transforming the human relationship to land points to those "incommensurabilities" that Tuck and Yang evoke in their description of "a dangerous understanding of uncommonality that un-coalesces coalition politics" in a land-centered decolonial mandate.[43] Competing claims among disparate communities can work to cross purposes: calls for social justice do not easily map on to Indigenous claims to land and sovereignty; the interconnections among the history of Indigenous land dispossession and the antiblackness that is the legacy of the Middle Passage and plantation slavery make sometimes competing claims on what critiques of state power and demands for land back and reparations may entail. Simultaneously, the uncommonalities among these political projects may drown out or occlude the histories and technologies of oppression and racial violence encountered by Latinx, Asian diasporic, Desi, Arab diasporic, Afro-Caribbean, and non–North American Indigenous groups. Decolonial agendas themselves sit uneasily between, as Tuck and Yang discuss, calls to decolonize the mind and the prioritization of land claims; between critiques of modernity that can risk idealizing premodern traditions and futurisms that can seem technologically and conceptually abstract and divorced from the contingent demands of decolonial projects rooted in place.[44] The critical decolonial theory being developed by thinkers like Deloria, Manuel, and Wynter proposes a "common soil" or shared idea of land "underlying this forest of legitimate differences" as a way to begin exploring solidarities in struggle, but these solidarities can be blocked by frictions in decolonial labor itself. What I am calling the 1970s precursors to critical decolonial theory point to a particular history of this effort to work from a common soil that was hopeful in terms of the prospects for global solidarity based in a shared idea of land. It is the history of this hope that guides *Angry Planet,* although I revisit, in the conclusion, the impasses of decoloniality, solidarity, and ontology that shape critical thinking and revolutionary praxis today.

Between the Third and Fourth Worlds

In Linda Hogan's 1995 novel *Solar Storms,* Angel Jensen returns to her family home from an adolescence in foster care to find the land—already once "worn out," "destroyed" and "used-up" by the fur trade—

being reexpropriated for state-funded hydroelectric infrastructure.[45] In *Solar Storms,* Hogan tracks how Fourth World terrain and intelligence is remade into landscapes of what this project calls American Third World toxicity and blight. In angry planet fiction, this developmental process absorbs Indigenous culture, and in the process shifts claims based in grounded normativity into the analytic of U.S. racial complaint. This attention to how land use negotiates between the production of knowledge and of racial difference addresses, to slightly modify a paradigm articulated by Jodi Byrd, how "the [materialist] colonialist traces of the transits of Indianness . . . haunt theorizations of race in the United States."[46] In *Solar Storms,* Angel describes infrastructural development producing the conditions of Indigenous knowledge erasure when she and her relatives take their fight against dam developers to court, and she sees an elder's "beauty turned into some kind of homeliness contained in the cold halls of stone that came from the illegal quarries of our world."[47] In these halls that turn living stone into the physical expression of First World judgment, Indigenous knowledge is "relegated to the jurisdiction of ethnographic locality" and thus into the register of complaints made by special interests.[48] "It seemed now that his wisdom was nothing more than a worn-out belief," Angel thinks as she sees her elder's expression of grounded normativity distorted: a belief "that had no place in this new world where the walls themselves came from the lost lives and worlds of men like Tulik."[49] The lost worlds that Angel evokes here are those that Manuel envisions recovering with the Fourth World, which struggles for space at the end of the twentieth century with the racially coded contest between post–Cold War First World capitalist development and Third World difference, all of which meet over the colonial map of the North American settler state.

The following project uses the term *American Third World* with deliberate ironic force. Wynter designates this zone of exile as an "archipelago of Human Otherness" made up of slices and pockets of the nation's cities, suburbs, university campuses, factories, farms, borderlands, rural areas, and reservations that share more in common with the struggles of populations around the world dispossessed in modernity's wake than they do with the affluent First World citadels of recognizably American imperial power.[50] Now a stigmatized term, "Third World" had a currency in the post–civil rights era among American social movements, including the Black Panther Party, the Chicano Movement, the American Indian Movement, and queer women-of-color feminisms, that identified with the global struggle against colonialism, capitalism, and the "racial grammar and lexicon" that is the necessary product of this developmentalist mandate.[51] But even in its early Cold War–era iteration, "Third World" possessed an uncomfortable triple valence. For U.S. artists, activists, and critics, it could be both pejorative and generative. The term designated the conditions produced by racial capitalism, which partitions American lives into extremes of security and precarity. With no small measure of ambivalence, then, the term was also made to express solidarity, among racialized and exploited U.S. populations, with the revolutionary potential of postcolonizing nations, which drew on their own histories of struggle in imagining and creating alternatives to the capitalist vs. communist world order.[52] American Third World activists and artists saw themselves aligned with the global struggle for, as Jodi Melamed writes, "psychic decolonization, nonexploitative ethico-economic orders, an internationalism aligned with the third world, and new powers for new collectivities."[53] In the mid-to-late twentieth century, an elision of the specificities marking race- and class-based struggle in favor of identification with and as the Third World represented the potential for a position of structural difference and oppositional strength against the ascendant global hegemony of U.S. economic and military power.

For Indigenous peoples, on the other hand, the term "Third World" stood for what the continent was emphatically *not:* not decolonizing and not understood in the context of international law as a site of struggle for distinct Indigenous nations seeking the rights of self-determination. George Manuel develops his concept of the Fourth World as an alternative not only to the colonial-capitalist First World but to emergent Third World nation-states that "believe that their paper constitution is their proof of identity, their ticket on the train to the next world."[54] This is not to say that solidarities did not flourish. For Elizabeth Cook-Lynn, Third Worldism created space for nationalist identifications that were otherwise collapsed into "people of color" and "multiculturalis[t]" modes of state-sanctioned melting-pot recognition politics as the United States moved through the Cold War decades.[55] In a global context, Third World struggle spoke persuasively to the North American Indigenous right to nationhood. Such parallels could thus draw attention to powerful political incommensurability while bringing together distinct sites of struggle in the American Third World that also presented the challenge of working beyond these distinctions.

In angry planet fiction, allyship based in the angry earth is claimed by Indigenous peoples and settlers of color; communities of multiethnic anticapitalists and black Americans living in the afterlives of slavery. From the gated communities whose walls cannot hold in Octavia Butler's 1993 *Parable of the Sower,* to the borders between nations and neighborhoods that cannot stand in Karen Tei Yamashita's 1997 *Tropic of Orange,* the American Third World emerges as one of the Cold War's hot zones: an antagonistic terrain of colonial warfare and capitalist exploitation that needs to be reconfigured at a basic material level. Simultaneously, however, the slippage between the destruction of colonial-capitalist state power and the satisfied demands of specific marginalized communities marks a set of impasses that arise both on the threshold of decolonization and in contemporary decolonial thought more broadly: a shared idea of land can be a model framework for "living our lives in relation to one another and our surroundings in a respectful, nondominating and nonexploitative way" as Coulthard argues, but that doesn't mean that everybody gets what they want.[56] If the American Third World clamors for inclusion, freedom, and an end to racial injustice, this does not necessarily equate to the radical transformation of land and property relations that would constitute the journey to the Fourth World.

This tension between a shared idea of land, and the complexity of specific sites of struggle against capitalism, racism, and colonialism, shaped critical decolonial theory as it was involved in the first attempts to bring together environmental and antiracist activism in the 1980s and 1990s. In these decades, post–civil rights era Third World social movements from Mexico's Zapatistas to the black radical MOVE organization in the United States made connections between racial oppression and environmental devastation that aligned these movements with global Indigenous and people of color organizing. Significantly, Cook-Lynn characterizes these social movements as producing "essentially literary events," that is, events of textual production in which documentation was created that demonstrated the connections between the colonial-capitalist exploitation of the planet and of its Indigenous and racialized others.[57] The first versions of the United Nations Declaration on the

Rights of Indigenous Peoples (UNDRIP) were drafted in 1985. The document placed an emphasis on the need for Indigenous control of natural resources, which was one of the key points of contention preventing its adoption for over two decades. Drafting and redrafting this declaration required a tremendous output of labor by Indigenous peoples, both in their own communities, where similar assertions of localized sovereignty were being opposed by settler governments, and at the annual meetings of the Working Group on Indigenous Populations in Geneva.[58] In 1987, the term *environmental racism* was coined by the United Church of Christ's Committee on Racial Justice, marking a moment at which social and environmental justice movements came together to "explicitly locate environmental concerns within the context of inequality and attempts to alter dominant power arrangements."[59] Actions such as the 1990 letter sent by the Southwest Organizing Project to the "Group of Ten"—environmental groups including the Nature Conservancy and the National Audubon Society—called mainstream environmentalists to account for conservationist agendas that ignored the concerns of, and even negatively impacted, poor communities of color.[60] In 1991, the First National People of Color Environmental Leadership Summit in Washington, D.C. addressed the globalizing effects of industrial pollution and toxic working environments as they disproportionately target communities of color.[61] What these movements shared was the demand for a fundamentally different human relationship to land and to the planet than that which is afforded by colonial-capitalist social order, but the multiplicity of sites of struggle, both local and global, also drew out the scope of the macrostructures of power against which these movements fought: as Hogan demonstrates in *Solar Storms,* arguments about environmental rights, couched in the language of recognition politics, allowed colonial-capitalist state governments to frame environmental concerns as special interests and even threats to First World democracy. The shared idea of land that united Third and Fourth World revolutionary struggle also became one of the colonial-capitalist state's first and best excuses for ignoring climate crisis.

The activist rubric of environmental racism may have produced blockages to realizing the generative possibilities of global Indigenous solidarity and interethnic coalitional struggle. Nonetheless, cultural producers found the concept useful for documenting the terrains of the

American Third World as well as the ways that it both stands in for and overshadows the realization of the Fourth World or Indigenous sovereign statehood. The "struggle for an 'Indian' identity" narratives of this post-AIM period, such as *Green Grass, Running Water* and *Solar Storms,* demonstrate the settler naturalization of Indigenous erasure as demands for land and sovereignty are absorbed into the U.S. activist rubric of social justice.[62] In these narratives, journeys to reconnect with land and tradition are often qualified or smothered by resource extraction projects that destroy sacred sites of knowledge production as Indigenous protagonists approach the threshold of reconnection. Environmental racism also became a core analytic of Third World American literature during this period, including Ana Castillo's *So Far From God* (1993), Helena María Viramontes's *Under the Feet of Jesus* (1995), T. C. Boyle's *The Tortilla Curtain* (1995), and Ruth Ozeki's *My Year of Meats* (1998). These novels trace, as Stacy Alaimo demonstrates in her reading of Castillo's work, how global patterns of exploitation come to be felt and experienced through the ways that "human bodies, human health, and human rights are interconnected with the material, often toxic flows of particular places."[63] These particular places, like the dammed watersheds, *maquiladoras,* freeway underbellies, factory farms, ranches, and homeless encampments that the above novels address, spatialize the American Third World as the naturalized site for the disposal both of First World effluvia and Fourth World difference.

Angry planet fiction emerges as an undercurrent unique within the larger body of literature addressing environmental racism because of its narrative ontology, which attempts to use earthly motion as a vehicle for resisting these intolerable material conditions. How might contingent events and tectonic processes take the shape of arguments about being-in-the-world, delineations of conditions of possibility, or forms of historical consciousness drawn like precious minerals from the perspectival substratum of the planet? Change the way we understand the *being of* the planet, these novels propose, and we can change our way of *being on* the planet. The narrative argument of this literary undercurrent—its speculative gambit and proposal to readers—is both descriptive and prescriptive. It describes the infrastructures of North American colonial-capitalist modernity as a material legacy of racial violence and dehumanization, rooted in the history of colonialism, plantation slavery, and Indigenous land expropriation and genocide. Taken as a whole, this legacy is that of *colonial terraforming.* Terraforming is a term from speculative fiction—a genre with which angry planet fiction closely overlaps—used to describe the technological processes whereby an alien planet may be made habitable for human life.[64] Colonial terraforming, then, makes the planet habitable for European colonial settlers, settler-adjacents, and domesticated nonhumans—one particular constellation of lifeforms—creating, in a very material sense, breathing room for these lifeforms to flourish. Simultaneously, colonial terraforming creates the conditions —what Christina Sharpe provocatively calls "the weather"—of racial capitalist partitioning for those lifeforms that become suffocated, dehumanized, and illegible as life in this terraformed space.[65] The history of colonial terraforming is the history of what Alexander G. Weheliye calls "racializing assemblages," "etching abstract forces of power onto human physiology and flesh in order to create the appearance of a naturally expressive relationship between phenotype and sociopolitical status."[66] Thinking of terraforming in terms of its colonial history rather than its speculative futurity allows us to follow thinkers like Sharpe and Weheliye in understanding how racialization is produced and inflicted on bodies environmentally rather than grown out of embodiment proper.

As colonial terraforming clashes with terrestrial instability in the American Third World, angry planet fiction prescribes an antagonist narrative ontology that refuses to accept these conditions as totalizing. This is the ontology of shattered grounded normativity, in which knowledge of being-in-the-world is often recognized through the human affect of rage. In *Solar Storms,* the development of dam infrastructure produces an "angry land" that "would try to put an end to the plans for dams and drowned rivers. An ice jam at the Riel River would break loose and rage over the ground, tearing out dams and bridges, the construction all broken by the blue, cold roaring of ice no one was able to control."[67] Silko's *Almanac of the Dead* similarly represents tectonic motion as in furious alignment with the novel's revolutionaries who resist colonial resource exploitation and infrastructural development.[68] "You think there is no hope for Indigenous tribal people here to prevail against the violence and greed of the destroyers," one of the novel's revolutionaries warns, "But you forget the earth's outrage and the trembling that will not stop. Overnight the wealth of nations will be reclaimed by the Earth."[69] From the position of this narrative ontology, the racializing infrastructures that make up the built environments of colonial modernity are always on the brink of destruction, their materials poised to be reclaimed by the earth from which they were extracted and made to organize "Human Otherness" by colonial terraforming. And it sees this reclamation in the motion of earthquakes, of droughts and lightning and insect swarms, and in inexplicable technical malfunctions, hard-to-explain disasters like car crashes, and towns that tumble into the sea. In its grounded normative focus on knowing through and acting with these physical processes, angry planet fiction's narrative argument is built on what this book posits as a *decolonial ontology.*

Decolonial Ontology

In angry planet fiction, ontology is always political. Thomas King demonstrates that ontological struggle is at the heart of defining the antagonistic interplay of the two ideas of land that separate colonial and decolonial reason through the relationship between Clifford Sifton and Eli Stands Alone. For Sifton, the dam is as natural as the settler-colonial state and the white, male, property-owning settler-consumer. Sifton asserts that dams "don't have personalities, and they don't have politics."[70] By this he means that the dam, like the settler-consumer, is the naturalized zero point of modern political life. Amidst the racializing infrastructures of colonial capitalism, to be "natural" is to be the unmarked subject against which all other objects of knowledge are defined. But as the dam begins to move, it defamiliarizes Sifton's "natural landscape." King could be thinking here of one of Deloria's critiques of colonial logic, which he calls, riffing on Alfred North Whitehead, "the grievous sin of the Western mind: misplaced concreteness—the desire to absolutize what are but tenuous conclusions."[71] Misplaced concreteness appears in this scene when the dam—quite literally misplaced concrete that Sifton absolutizes as stable and predictable—becomes strange and rebellious. Dam and water and earth reveal the persistence of terrestrial qualities embedded in dam infrastructure that the dam developer has tried to suppress. Property owners on the short-lived lake watch their "shoreline disappear" as "below, in the valley, the water rolled on as it had for eternity."[72] When the earth flexes its tectonic muscles, its motion exposes the dam as a reluctant servant of the settler-colonial state and its racial capitalist parsing of human and nonhuman, valuable and disposable life. The dam burst expresses the planet's powerful capacity to sever ties with human attempts to naturalize it as a controllable, meaning-making, value-producing structure. Despite Sifton's confident assertion, it turns out that the dam does have a personality, and it does have a politics. Deep in its steel and concrete bones, the Grand Baleen is rooted in—and grown from—the bedrock of an angry planet.

The two ideas of land that clash in this standoff emerge as not only irreconcilable and antagonistic but also as unequal in their ontological rigor. Manuel proposes that the idea of land that draws knowledge of being-in-the-world from the earth—Coulthard's grounded normativity —is an ontologically correct description of material conditions:

> The traditional relationship of Indian people with the land, the water, the air, and the sun has often been praised because of its spiritual nature. People seeking their own roots have praised it because it is a tradition they can grasp. But its real strength historically for our people, and its growing appeal today both for our own young people and for non-Indian people concerned for the generations still coming toward us, is not a romantic notion. Its strength lies in the accuracy of the description it offers of the proper and natural relationship of people to their environment and to the larger universe.[73]

In this passage, Manuel uses "natural" in the opposite sense to that of the colonial-capitalist developer ventriloquized by Sifton. In the ontological framework of grounded normativity, "natural relationship" is based on what land knows and teaches "as the ultimate reference point."[74] When Eli Stands Alone tells Clifton that "you can't hold water back forever," he is making an ontological statement drawn from what the ground beneath his feet is telling anyone who will listen about its relationship to the dam. What is normative here is not the dam's stability, but rather its movement back into and toward the earth and its tensile capacity to both hold water and to crack and leak and snap in response to water's eternal and relentless movement. Grounded normativity as an ontological framework drawn from the land is therefore anticolonial as well as supportive of the correctness of the decolonial mandate. The grounded normativity that King describes in *Green Grass, Running Water* directs us to the ways in which the earth resists the imposition of colonial and capitalist infrastructure *and* to this infrastructure's own resistance to serving as a stable avatar of colonial-capitalist power.

Authors writing in this decolonial ontological register are keenly aware of how every seemingly neutral description of being-in-the-world is deeply inflected by history, geolocation, and what the editors of a special issue of *Theory & Event* call "colonial unknowing."[75] Statements issued in the ontological register tend to not only map onto those markers of time and space specific to European coloniality but to do so in ways that "unknow": delegitimizing and marginalizing other genealogies of knowledge production and therefore other ways of being human and of understanding nonhuman being. As Tiffany Lethabo King writes, "The problem with the human is its scaffolding, not the category itself."[76] While Eurowestern modes of ontological inquiry often argue that ontology is the study of being, proper, and therefore not materialist in any necessary sense of the term, the decolonial mandate insists on the irreducibly historical, embodied, and material stakes of any ontological claim. The framework of grounded normativity is how the earth thinks, if we can imagine (as do these authors) that an ontological proposition can be stated through movement, and proven by planetary processes.

In the late twentieth century, academic reframings of ontological inquiry—the desire of the Eurowestern world to "catch up" with what the Indigenous world has been saying for centuries—emerge out of the intellectual search that Manuel describes when he marks the "growing appeal today" of the Indigenous relationship to land "both for our own young people and for non-Indian people concerned for the generations still coming."[77] In the 1970s, Manuel is describing the move of postmodernist and postcolonial thought away from European Enlightenment knowledge traditions and the violent century they have produced. Manuel's searchers were conversant with poststructuralist and postcolonial projects in that they followed their provincializing critiques of Western Enlightenment rationalism. But they were dis-aligned with both projects in their refusal to, as Bruno Latour phrases it, dissolve reason in the "acids" of "naturalization, sociologization, discursivization, and finally the forgetting of Being."[78] For this materialist undercurrent, ontology could not be discarded along with Enlightenment mores because of that accuracy of description Manuel evokes.

Two unique streams of ontological inquiry that resisted postmodern claims of ontological indeterminacy began to emerge in the 1970s and set up the intellectual trajectories that lead to the encounter between ontology and decolonial thought in angry planet fiction. The first is representative of the emergent engagement with a critical decolonial theory that we have already seen in Deloria, Manuel, and Wynter. Although not directly affiliated with Indigenous thought, the grounded normativity of the plantation-plot dichotomy that Wynter sketched in 1971 developed out of the context of colonial terraforming that forcibly welded African slaves to the land and to freedom struggle tied to decolonization. By 1984, Wynter is publishing on what she describes as "an overall crisis of the episteme/organization of knowledge."[79] Wynter argues that the most significant legacy of colonial conquest is its dissolution of the human as an ontological category in favor of its culturalization and biologization under the rubric of racial difference. It was during the era of colonial conquest and its "complementary *non-discursive* practices of a new wave of great internments of native labors in new plantations orders" that Eurowestern "Man" became instantiated as the standard for what qualifies as human life.[80] Within the process of colonial ontological conquest that Wynter describes, a particular genre of the human becomes standardized as a universal norm, an "ethnoclass (i.e. Western bourgeois) conception of the human, Man, which overrepresents itself as if it were the human itself."[81] Wynter extends her analysis of this genre problem to the development and ordering of the physical environment. It is at the level of "non-discursive" material practices that colonial power ontologizes race and forces "the human itself," as an ontological category, into the state of permanent crisis, for people and for planet, that defines the present.

Wynter's work is representative of a stream of developing critical decolonial theory that is not always based on Indigenous intellectual traditions but that shares an attention to the persistence of colonial conditions in the ostensibly postcolonial world and that speaks against the ongoing developmentalist agendas of racial capitalist state power. The thinking that emerges here offers us the burgeoning contours of a critique of colonial ontology that echoes foundational texts like *God Is*

Red and *The Fourth World*. Similar projects emerge out of the U.S. Third World feminisms developed by Anzaldúa's *pensamiento fronterizo* (borderlands thinking) (1987) and Chela Sandoval's "oppositional consciousness" (1991). Both of these projects describe the ways in which dominated social subjects might "break with ideology" and operate as mobile agents moving strategically among multiple registers of opposition and dissent.[82] The interrogation of the relationship between colonialism and ontology also finds Wynter's and Anzaldúa's work intersecting with the Latin Americanist modernity/coloniality/decoloniality [MCD] project, which makes its first intervention with Aníbal Quijano's articulation of the "coloniality of power" in 1991.[83] Led by Latin American and U.S. scholars including Quijano, Walter Mignolo, Arturo Escobar, José David Saldívar, and Nelson Maldonado-Torres, this project focuses on how knowledge is colonized—turned into a universal and homogenous thing called *rationality*—during the era of European empire building.[84] The contributions of this group are valuable for the work that they do couching this process in terms of what Nelson Maldonado-Torres calls the "coloniality of being," which misrecognizes the planetary surface as inert, as background, or as perhaps once lively but now fully subordinated to anthropogenic agendas.[85]

The routing of decolonial ontological inquiry around Indigenous contexts is representative of the other stream of ontological inquiry seeking alternatives to the often-dematerialized discourses of poststructuralism and postcolonialisms in these same decades. This stream is identified by Manuel as that of those "non-Indian" roots seekers that he calls "discoverers": hippies and anthropologists searching for insights from Indigenous communities and traditions in the post–civil rights era.[86] Briefly cited above, Latour's critique of modernity is paradigmatic of this stream. At the same time that Manuel is writing *The Fourth World*, Latour is conducting anthropological and ethnographic fieldwork in Ivory Coast, producing a 1974 report on barriers in neocolonial industries to replacing European management with Indigenous Ivoirian leadership.[87] "The shock felt by Latour at discovering the effects of colonial domination in his fieldwork," writes Jérôme Lamy, "partly contributed to his changing directions back to [interrogating the relationship between] rationality and modernity," an experience that laid the groundwork for the critical insights that structure *We Have Never Been Modern*.[88]

However, by its publication in 1991, any attention to the legitimate differences produced by Indigenous intelligence has been reduced to passing ironic references to "the poor premodern collectives," accused by colonial empires of "making a horrible mishmash of things and humans, of objects and signs."[89] The "premodern" then becomes the generalized foil against which Latour launches his takedown of Enlightenment modernity and its foundational ontological error: the "Great Divide" of nature and culture that produces all the miseries of environmental and human exploitation that become freshly visible in the wake of the Cold War. "Nature," Latour writes, describing the contours of the emergent angry planet, "over which we were supposed to gain absolute mastery, dominates us in an equally global fashion, and threatens us all. It is a strange dialectic that turns the slave into man's owner and master."[90] The planet in crisis, Latour argues, pushes us to break down the illusory divisions in modernity in deference to the profound and ever-shifting relationality among all actors (or "actants"), human and nonhuman, that structure social and spatial order.

What is significant about this stream of inquiry is that it manages to "discover" its critique of Enlightenment modernity with virtually no reference to other knowledge traditions. In the process, scholars like Latour lay the foundations for some of the major critical conversations of the twenty-first century and for the frictions that have sprung up in many fields among new materialism and critical theories of race and ethnicity. The work of other "non-Indian" discoverers includes Louis Althusser's 1982 "Underground Current of the Materialism of the Encounter," Donna Haraway's 1985 "Cyborg Manifesto," Jane Bennett's 1987 *Unthinking Faith and Enlightenment: Nature and the State in a Post-Hegelian Era*, and Nick Land's 1988 "Kant, Capital, and the Prohibition of Incest: A Polemical Introduction to the Configuration of Philosophy and Modernity." While these projects emerge out of disparate fields of inquiry, they share a commitment to an ontological critique of Enlightenment rationality that remains firmly rooted in Eurowestern intellectual traditions. This "discoverer" stream draws instead on the "undercurrents" that Althusser identifies in Western thought: from the atomism of Epicurus and Lucretius, to Heidegger's phenomenology and the process philosophy of Alfred North Whitehead (also a favorite of Deloria's), to Deleuzian transcendental empiricism. Even in its most postcolonial moments, however, the field remains distinctly silent on potential indebtedness to Indigenous or non-Eurowestern knowledge traditions.[91]

It is against the backdrop of these coevolving decolonial ontologies that angry planet fiction develops and emerges as an important precursor to many of the preoccupations of contemporary critical theory and fiction. In telling stories that spatialize the ontological priority of land, angry planet fiction narrates grounded normativity, looking to terrestrial motion as a model for what it can "teach us about living our lives in relation to one another and our surroundings in a respectful, nondominating and nonexploitative way" while also attending to how shattered grounded normativity can produce lessons in revolution.[92] In its descriptions of planetary motion and material contingencies, angry planet fiction follows Leanne Simpson's description of Indigenous intelligence drawn from the earth's "algorithms": "Moss reminds us," she writes, "Moss, like pine trees, or maple trees, or geese, is an algorithm, a practice for solving a problem."[93] In spatializing these algorithms, this narrative ontology contributes to the work of critical cultural and decolonial geographers like Katherine McKittrick and Sarah Hunt who face "the task of confronting the epistemic violence entailed in closures established around geographic knowledge."[94] Angry planet fiction approaches this task by following Kathryn Yusoff below the topographic surface to think geologically about the stratigraphic inscription of racialization through the geo-logic of resource extraction, "whereby extraordinary possibilities in relation to the earth were wiped out."[95] Angry planet fiction pursues those extraordinary possibilities, seeking to reinscribe them back into the frame of the knowable world.

Angry planet fiction is attentive, along with materialist and elemental ecocritics, to the force of the elements as they "disrupt human endeavors by refusing to be reduced to tidy equations and known-in-advance formulae."[96] It is interested, like feminist materialisms, in what happens when "nature 'punches back' at humans and the machines they construct."[97] It answers Amitav Ghosh's call, prompted by understanding climate change through the colonial context, for a realignment of narrative representational practices toward the real of catastrophe, returning uncanny and improbable events to "the mansion of serious fiction."[98] This attempt to think the nonhuman independence of the physical environment is consonant with the work of object-oriented ontologists including Graham Harman, Quentin Meillassoux, Levi Bryant, and Timothy Morton, who describe the physical world as "existing in itself regardless of whether we are thinking of it or not; that outside which thought could explore with the legitimate feeling of being on foreign territory—of being entirely elsewhere."[99] Along with infrastructural theorists, angry planet fiction is attuned to how the disruptive force of this "foreign territory" invades seemingly subdued urban space and civic infrastructure, drawing out the paradox of urban ecologies where material life can appear as both overdetermining and insubstantial or precarious.[100] Angry planet fiction also tells stories about the ways in which bodies are "trans-corporeal," "immersed," in Alaimo's words, "within incalculable, interconnected material agencies that erode even our most sophisticated modes of understanding."[101] While the political agenda here recuperates terrestrial agency, the angry planet analytic marries together posthumanist and aspirationally humanist materialisms by always returning to the human body, narratively recalibrating which forms of human being and expression are legible depending on where we find ourselves in the battle for ontological authority.

This book's efforts to stage this battle against the backdrop of end-of-millennium planetary rage contributes to the growing field of literary study that addresses the intersections of racial capitalism, decolonization, and ontology in American literature. The authors gathered in the coming chapters arrive from black American, Anishinaabeg, Laguna Pueblo, Guatemalan-American, Japanese-Brazilian-American, and Anglo-European-American backgrounds. However, their narrative commitments speak in what I believe are generative ways to the pursuit of grounded normativity as an ontological framework that supports a land-focused decolonial mandate. Their description of the possibilities for creating different worlds begins with, as one character in Whitehead's *The Intuitionist* says, "a renegotiation of our relationship to objects."[102] In angry planet fiction, this renegotiation requires us to take nonhuman agency seriously; to pay attention when the world moves in ways that baffle rationalist frameworks and to understand this motion as pointing toward other ways of being-in-the-world that reject the racializing logic of capitalism and the expropriative logic of settler colonialism. These are all first principles, what Deloria calls "a more realistic knowledge," locatable within the framework of even a shattered grounded normativity.[103]

In the narrative act of claiming ontological authority, angry planet fiction anticipates the intersection of new materialist analysis and cultural studies. In the early 2010s, this "turn" is led by the work of feminist and ecocritical scholars including Karen Barad and Stacy Alaimo, who make the connection between breaking the heteropatriarchal logic of objectification and renegotiating our relationship to being human. For the first Americanist projects taking up new materialism, engaging with nonhuman agencies and movements clearly initiates an exploration into the subject agency and mobility of racialized subjects. As Bill Brown's articulation of "thing theory" demonstrated in the early 2000s, there can be no discussion of objects or ontology in American literature without accounting for the "ontological scandal" of slavery.[104] The first publication that explicitly takes up the language of new materialism, speculative realism, and object-oriented ontology in a literary critical capacity is Ramón Saldívar's work on postrace aesthetics, published in 2011.[105] In 2013, Matthew Taylor's *Universes Without Us: Posthuman Cosmologies in American Literature* historicized the intersection of race and ontology in nineteenth-century American literature.[106] Taylor argues that Charles Chestnutt and Zora Neale Hurston narrate a "conjure cosmos," which draws on "an African diasporic spiritual tradition that explodes [Enlightenment] metaphysical justifications" for racial difference, evoking instead "the continuity of earth, only the literal, mortal equality of common ground."[107] The African diasporic cosmos that is woven throughout American literature directs us to the ways in which grounded normativity creeps into infrastructural relationships, destabilizing their status as good avatars of state power.

That thinking through a renegotiation of our relationship to objects brings American literary scholarship into inevitable confrontation with the history of racialization in the United States reprises the insight of Indigenous intelligence that acknowledging the ontological priority of land forces us into engagement with the decolonial thought. It makes sense, then, that the radical flattening of ontological order Taylor describes in the African diasporic cosmos, and that is found in epistemes grounded in the assertion "that the universe is alive," is welcomed by those who have never been the beneficiaries of colonial modernity's historical form of onto-privilege but is processed as a kind of existential terrorism by the privileged and vulnerable subject of human exceptionalism.[108] It is perhaps for this reason that new materialist theory has a complicated relationship to scholarship on racial formation and colonialism. Via Latour's infamous 2004 essay, "Why Has Critique Run Out of Steam?," branches of new materialist theory have become associated with a postcritical trend eager to do away with the *mood* (to use Rita Felski's term) of suspicion central to the demystifying labor of historical materialist analysis. This postcritical turn uses Latour's attention to networks and material entanglements to produce ecstatic descriptions of the agency of texts, accessible to those modest readers willing to "trudge along like an ANT, marveling at the intricate ecologies and diverse microorganisms that lie hidden among the thick blades of grass."[109] The payoff of such a reading practice is the ability to see our relationships with objects as gentle, affectively intimate, and capable of circulating inside or beyond the global networks of colonial modernity and racial capitalism. The project of *Angry Planet,* conversely, engages the agency of the nonhuman world as a pathway to deepening the critical labor of demystification. When we demystify intricate ecologies, we notice the ways in which grass grows on expropriated Indigenous land and out of the racialized bodies whose exploited labor and violent deaths feed the terraformed earth and its insect life. Angry planet fiction, as we will discover, is full of grass, and like ontological assertions, no blade of grass is neutral.

The postcritical face of the new materialist turn is a turning away from the (uncomfortable for some, painful for others) confrontation with the bloody history and shattered grounded normativity of colonial-capitalist modernity. It expresses not only the disciplinary but ontological anxiety that scholars of color identify, among its many names, as white fragility and as "settler moves to innocence" produced when self-contained subjects find themselves overexposed to the previously objectified other, suddenly sprung, to borrow a phrase from Bill Brown, into uncanny motion.[110] Nowhere are these moves to innocence more clearly on display than in new materialism's reluctant indebtedness to Indigenous ontologies. That ontology is a site where colonial power can sustain an injury—and is thus closely guarded—is Kim TallBear's point in her critique of new materialism's failure to acknowledge its clear precedents in Indigenous thought:

Indigenous people, our movements and our voices are the others it seems the new materialists—indeed most of Western thought—cannot fully comprehend as living. They may hear us like ghosts go bump in the night. Once forced to see us, they may be terrified by the claims we make on their house. The invisibility of our ontologies, the very few references to them in their writing, and references to Indigenous thought by other theoretical traditions as "beliefs" or artifacts of a waning time to be studied but not interacted with as truths about the living world—all of this is to deny our vibrancy.[111]

In TallBear's formulation, the force of Indigenous ontologies is not only anxiety producing but also appears to the Western subject as a haunting, a horror show: the rebelling slave at the gates of the Plantationocene. By grounding its decolonial ontological argument in Indigenous and non-Western traditions of knowledge production, angry planet fiction anticipates the new materialist turn and offers contemporary critical theory an alternative genealogy grounded in the work of making visible these ontologies and deploying them as powerful tools for radical decolonial critique. Again, we can return to the protagonists of this fiction who follow the revolutionary decolonial imperative to raze colonial modernity and start again. "The claims we make on their house" are rightly terrifying. We are here to burn it down.

Narrative Defiance

In Linda Hogan's *Solar Storms,* moments of radical terrestrial autonomy realize decolonization as a deeply physical praxis; an activity of what the modernity/coloniality project calls *delinking,* or pulling away from colonial capitalist modernity. Angel describes an incident when the James Bay Project's transformation of a drainage basin the size of New York State causes a chunk of land to "split off from all the rest and move through the rain down toward the new river."[112] "It was frightening and sad to see," Angel thinks, "but there was also a kind of defiance in that splitting, one that couldn't be spoken except in the language of the earth, and it was a sign we couldn't decipher, a meaning not known to us."[113] In angry planet fiction, the earth expresses defiance in an unknowable language, this very "meaning not known to us" its assertion of radical autonomy. Against all the force of colonial terraforming, and even in part because of that force's own shattering of the planetary body, the earth contains the ontological capacity to *withdraw,* a state whereby nonhuman being demonstrates its ontological difference from anthropogenic intention and development.

As the chunk of land floats away from its hydroelectric confinement, its indecipherable language physically expresses the fact that the human and the nonhuman, the material and the semiotic, the built and the organic environment do not easily merge into each other. Despite new materialist proponents of the rich critical reservoir opened by theories of quantum and sociological *entanglement,* colonial-capitalist development has to work hard to naturalize this form of entanglement in the registers both of language—those forms of linguistic imperialism that silence not only colonized populations but that "language of the earth" that Angel describes—and of land. At the same time, the earth physically performs the activity of what decolonial Indigenous scholars call *resurgence,* seen here in the river's capacity to "break loose and rage over the ground, tearing out dams and bridges."[114] This moment emphasizes that Indigenous resurgence is simultaneously a human process of re-engagement with tradition and territory, and bound to the rebirth of land and the land's own reconfiguration of social and spatial orders. As it moves and grows toward the long-buried Fourth World, planetary motion defamilarizes those characteristics of colonial warfare that otherwise appear as the everyday conditions of normal, rational modern life in the American Third World, and reasserts its own ontological priority.

Throughout *Angry Planet,* ontological assertions that I identify as emerging from grounded normativity structure relationships between the planet's modeling of decolonial movement and human decolonial struggle, which manifests in anticapitalist, antiracist, antiheterosexist, and environmentalist action. Each of these assertions can be expressed through language used by critical decolonial theorists drawing on grounded normativity and by new materialist discoverers, and each reveals potential nodes of allyship and of friction among these streams of ontological inquiry. In the following chapters, I draw in particular on the new materialist concepts of *entanglement* and *withdrawal,* as well as the decolonial concepts of *delinking* and *resurgence.* These concepts are key to *Angry Planet's* exploration of grounded normativity in two registers. First, they each describe a terrestrial motion modeled in these narratives as a conduit to repairing the ontologically damaged relationship between humans and the physical environment. Second, however, each concept also finds angry planet fiction running up against a kind of limit point to what the earth can offer as a model for global solidarity. A shared idea of land only takes us so far in this narrative universe, which never quite arrives at the decolonial future it anticipates.

Through eight novels read comparatively across four chapters, *Angry Planet* tells a story about the colonial occupation of Turtle Island and how the conditions of colonial warfare persist through the twentieth-century rise of modernity. This is also the story of the United States as a global superpower and of how poised that superpower appears, from the perspective of its Third World, at least, to collapse entirely into the Fourth World churning beneath its surface. This story begins in chapter 1, "Terraforming the New World: Thomas Pynchon's *Mason & Dixon* and Colson Whitehead's *The Intuitionist.*" Each novel identifies a moment in U.S. history in which colonial terraforming builds its spatial logic into the continent with particular intensity, its capitalist mode of production becoming *entangled* with the surface of the continent. Pynchon and Whitehead describe how colonial-capitalist ontological order breaks down the category of the human as it expands infrastructurally: its frontier moving west in the eighteenth century and developing vertically through the rise of skyscraper cities in the late nineteenth and early twentieth centuries. In their telling, these histories also describe the formation of the Du Boisian color line, which turns the racialization of space into a black/white binary that strategically deploys competing claims to suffering the foundational colonial wound as each group is dehumanized through its relationship to/as property. In these historical novels, the new materialist fact of quantum entanglement emerges as racial entanglement, spatializing how the *longue durée* of what Deloria calls "playing Indian" informs modes of differential racialization that shore up the partitioning function of racial capitalism as it develops in the North American settler-colonial context.

In chapter 2, "First World Problems: John Edgar Wideman's *Philadelphia Fire* and Karen Tei Yamashita's *Tropic of Orange,*" the angry planet is at work resisting colonial-capitalist entanglement. Shattered grounded normativity appears here as ontological *withdrawal,* a concept described by object-oriented ontology. For object-oriented ontologists, the object world withdraws in the sense that its qualities are always in excess of human *and* nonhuman grasp. This approach to materiality is, Harman contends, "a *weird* realism in which real individual objects resist all forms of causal or cognitive mastery."[115] The earth withdraws in *Philadelphia Fire* and *Tropic of Orange* as it models its difference from the social structures and material infrastructures shaping the neoliberal multicultural 1980s and 1990s. Centering on segments of the American Third World in Philadelphia and Los Angeles, respectively, Wideman and Yamashita represent the violence inflicted on economically disenfranchised communities who are not the beneficiaries of the neoliberal state's class-qualified race-liberal order. In the novels, these communities enter into creative alliances with their physical environments to combat the everyday precarity they experience, and they find new modes of building and dwelling within urban spaces—abandoned lots, freeways, decaying suburbs—produced by this antagonist relationality. But it is their very engagement in interethnic solidarities forged through reasserting the ontological authority of property that exposes the fraught relationship between property, wealth, and uplift that shapes antiracist struggle while foreclosing otherwise generative pathways to decolonial futures. Instead of a transformation of material conditions, the acts of withdrawal in these novels reveal the violence the state will employ to protect its ontological authority. *Philadelphia Fire* and *Tropic of Orange* take us to the brink of a decolonial future, only to find its borders policed by a militarized state that will go to any lengths to reconsolidate its social-spatial dominance.

But the planet is on the move now and only getting more disruptive. In chapter 3, "Third World Liberation: Leslie Marmon Silko's *Almanac of the Dead* and Héctor Tobar's *The Tattooed Soldier,*" the angry planet bursts onto the scene as an agent of chaos that can do much more than provoke state violence. In *Almanac of the Dead* and *The Tattooed Soldier,* the shattered grounded normativity of *delinking* models the potential for angry people to break with the settler state and its everyday violence. Delinking is a concept used by the MCD project to describe economic and political strategies whereby a postcolonial nation may sever ties with its imperial state. Walter Mignolo expands our understanding of delinking to refer to a "decolonial epistemic shift [that] brings to the foreground other epistemologies, other principles of knowledge and understanding and, consequently, other economies, other politics, other ethics."[116] In *Almanac of the Dead* and *The Tattooed Soldier*, delinking describes planetary motion that physically extracts itself from colonial systems of entanglement. If climate change, urban decay, racial violence, endemic poverty, and state neglect of social welfare are the new normal of what Antonio Negri calls "the crisis state" in these novels, delinking becomes an ontological event when altered material conditions produce not only a different relationship to the planet but a different mode of being human.[117] At both the macro and micro scales of unruly tectonic motion, the angry people of *Almanac of the Dead* and *The Tattooed Soldier* follow the delinking movement of the angry planet in an effort to quit colonial-capitalism for good.

It is finally in chapter 4, "The Fourth World Resurgent: Gerald Vizenor's *Bearheart* and Octavia Butler's *Parable of the Sower*," that we begin to explore what seem to be fully realizing visions of decolonial futurity in which *resurgence* appears as a characteristic of healing grounded normativity. Chapter 4 reads these novels, critically characterized as operating in the apocalyptic and dystopian registers, through Indigenous resurgence theory as decolonization narratives in which the angry planet overturns the apocalyptic conditions produced by colonial capitalism. Resurgence politics are central to Indigenous decolonial thought in North America, which focuses on redirecting Indigenous politics as well as everyday life away from the settler-state-sanctioned processes of recognition and inclusion and toward a materialist politics based on land and kinship.[118] Chapter 4 stresses that the resurgence of human community also requires the resurgence of the land itself, and *a politics of terrestrial sovereignty* based on rebuilding human community through the model provided by planetary motion. This chapter uses the narrative arguments embedded in *Bearheart* and *Parable of the Sower* to develop a theory of terrestrial sovereignty that articulates the planet's right to be in motion. In *Bearheart* and *Parable of the Sower*, the angry planet's transformative terrains are brutal and uncompromising—humans trapped in old ways of thinking about social and spatial belonging are not long for this world—but these terrains also offer freedom to those for whom bodily precarity and social disenfranchisement were the norm under the old order of things. Vizenor and Butler model ways of being human after the end of the world that stress the fierce autonomy of the planet, but this chapter also arrives at the limit of what interethnic solidarities based in a shared idea of land can offer. As private property dissolves, new forms of possessive individualism arise, suggesting the ways in which decolonial futurity itself can become inflected with the human impulse to claim and own the decolonial means of production.

These four chapters tell a story that is ontologically defamiliarizing in order to foster consciousness of a planet that struggles against the legacy of colonial terraforming. There is, however, no complete decolonial project in the angry planet universe. In conclusion, I connect this project's late twentieth-century moment to our present to ask how it anticipates—and whether it offers any insight into—the tensions and questions shaping the relationships between decoloniality, solidarity, and ontology today. In the era of Idle No More and Land Back, Black Lives Matter and MeToo, what solidarities have become impossible or less possible, and why? How do problems of literary production rooted in the fraught relationship between genre and narratives of human difference block the way to imagining decolonial futurity? What might contemporary models of racializing erasure like the Anthropocene learn from the angry planet, not only about accounting for difference but about the failures of totalizing models of global solidarity in the face of climate crisis?

My hope is that telling the story of the angry planet also serves to archive one of the many American imaginaries that were suppressed and discredited by the U.S. government's response to 9/11. Before September 11, 2001, a worldwide movement of resistance to neoliberal economic globalization targeted urban areas and freeways as sites that could be radically disrupted in service to social, environmental, and racial justice. As Naomi Klein writes in *No Logo,* these activists refused "to write off the city or the present" as locations ripe for profound social and spatial transformation.[119] After 9/11, creative attacks on city space became taboo, as did grassroots political action that seemed optimistic about what different futures, geographies, and ways of belonging might appear if all our ordered streets and buildings were to suddenly, spectacularly, collapse. But when we make our cities sacred sites of stability and order, we also miss the lesson of angry planet fiction, which is to look for the earth rumbling beneath the pavement. And this allows for the kinds of colonial unknowing and moves to innocence that leave us freshly shocked by Hurricane Katrina; Deepwater Horizon; contaminated drinking water in Flint, Michigan; and by tanks rolling through the streets of Ferguson, Missouri and across antipipeline barricades on Indigenous land. These novels begin with planetary agency in order to confront the politics of representation, punch through boundaries of mediation, and shape the contours of a different physical terrain upon which to register their ontological claims. In this way, the demystification performed by critique is rendered as a material, physical activity that nonhumans might engage in as fully as humans in the struggle to imagine and to build a different world.

1

TERRAFORMING THE NEW WORLD

THOMAS PYNCHON'S *MASON & DIXON* AND COLSON WHITEHEAD'S *THE INTUITIONIST*

On September 11, 2001, Mohawk ironworkers setting steel girders high atop new construction projects in Brooklyn and Manhattan saw American Airlines Flight 11 and United Airlines Flight 175 crash into the North and South World Trade Center Towers. Like many ironworkers who had a bird's-eye view of the attack, Mohawk riveting crews headed for Ground Zero to help with rescue efforts.[1] Some of these riveters had been involved in building the Twin Towers between 1966 and 1974.[2] Mohawks have been working high steel in New York since the 1920s, commuting across the settler-state border from the Kahnawà:ke reserve in Québec six hours away. The first generation of Mohawk ironworkers was trained in 1886, when the Dominion Bridge Company (DBC) agreed to employ Mohawks in exchange for permission to build a train bridge on tribal land. Dissatisfied with grunt work, the "members of the tribe would go out on the bridge during construction every chance they got."[3] The DBC quickly idealized the young Mohawk men's sure-footedness. "These Indians were as agile as goats," writes a DBC official, and "seemed immune to the noise of riveting."[4] Based on these seemingly supernatural abilities, the company began to employ the "fearless" men as riveters.

So goes the narrative of the Mohawk "skywalkers," urban warriors that early observers describe navigating the dangerous heights of skyscraper modernity with "a natural balance and agility."[5] But as historians point out, this supposedly "natural" ability did not protect Mohawks from injuries and death. In 1907, the collapse of the Québec Bridge construction project killed thirty-three Kahnawà:ke ironworkers.[6] After this disaster, the workforce decided to "boom out" in order to prevent future mass deaths.[7] The community's strategic redistribution of their labor pool sent the skywalkers across the United States to St. Louis, Chicago, and Minneapolis. The need to protect their numbers against another catastrophic disaster led to the Mohawks' instrumental role in developing the New York City skyline and in cleaning up and rebuilding after its partial destruction on September 11.

The date 9/11 is important for *Angry Planet* because it marks the end, or at least the retreat, of a particular U.S. political imaginary, tracked in the following chapters, that envisioned social change coming about through a dramatic transformation of the physical environment. Like the antiglobalization activism that disappeared as September 11 was, in Phillip Wegner's terms, "effectively hegemonized by the U.S. neoconservatives," narrative visions of an angry planet shaking the city apart at its roots go increasingly silent in the first decade of the twenty-first century.[8] Post-9/11, the breakdown of social and symbolic space becomes a tragedy, what Don DeLillo, in *Falling Man* (2008), identifies as "the processing of white panic data" that occurs when the order of things in settler society starts to look not quite white enough.[9] September 11 was a moment when the well-established boundaries between the American First and Third Worlds seemed unstable. But the Mohawk ironworkers at Ground Zero that day embody the entanglements of race and space in U.S. history that the World Trade Center attacks did not break down but rather fiercely reconsolidated.[10]

The presence of Mohawk skywalkers in the U.S. infrastructural imaginary delineates the fraught status of racialized colonial embodiment. The skywalker narrative renders Mohawk presence in the city fantastic, even mythic: "a material metaphor of survivance," Gerald Vizenor writes of the representation of Indigenous steelworkers in David Treuer's 1999 novel, *The Hiawatha,* that "once grounded," leaves its subjects "separated, dissociated, tragic, and enervated by cultural dominance, nihility, and victimry."[11] Vizenor identifies the slipperiness of metaphorizing the materiality of labor, which in this case absorbs Mohawk workers into an uplift narrative that idealizes Indigenous urban presence while occluding the other forms of "hard labor" that shape the reality of Indigenous life on the ground.[12] These ironworkers, moreover, not only walk the high beams of skyscraper infrastructure, they labor for their mobility, engaging in the regular negotiation of an international border that does not technically apply to them as members of a sovereign polity preexisting settler state formation but that nonetheless processes them as "aberrant because they interpret and deploy their own sovereignty in ways that refuse the absolute sovereignty of at least two settler states," writes Audra Simpson, "and in doing so they reveal the fragility and moral turpitude of those states."[13] Simultaneously, the extreme danger of the riveting profession and its antecedent high salaries, along with the partial protection from racial violence conferred by membership in the ironworkers union, are the very practical realities that have driven six generations of men from Kahnawà:ke to take on work that, beneath the romance of skyscrapers, reproduces the racial capitalist partitioning of many other forms of high-risk wage labor.[14] Mohawk ironworkers take well-earned pride in this history of labor, but their position at the juncture of fantasies of magical skywalkers and realities of precarious labor indexes the ways in which racial difference (and Indigeneity itself *as* a form of racialized difference) is produced and policed infrastructurally, even as it is made to mean discursively and imaginatively, as though nation-building were the pure labor of mythopoesis rather than the colonial expropriation of territory and its development into the partitioning machinery of racial capitalism.

The problem of how bodies become physically entangled by racialization within the infrastructures of colonial-capitalist social order preoccupies Thomas Pynchon's *Mason & Dixon* (1997) and Colson Whitehead's *The Intuitionist* (1999). Both historical novels offer up visions of the violence of colonial entanglement as a network of material relations that produce and entrap bodies as racial objects in the process of terraforming the physical environment into the colonial idea of land that, George Manuel writes, "can be speculated, bought, sold, mortgaged, claimed."[15] This colonial terraforming physically instantiates what Jodi Melamed, in her description of racial capitalism, defines as the "social separateness—the disjoining or deactivating of relations between human beings (and humans and nature)—needed for capitalist expropriation to work."[16] And both novels stress that this terraforming is achieved through and upon laboring bodies that become racialized through the labor of colonial-capitalist development and its "thirst for geological materials," which, in Kathryn Yusoff terms, "unleashed certain notions of what and who could be a subject (and in parallel, what and who could be inhuman as both property and possessing valuable properties to be extracted)."[17] It is during this wave of extractive colonial development that, Aníbal Quijano argues, "'race' (biology and culture or, in our present terms, 'race' and 'ethnicity') was placed as one of the basic criteria to classify the population in the power structure of the new society, associated with the nature of roles and places in the division of labor and in the control of resources of production."[18] By focusing on how racialization and capitalism are co-constituted and congealed through the laboring body, *Mason & Dixon* and *The Intuitionist* tell the story of what the following chapter calls the colonial-capitalist transaction. Through this transaction, the particular material relations defined by colonial capitalism become realized ontologically as a feature of the continental surface.

As the high beams and rigid borders navigated by Mohawk ironworkers suggest, the idea of land ontologized by colonial terraforming has a particular geometry: what Tiffany Lethabo King, drawing on Linda Tuhiwai Smith, calls "the geo-epistemology of the 'line.'"[19] "Within humanist cognitive frames, lines emerge in response to chaos," King writes. "The line, which seeks to separate 'order' from 'chaos,' falls into formation with what Sylvia Wynter identifies as 'the structural oppositions' that order humanist thought."[20] In this humanist ordering, white-coded humanity is defined and defended by linear spatial organization, while "chaos" defines the spatiality of threatening, racially coded inhuman and subhuman others. From the very un-geological borderlines that carve up what Lenape, Iroquois, and Anishinaabe peoples call Turtle Island to the skyscrapers that equate vertical trajectories with power in urban modernity, linearity as a rational structuring principle for maximizing operational efficiency and therefore capital gain is terraformed into the surface and subsurface of the continent. The geometry of the line appears in the form and definition of borders, property demarcations, the assembly lines of Fordist factory production, and shipping routes; in the rectilinear infrastructures of prison- and military-industrial zones, vertical housing development, and grid-system approaches to urban planning such as Le Corbusier's Radiant City; in U.S. nationalist narratives of westward expansion and teleological progress; and in social order paradigms like the Du Boisian Color Line and the Thin Blue Line taken up by anti–Black Lives Matter policing rhetoric. To make Turtle Island into North America is a process of building the surface of the earth into a mechanism that serves the needs of white capital development by ordering the "'chaotic' realm of the dead Indigenous and Black 'nonbeing'" into the racialized division of labor.[21]

As the above examples suggest, linear infrastructures that speak the language of productivity and progress offer a rationalizing spatial overlay to what are in fact the deeply messy material entanglements of racialization and capitalist productive forces. To think the racialized content of entanglement directs us toward the political content of a concept that is deployed by new materialist thinkers in staunchly ontological terms. In many branches of new materialist theory, entanglement is a fascinating description of being-in-the-world. For Jane Bennett, material being "is a flow, an indivisible continuum of becomings whose protean elements are not only exquisitely imbricated *in* a flowing environment but also *are* that very flow."[22] And this is not only a fact of matter but a fact of the social. As Bruno Latour puts it, "the social" is a constantly shifting phenomenon of networks and assemblages, not "a particular sort of thing" but "a very peculiar movement of re-association and re-assembling."[23] Latour means that the social, or *society,* is never a stable or fixed quantity, but what remains stable in both Latour's and Bennett's formulations is the fact of entanglement itself. Timothy Morton emphasizes that this facticity generates a sense of "meaninglessness and disorienting openness" as humans realize how very unspecial we are in the absolutely deindividuating and ever-shifting mesh of existence.[24] Understanding entanglement can reshape our politics, as Latour argues, by asking us to understand political constituency as made up of this interconnected mesh of human and nonhuman actors.

But these theorists rarely address the question of what kind of politics forms out of this mesh. New materialists are reluctant to connect the ontological entanglements of "human and nonhuman, material and discursive, and natural and cultural factors" to colonialism or its capitalist mode of production because entanglement is, as Karen Barad argues, more properly quantum fact than historical materiality.[25] As in the case of many new materialist "discoveries" of this type, entanglement theory repeats the insights of more clearly politicized ontological premises. Of particular significance is the Indigenous first principle of relations, drawn from the grounded normative understanding of the deeply networked connections and modes of kinship that structure social relationships, knowledge production, and ethical engagement among humans, nonhumans, time/history, and space/place.[26] In grounded normativity, entanglement is entirely about obligation and the maintenance of right relations among what Leanne Simpson defines as the "networked series of international relationships" that need to be maintained among interlocking communities of "plant nations, animal nations, and the spiritual realm."[27] By designating these relations as international, Simpson stresses that entanglement requires diplomacy; it is not incidentally political but rather the basis of politics.

New materialist theories of entanglement also celebrate its rich theoretical implications without reference to Karl Marx's still-revelatory articulation of capitalism as a particular relation of production that generates entanglements not of reciprocity and respect but of mobile and flexible accumulation, domination and alienation, "a complete separation between the workers and the ownership of the conditions for the realization of their labor."[28] These conditions for the realization of labor are, in this context, land itself and a direct relationship between land and laborer. The politics of relationality of the capitalist mode of production that generates this alienation are those of force, the forcible partitioning of human bodies from a primary relationship to land, "in effect," as Taiaiake Alfred writes, "alienation from nature."[29] Marx's point in insisting on land expropriation as the original condition for the realization of a capitalist totality demonstrates that ontological entanglement is also irreducibly tied to economic orders, which are not created equal. Manuel makes this point when he describes the noncapitalist economic order of the Fourth World, in which "The economy is an accurate reflection of the environment. It has a plan, in the sense that it is highly organized. At the same time it is not something that must be continually reconstructed in your mind in order for it to go on working. It is something that you simply live with, like your own body. Nonetheless, economic organization is just as much a part of the total environment as in the most highly industrialized societies . . . the economy is the total environment."[30] This is an apt description of an economic order based in grounded normativity, where the global economy is no less a totality than in the capitalist mode of production, but the totality is that of the physical environment itself as well as environmental conditions shaping relations of production rather than vice versa. What both Indigenous and Marxist thought add to the new materialist understanding of entanglement is just how profoundly nonabstract and nonabstractable it is as a material condition. The colonial-capitalist idea of land and the qualified humanist thought that it produces does not ascend to power as an idea. Rather, this idea of land achieves its authority through the ontological transaction of land development, in which the complicity between infrastructural linearity and racialized entanglement is produced not as a by-product but as the commodity itself.

The following chapter uses Pynchon and Whitehead's histories of colonial terraforming to explore how the modes of ontological entanglement that new materialists theorize today are deeply tied to the legacy of colonial-capitalist development, which conceals its messy violence behind the discursive force of its rationalist lines. In light of the violence and messiness of colonial-capitalist entanglement, linearity emerges as a kind of red herring, a performance of the ordered and rational operation of a system that in fact thrives on its own capacities to sprawl disastrously and to conceal the ways in which it creates value through the strategic racialized partitioning and annihilation of human bodies. This is the narrative ontological argument that structures *Mason & Dixon* and *The Intuitionist,* which both address a particular moment in U.S. history—the survey of the Mason-Dixon Line in late eighteenth-century Pennsylvania, and the rise of the skyscraper in early twentieth-century New York, respectively—that is foundational to the development of the modern colonial-capitalist state. While this development is always ongoing, both authors frame these moments as, to use a phrase from Wynter, a "phase of objectification": a moment in history "in which events and their functioning spin out of the control of human motivation and purpose."[31] Pynchon and Whitehead identify their respective historical moments as flashpoints of intense infrastructural development in which the spatial logic of colonial capitalism is terraformed into the land and concomitantly imposed upon human bodies. As narratives addressing the very basic spatiality of this logic, these novels question the line's role as an avatar of spatial dominance. Pynchon and Whitehead suggest that the stories we tell ourselves about "despotic discursive lines" may have a greater hold on us than linear infrastructures themselves, which instead become the un-metaphorizable limit of colonial-capitalist violence.[32] In these novels, the racializing infrastructures of boundary line and elevator trajectory fail to operate as obedient containers for colonial-capitalist order, and this failure directs each narrative toward the more unruly ways in which power proliferates through physical space.

This chapter is organized around three distinct registers in which Pynchon and Whitehead challenge the power of the linear: those of metaphor, materiality, and racialization as the meeting point at which metaphor and materiality encounter the angry earth. First, I describe each novel's consideration of how linearity operates in U.S. literature as a spatial metaphor for fascist power. For Pynchon, this means confronting his own body of work and its overrepresentation of linearity as the ideal allegorical vehicle for spatial systems of control in novels like *The Crying of Lot 49* (1965) and *Gravity's Rainbow* (1973). For Whitehead, conversely, this means wrestling with the Black modernist literary tradition, in which the linear trajectory operates as a key spatial allegory for gauging the socially deterministic factors that constrain the agency, mobility, and survival of Black Americans in modernist novels ranging from Nella Larsen's *Passing* (1929) to Ralph Ellison's *Invisible Man* (1952). Second, I argue that each novel defuses the linear allegory, of boundary line and elevator trajectory, to redirect our attention toward the far messier operations of colonial capitalism that materialize through its continental terraforming. By writing against what Brian McHale has defined as "the poetics of Pynchon-space" established in his earlier work, Pynchon exposes the linear as a geometry of distraction that discursively conceals how the colonial-capitalist transaction replaces the agency of the land with the agency of capital.[33] *The Intuitionist* opens on a moment at which this ontological order is being intensified by the vertical development of skyscraper cities. As the narrative progresses, however, a physical world with an explosive inclination to chaos, "a secret scofflaw city within the known city" emerges, giving expression to the angry planet rumbling beneath the city's concrete surfaces.[34] Finally, I suggest that by narratively rematerializing the significance of infrastructure in the development of the colonial-capitalist state, each novel confronts how race and space become entangled as stigmatized racial identity and privileged white nonidentity are spatialized through colonial infrastructural development. In these terms, *Mason & Dixon* is an elegy for human agency that is preoccupied with the dehumanization of racialized bodies to the degree that it lays the groundwork for the permanently embattled white masculinity that Charles Mason and Jeremiah Dixon find themselves taking on as they participate in redeveloping the continent to serve colonial capitalism. Conversely, Whitehead's protagonist, Lila Mae Watson, finds forms of agency and mobility that open up for Black female subjects through claiming space in a physical environment reluctant to serve the state and its partitioning of lives into First and Third World spaces. In both cases, definitions of non-Indigenous American identity navigate among the poles of what Gerald Vizenor calls "victimry" and "survivance," suggesting that racialization is itself produced against a background of competing claims to American indigeneity that are won through the erasure of Turtle Island and the assimilation of Indigenous land claims into the U.S. ontology of racial difference.

Diffusing Colonial Allegory

In *Mason & Dixon,* Thomas Pynchon describes capitalism's rise as a force that swells with agentic power as it suppresses the continent's precontact environmental order. In a sense, the novel tells the story of Manuel's "struggle of the past four centuries . . . between these two ideas of land," one an environmental totality, the other a capitalist totality made up of the racializing linear partitioning of landed property.[35] However, Pynchon tells the story from the perspective of the colonialist laborer, for whom this struggle is ultimately most tragic in its production of white masculinity as both monstrous and helpless in the face of its own monstrosity. Phillip Wegner argues that Pynchon's novel is fundamentally "about the 1990s," and about linking that decade to "an earlier moment of globalization and spatial mapping."[36] Both Pynchon's 1990s and Mason and Dixon's 1760s are moments in which capitalism is taking shape, in Neil Lazarus's terms, as "an unstable, unsteerable, rampaging juggernaut which it is quite beyond the capacity of any human agency to temper or domesticate."[37] While Lazarus ventriloquizes this position to question its "fatalism and technological determinism," *Mason & Dixon* takes the possibility of history and humanity's end quite seriously.[38] Pynchon often populates his novels with agentic nonhumans.[39] *Mason & Dixon,* however, is the first novel in which he explicitly pits land and capital against each other, and has that "great single Engine" of capitalism emerge the undisputed victor.[40] As a decade that anticipates the American expansionism of the neoliberal 1990s, Pynchon's 1760s become the moment at which colonial-capitalist land development sets in motion the mechanism for a terrible species of historical materialism without dialectical movement; a bleak end to history in which capital circulates endlessly and humanity loses the capacity to function as a historical agent (yes, white men, too).[41]

Focusing on the 1760s, Pynchon highlights the intense land development occurring at the time that Charles Mason and Jeremiah Dixon cut the boundary line between Penn and Calvert territory. This period of heightened development burst out of the geopolitical shifts caused by the Seven Years' War in Europe and the French and Indian War in North America that unfolded from 1754 to 1763. In North America, the global conflict ended with a massive expansion of British colonial territory and an antecedent drive to settle internal boundary disputes and to push the frontier west. But while it is his most line-obsessed novel, *Mason & Dixon* also stages Pynchon's confrontation with the failure of linearity to effectively track and make sense of the colonial-capitalist entanglements that ensnare human agency. *Mason & Dixon*'s readers frequently interpret the Line's plot-structuring function as an allegory for American westward expansionist violence.[42] This interpretive strategy is consonant with Gordon Teskey's articulation of the relationship between allegory and violence, in which meaning is created, "not as a representation of what already is but as the creative exertion of force."[43] These readings map satisfyingly onto Pynchon's earlier work, in which he is at pains to describe the linear trajectories connecting global warfare to the spectacular rise of the American military-industrial complex. As McHale suggests, in *Gravity's Rainbow,* Pynchon "affiliat[es] the verticality of rocket flight . . . with fascism, the Elect, the spurning of earth and the yearning for transcendence."[44] A similar complex of associations structures *The Crying of Lot 49,* in which Oedipa Maas is trapped by the "hard, strung presence" of freeways, railroads, and power lines that "laced, deepened, authenticated the great night" of twentieth-century America.[45] Throughout Pynchon's body of work, white American subjectivity is positioned as under threat by the very linearity that naturalizes and rationalizes its privileged spatiality, and *Mason & Dixon*'s Boundary Line appears as the apotheosis of this engagement with rectilinearity as an allegory for oppression.

But as Pynchon plots the Visto's cutting, a massive project that takes years to carve deep into the earth's terrestrial surface, he also arrives at the limits of what the Line can offer as an allegory for the oppressions fixed into the continent by colonial-capitalist terraforming. It is as if the more he writes about the continent's disappearance as an environmental totality, the less a line of any size or length can suffice to explain the injury. Even as the Line is made to stand as an "Agent of Evil," "Tellurick Injuries," and "Bad Energy," it conceals the ways in which the structures of power that it symbolizes function through messier, more flexibly accumulative transactions.[46] Having spent "twenty-four years in the making" of the novel, the author finds that the flood of signification that it produces is not a loyal servant to his explanatory models.[47] Like Walter Mignolo, he wants "a new logic to tell the story" of colonial modernity.[48] Pynchon breaks the allegorical contract by rendering the Mason-Dixon Line in ways that frustrate the hermeneutic anxiety and interpretative play—that desire to solve the symbolic puzzle—that are central to allegory's aesthetic effects. Thomas H. Schaub identifies this break in form: "In *Mason & Dixon,* by sharp contrast with his earlier novels, the status (as well as the meaning) of the allegory is always in sight, while doubt itself becomes a recurrent theme, rather than the experience of the reader, who never works very hard to identify Pynchon's intentions or (for example) the meaning of that Line which Mason and Dixon are surveying."[49] Hermeneutic overload takes place as the symbolic function of the Line is so imposed on readers as to truncate opportunities for hermeneutic anxiety. By oversaturating the Line's interpretive possibilities, Pynchon redirects his spatial poetics toward colonial conquest's more entangling material processes, which trap and constrain the futurity of colonized and colonizer in what the novel problematically frames as equal measure.

Pynchon's attempt to diffuse colonial allegory delineates the problem with material-semiotic entanglement confronted by angry planet fiction. The more entangled with signification the Line becomes—draw "a Line, in particular a Right Line," one character warns, "all else will follow as if predestin'd, unto War and Devastation"—the more power it seems to possess as an explanatory model for the colonial-capitalist takeover of the continent.[50] And yet, as Pynchon's oversaturation of the Line's allegorical function suggests, insisting on material-semiotic entanglement may shore up colonial meaning-making practices at the expense of confronting the real physical labor involved in building the colonial-capitalist state. In other words, material-semiotic entanglement emerges here not as an ontological fact but as an explanatory power grab in which "'colonization' as a metaphor for oppression" allows all subjects within the purview of colonial lineation to claim the injury.[51] In Pynchon's framework, focusing on empire building's discursive operations distracts from the ways in which colonial power is realized most violently and forcefully, that is, through material practices.[52]

Materializing Colonial Infrastructure in *Mason & Dixon*

The material practice of boundary cutting is central to what this argument identifies as the colonial transaction whereby the life of the land, "one and indivisible," is exchanged for the life of capital.[53] Lazarus's "juggernaut" comes alive in *Mason & Dixon* as the Line takes shape as an infrastructure "cut and beaten out of the wilderness," eight yards wide and 244 miles long.[54] The more the surveyors persist in convincing themselves that they are engaged in a detached and rational act of scientific measurement, the more they experience a sense of being harried by a "something invisible" that pursues them with increasing force as the Line progresses.[55] This "something invisible" is the problem of invisibility itself, the way that the Line voids the land beneath it of its presence, power, and "whatever the Visto was suppos'd to deny,—the covetousness of all that liv'd . . . that continued to press in at either side, wishing simply to breach the long rectified Absence wherever it might,—to insist upon itself."[56] Pynchon uses the complex figure of a "long rectified Absence" to identify the Line as a project that does not just signify but terraforms invisibility into the earth's surface. Boundary cutting entails deforestation and habitat destruction, the imposition of a rectilinear shape—"the very shape of Contempt"—onto nonlinear terrain, all of which work to transform the vibrant, populous continent into *terra nullius*.[57] Simultaneously, agents of conquest must contend with the land, which probes for opportunities to "breach" the Line's integrity as a stable structure and "to insist upon itself."

No small part of the labor of the colonial transaction, then, is that of learning to drown out, ignore, and suppress the relational assertions of grounded normativity. Struggling against the terrestrial insistence on itself, Pynchon's colonial laborers need to work doubly hard to assure *themselves* of the Line's meaning and power, even as they give it physical form. It is almost as if the Line's earthy being is crying out, "Look at me! I'm hiding something!" and its surveyors must persist in conversing about its terrible powers in order to drown out this nonhuman appeal. The sense of hermeneutic anxiety plaguing the novel's surveyors is not only that of being too easily able to interpret the allegory that they are constructing; it indicates the greater fear that they themselves are becoming allegorical, transforming into the avatars of the monstrous white masculinity that supports the rise of capital as a sentient and sinister machine.[58] The "something invisible" that grows all around them generates what Timothy Melley designates, in relation to Pynchon's other novels, as "agency panic . . . intense anxiety about an apparent loss of autonomy or self-control—the conviction that one's actions are being controlled by someone else, that one has been 'constructed' by powerful external agents."[59] While Melley identifies the rise of post–World War techno-capitalism as the historical moment that produces Pynchonian agency panic, *Mason & Dixon* relocates the origins of this version of DeLillo's "white panic data" to what Yusoff calls the colonial-capitalist "*cut* of property" that redefines space along racial capitalist relations of production in the early eighteenth century.[60] Like the stories told about Mohawk skywalkers, the stories that the surveyors tell about the Line lend it a mythic power that does not actually exist in order to deny the right relations of existence prescribed by grounded normativity "that continued to press in at either side" of the Line's cut.[61] It is in the *"cut"* created by these material entanglements that the sense of lost agency Mason and Dixon intuit breeds invisibility for the colonized world and anxiety for the colonizer.

As Pynchon eschews rectilinear allegory in favor of tracking the messy sprawl of colonial power, his description of carving the Boundary Line becomes a deliberately Marxist account of how creating the racial capitalist means of production became central to colonial conquest. Dixon makes this point when he complains that the Line allows capital to sprawl across the continent, "of use at Trail's End only to those who would profit from the sale and division and resale of Lands. 'Guineas, Mason, Pistoles, and Spanish Dollars, splendorously Vomited from Pluto's own Gut! Without End! All generated from thah' one Line.'"[62] Through Dixon's identification of surveying as a labor that creates the spatial conditions for the coming global marketplace, Pynchon equates the colonial act of surveying with the capitalist act of value creation. In this colonial transaction, the construction of the Line absorbs labor and generates surplus value from the racialization of that labor, which also becomes the racialization of indigeneity both in terms of the construction of the first nations of Turtle Island as expropriable nonwhites, and, as I argue below, of whiteness that claims indigeneity through a fantasy of victimry.

Pynchon proposes that the mid-level physical labor of line cutting is integral to this transaction by beginning the novel with the infrastructural violence of enclosure as it erupts in Britain in the eighteenth century. The novel's narrator, Wicks Cherrycoke, tells the story of the Line from post–Revolutionary War Philadelphia. Cherrycoke is exiled from Britain for anonymous postering against the "Crimes" of "enclosures, evictions, Assize verdicts, Activities of the Military."[63] The dating of his exile, 1760, is the novel's real opening moment, a year also identified by historians as the beginning of enclosure's peak period in Britain.[64] Like a good proto-Marxist, Cherrycoke also connects enclosure to the "Activities of the Military" engaged in expropriating Indigenous populations on a global scale.[65] By beginning with enclosure, the novel explicitly links Enlightenment scientific rationalism to the physical labor of imperial warfare.[66] Cherrycoke reports first meeting Charles Mason and Jeremiah Dixon on the HMS *Seahorse,* which boarded in late 1760, commissioned to deliver the surveyors to the southwest coast of Sumatra, where they would observe the 1761 Transit of Venus. The *Seahorse* is a naval ship enlisted for recording the transit, a scientific enterprise thought at the time to be central to the "quest for longitude" so valuable to streamlining imperial trade routes.[67] This government-funded scientific endeavor's military-imperialist subtext is dramatized when a French frigate attacks the ship. The incident evokes the Transit, one of the first globally conceived scientific projects, as inextricably imbricated in the contexts of colonial warfare. As Jodi A. Byrd notes, "the paired transits of Venus across the sun . . . served in 1761 and again in 1769 as global moments that moved European conquest toward notions of imperialist planetarity. . . . At its center were discourses of savagery, Indianness, discovery, and mapping that served to survey a world into European possession."[68] Byrd's insight draws out the form of entanglement that *Mason & Dixon*'s opening evocation of enclosure tracks: the localized, muddy act of the property survey and the global, astronomical act of fixing longitudes engage in the same labor processes enacted at different scales. Imperialist planetarity's difficult-to-conceive scales—those of islands and continents and populations—take shape and force through surveying's small physical labors, which entail "Staring yourself Blind," as Dixon's mentor says derisively, "Chaining through the Glaur."[69] Colonial force enacts its terraforming agenda by pitting mid-level scientific laborers against mud.

Pynchon's destabilization of the Line's place in narrative allegory suggests that the problem with the Line's ontology is that it is discursively quite stiff as ballast for theories of meaning and power, but its real material operations are far murkier. In the novel, despite the Line's frequently cited power to divide populations and command social and environmental orders, the only thing that ever gets properly trapped on it is a chicken, "seemingly fallen into a Trance" at the center of the Visto.[70] The chicken spurs a lively discussion among the surveying party as to "History's assessment of the Good resulting from this Line, vis-à-vis the not-so-good."[71] The debate is paradigmatic of what I see as Pynchon's joke on himself here: why did the chicken cross the road? It didn't, and all else followed "unto War and Devastation."[72] The joke suggests that rather than looking to the chicken for the Line's good and bad effects, we might look to the rest of the material history that sprawls around the Line's discursively stable boundaries, demarcated here by the most generic American punchline. Pynchon maps an entire web of colonial transactions that spread out around the Line: Black and Indigenous slavery and Indigenous genocide; lead mines, coal mines, iron plantations, textile and powder mills; Newtonian physics to subdue "the Attraction of Mountains"; "the Flow of Water through Nature . . . re-shap'd to drive a Row of Looms."[73] These are the transactions that build colonial capitalism's ontology into the land. This is not an allegory.

The Ontology of White Male Victimry in *Mason & Dixon*

Mason and Dixon's sense that they are navigating a world to which they are growing increasingly blind tracks the novel's elegy to the loss of white male subject agency. The deeper the surveyors go into the labor of colonial terraforming, the fewer the agentic beings that are visible to them, and the more they are themselves compromised by these conditions. Despite readings of the novel that laud Pynchon's indictment of the colonial "history of ethnic cleansing," for Mason and Dixon, it is not the violence done to colonial capitalism's others that is at issue but rather how this violence contributes to compromising their own agentic force as ahistorical, universal (read: white male) subjects.[74] As they cut the Line into the land, the surveyors' refusal of grounded normativity limits what they understand about their physical environment. The Boundary Line's borders begin to define what exists—the types of identifiable and permissible modes of being-in-the-world—and Mason and Dixon struggle against a force they come to call "the Presence itself, unbounded"; "the great Ghost of the woods . . . whispering to them,— tho' Reason suggests the Wind,—'No . . . no more . . . no further.'"[75] This is a force they have encountered before, observing the Transit of Venus in South Africa, where the "Ghost of the woods" was "a Collective Ghost of more than household Scale," as Cherrycoke relates, "the Wrongs committed Daily against the Slaves, petty and grave ones alike, going unrecorded, charm'd invisible to history, invisible yet possessing Mass, and Velocity."[76] As the physical development of the line makes invisibility a material substance with mass and velocity, the novel narratively explores how racialization is transacted by colonial land development. Yusoff describes this transaction as a "pincer movement," whereby geologic dispossession "determined the geographies and genealogies of colonial extraction in a double sense: first in terms of settler colonialism and the *thirst* for land and minerals, and second, as a category of the inhuman that transformed persons into things."[77] As imperialism and then capitalism use scientific reasoning to justify the superiority of white European ethnicity and the subjugation of nonwhite bodies, this same reasoning rationalizes the construction of environments like the Boundary Line that clearly demarcate racial and ethnic belonging. As the land is terraformed into a host that will accept the privileged white body, that body must engage in the discursive labor of convincing itself that it belongs by becoming increasingly affronted by how threatened it feels.

The pincer movement of this material-discursive labor entails both planting the white body into the land and displacing/replacing Indigenous embodiment. That the pincer's claws are those of line cutting emerges in the novel as Indigenous bodies dissolve into an ostensibly inanimate world that is antithetically always about to spring to dangerous life. Mason and Dixon leave the Line only with trepidation: "The Forest life ever presenting Mystery to them,—too much going on, night and day, behind ev'ry Trunk, beneath ev'ry Bush,—how many new Pontiacks may even now be raising forces, planning assaults."[78] Their journeys off the Line and through the forest echo the adventures of Nathaniel Hawthorne's Young Goodman Brown, for whom knowledge of "evil purpose" makes the forest a space of well-populated isolation: "The gloomiest trees of the forest . . . barely stood aside to let the narrow path creep through," Brown thinks as he enters the forest,

> and there is this peculiarity in such a solitude, that the traveller knows not who may be concealed by the innumerable trunks and the thick boughs overhead; so that, with lonely footsteps, he may yet be passing through an unseen multitude.
> "There may be a devilish Indian behind every tree," said Goodman Brown to himself.[79]

Like Mason and Dixon, Hawthorne's puritans depend on the paths they follow in a way that generates its own terror of subhuman otherness.[80] Brown's Christian metaphysics, like the surveyors' scientific rationalism, is a closed system. Stepping outside of that system exposes the colonial subject to perpetual opposition from the ontological slippage between the human and nonhuman forces—in both cases, the trees that may or may not be (concealing) Indians—that these closed systems create in asserting their own ontological integrity. It is only within an ontology that clearly separates subjects from objects that a collapse of these categories can generate such terror. The "unseen multitude" "behind ev'ry Trunk, beneath ev'ry Bush" directs us to why the colonial capitalist project must be so committed to infrastructural development. The market demands it, yes, but so does the ontological order that can operate only where it is terraformed into the continent, giving the white settler room to breathe while partitioning and suppressing environmental totality and the grounded normativity it models as right relations of entanglement. Significantly, it is the slippage between the pincers of land development and the production of inhumanity that makes the material-semiotic entanglement experienced by Mason and Dixon so threatening. When the terrain is simultaneously *terra nullius* and terrifyingly well populated, a great deal of discursive work needs to be done to shore up the subject's integrity vis-à-vis the protesting physical environment.

As Indigenous bodies are made both part of the landscape and illegible as landscape, the terms for registering distinctions between humans and nonhumans also shift in ways that center the white settler body while limiting its capacity to engage with its physical environment. What is on display here is a broken internationalism, to recall Simpson's definition, within grounded normativity.[81] On their journey, the surveying team comes across a case of "Kastoranthropy," a man named Zepho Beck who turns into a werebeaver during the full moon.[82] Lee Rozelle groups Zepho's "liminal" state among the novel's many "hybrid" creatures embodying a positive environmentalist message. "Ecocritically," Rozelle asserts, "hybrid 'monsters' . . . such as werebeaver Zepho Beck signify a profound reunion with all life."[83] But the idealism informing this "profound reunion" overlooks the conditions of its possibility. The novel portrays Zepho as crazed and alienated, rejected by beaver and human society alike. From the local Indigenous population's perspective, this hybridity is a troubling mode of relationality that does not signal interconnection but a tortured meeting of species: "These Indians are certainly no strangers to the idea of a Giant Beaver," Cherrycoke narrates, "he is a protector, sustainer, worker of Miracles. Zepho during the Full Moon, however, is not exactly what they had in mind."[84] What Zepho becomes, as Cherrycoke suggests, is a tree-felling monster that evokes the story of the Great Beaver, Ktsi Amiskw. According to Lisa Brooks, the Haudenosaunee story of Ktsi Amiskw changes in response to colonial capitalism's entry into the continent. As beaver pelts become integral to trade in the Northeast, Ktsi Amiskw's story becomes about "the danger of acquisitiveness," Brooks writes. "The Great Beaver gets greedy and uses his talent for building dams to hoard water, and everyone . . . suffers the consequences of his desires."[85] In this story, the figure of the greedy beaver is a corollary to the fur trade's excessive and destructive effects.[86] Beaver dams in the context of an environmental totality are closely tied to the production of life, "work[ing] continuously with water and land and animal and plant nations and consent and diplomacy to create worlds," Simpson writes, "to create *shared* worlds."[87] However, the colonial Ktsi Amiskw demonstrates that given the wrong ontological framework—bad diplomatic relations among animal, plant, and water nations—the point where the human and the nonhuman are profoundly entangled tips into violence and ecological imbalance. For the white colonial subject, to be united with "all life" is to be caught up in that network of dangerous relations that Morton describes as "meaninglessness and disorienting openness."[88] Zepho is united with nature, not in the American tradition of the Transcendentalists but in that of the cosmic posthumanism that Matthew Taylor identifies in the work of Adam Smith and Edgar Allan Poe, in which to merge with the earth is a gothic nightmare of dissolution.[89]

The question of the ontological charges that can be laid against an already-embattled whiteness emerges here as preoccupying Pynchon's oeuvre even more than the rectilinear allegory. In the figure of Zepho as Ktsi Amiskw, it is possible to track the sleight of hand whereby the colonial laborer claims indigeneity (he is the beaver), consolidates indigeneity *as* privileged white male subjectivity (he is the world builder), and is victimized by this status (he has built a world in which he is made monstrous). As Mason and Dixon develop the colonial-capitalist means of production, and they lose sight of humanness proper, their agency panic intensifies.[90] It is in finally realizing that they are completely surrounded by an imperialist agenda "murdering and dispossessing thousands untallied" that the surveyors are able to turn their generalized anxiety into the pertinent question, which is, predictably, about their own ontological status. Dixon poses the question to Mason: given their participation in this regime of terror, "What may they be willing to do to huz?"[91] *Mason & Dixon* thus offers a starting point for what Achille Mbembe identifies as the contemporary relationship between "paranoia . . . becoming the dominant language of power" and "the familiar tropes of white victimhood" deployed by that language.[92] On Mason's deathbed, he experiences a terrifying vision of what he thinks of as "a great single Engine, the size of a Continent . . . some of it is still invisible" but "day by day . . . more points are being tied in."[93] As Mason contemplates the rise of this terrifying network of relationality, he imagines himself into the position of victim to this system in the sense that *he* has been made monstrous by its production. Whiteness grows to occupy all the space of the colonial-capitalist transaction, both its monstrous creator and its victim as it becomes something done "to huz." He wins his claim to indigeneity through terraforming racial violence into the continent with one pincer and with the other catastrophizing the loss of his own subject agency in the face of the dehumanizing order he himself has produced.

Many readers see in *Mason & Dixon*'s sentimental deathbed conclusion a turn present in Pynchon's later work—Schaub calls it "an affective note worthy of Frank Capra"—toward the nostalgic and utopian comforts of hearth and home.[94] Reading with the angry earth, in this case a suppressed and ignored angry earth, draws our attention to how this affective note indulges the victimry of white, male, colonial subject agency. Victimry is not something to be resisted in this context as it is in Vizenor's definition of Indigenous survivance. While the novel traces the Black and Indigenous laboring bodies that are dehumanized in this era of intense colonial development, Pynchon's narrative ultimately concludes by reiterating the tragedy of compromised white male subjectivity that has occupied the center of the novel's sympathies throughout. These final discomfiting moments are the only price that Pynchon's mid-level colonial laborers pay for their complicity in building the Engine, a sense of loss at white masculinity's potential made monstrous. This dual sense of loss and of monstrosity—he is both the one who names the Mohawk skywalker and laments his own feet of clay—expresses what Tuck and Yang define as one of those settler "moves to innocence" that mitigate "settler anxiety," and do so in this instance by indulging settler paranoia.[95] Mason's agency panic in the face of the colonial capitalist juggernaut tallies the colonial transaction whereby he is able to dis-implicate himself as a central agency in the juggernaut's realization and replot his position as his own victim, the white laborer whose indigeneity to the terraformed continent is conferred by his alienated labor now become the foundational site of racial capitalist partitioning. All other competing claims to territorial and human belonging will be processed through the burgeoning racial logic that casts the white settler as its first victim. To experience white settler paranoia, in this sense, is to earn one's place as the tortured werebeaver embedded in the shattered grounded normativity of the continent. His foreclaws dig into the terrestrial surface, producing land alienation and dehumanization, a poisoned network of relations among the continent's human and nonhuman nations. They are toxic, these networks, but they are his, and he will guard them jealously.

Diffusing Racial Allegory in *The Intuitionist*

Colson Whitehead's elevator novel moves the angry planet forward a century and a half to arrive at another of those historical "phase[s] of objectification . . . in which events and their functioning spin out of the control of human motivation and purpose" that Sylvia Wynter describes.[96] At the turn of the twentieth century, colonial development has terraformed the continent's most temperate bioregions from coast to coast, rendering it ideally hospitable to white, male, bourgeois human life and its victimry narratives, and partitioning the lives of people of color into the slums, ghettos, other-sides-of-tracks, Freedmen's towns, reservations, and borderlands that make up the archipelagic geography of the American Third World. In *The Intuitionist,* we see the spatial logic of the colonial-capitalist property line turned on its side in the vertical rise of the city to form what Rem Koolhaas calls "the skyward extrusion of the Grid itself . . . *a frontier in the sky.*"[97] The skyscraper city is the focus of *The Intuitionist*'s narrative ontology, and it acts as a kind of bookend with *Mason & Dixon*'s Line because, even as the rise of the skyscraper in the late nineteenth and early twentieth century signals what Henri Lefebvre calls "the spatial expression of potentially violent power," it is also "the great metropolitan destabilizer," in Koolhaas's words, "promis[ing] perpetual programmatic instability."[98] Koolhaas suggests that the skyscraper—like Pynchon's Line—moves further out of the control of its architects the more massive it grows, injecting instability into urban form even as that form seems most certain of consolidating its violent entanglements. While *Mason & Dixon* shows us the foundations of colonial terraforming, *The Intuitionist* gives us its airy reaches both in terms of height and of colonial fantasies of dominion over the physical environment. But where Pynchon sees the caul of colonial capitalism closing over the continent, Whitehead injects the presence of the angry planet into his narrative ontology to draw out the instability that Koolhaas identifies in the most seemingly dominant infrastructural forms.

Just as Pynchon has staged a confrontation with his own narrative investment in using linearity as shorthand for structures of oppressive power, in *The Intuitionist,* Whitehead confronts the presence of linearity, with all its malevolent metaphorical heft, in the history of Black modernist writing. W. E. B. DuBois's use of the term "the color line" at the First Pan-African Conference in 1900 launched a century in which the figure of the Line would define both patterns of segregation in the United States, and the movements of racialized bodies through narrative space. In Nella Larsen's 1929 novel, *Passing,* the urban trajectories of women of color lead inevitably to the punishment of even invisible racial identities; Clare Kendry quite literally plunges to her death out of an open window to mark the rectilinear end of a narrative trajectory in which she has tried to pass as white on the streets of New York. A similar Line structures Ann Petry's *The Street* (1946), in which Lutie Johnson's one-way train ticket out of Harlem at novel's end spatializes the impossibility of the modern Black woman making it in "a white world which thrust black people into a walled enclosure from which there was no escape."[99] The same Line determines the fate of Ralph Ellison's *Invisible Man* in 1952, who "shoots up from the South into the busy city" only to be boomeranged by history back down through an open manhole into the underground that he will not escape within the space of the novel.[100] From South to North, up to down, the colonial Line that produced knowledge about race through the partitioning of laboring bodies is imbued by the modernist imagination with inexorable logic, flinging, thrusting, and shooting Black Americans toward inescapable fates.

The above examples share a sense of the way the Line cuts: vertically and horizontally, as historical and narrative trajectory, and as infrastructural form and force, carving the spatial logic of racial capitalism into the terraformed continent. Jodi Melamed defines racial capitalism as "manufacturing densely connected social separateness" to profit from uneven distributions of power and resources that make structural inequalities appear fair and rational.[101] Racial capitalism's lines delineate zones of possibility and precarity in the rigid city and define what encounters will and will not occur on the crowded streets. But in all these cuts, as we saw in *Mason & Dixon,* there is slippage between the allegorical and the physical operations of linearity. Whitehead's novel asks how narrative and spatial possibilities are reconfigured by this slippage as skyscrapers begin to populate the eastern seaboard in the late nineteenth and early twentieth centuries, the same phase of modernity during which the color line takes on metaphorical heft.[102]

In *The Intuitionist*'s thinly veiled iteration of early twentieth-century New York, the powerful Department of Elevator Inspectors rules over vertical development. The department's administration conceals the ways in which its bureaucratic agendas, corporate interests, and ties to organized crime are entangled in the quest for profit and power. Still, cosmopolitan order prevails until an elevator crashes in a newly developed civic building, and authorities scramble for someone to blame. Lila Mae Watson, the city's first Black female elevator inspector and the last to give the insubordinate elevator a clean bill of health, needs to figure out whodunit before she takes the, *ahem,* fall. The elevator crash signals the slippery interplay between linearity's discursive and material functions in the modernist city. The machine's crash explodes the promises of smooth upward trajectory, the signifying relay connecting upward movement and success, and the associated discourse of racial uplift, all of which dissolve in the wake of the crash to reveal a city less under the control of colonial capitalism's spatial logic than it at first appears.

This reading diverges significantly from other approaches to *The Intuitionist* because I argue that while the novel unfolds as a search for the meaning of the crash, the key to Whitehead's narrative ontology is that the crash has no meaning, at least not in the sense of its being an act perpetrated by some faction within the city's matrix of power relations. Instead, the crash slowly unfolds as having been a true accident: not an ideologically coded event but a message from the angry planet. And yet the novel is not read in these terms. *The Intuitionist* is instead vaunted for its allegorical dimensions, its elevator a fit vehicle for considering the rhetoric of racial uplift. Critics consistently evoke Walter Kirn's assertion that the novel is "the freshest racial allegory since Ralph Ellison's *Invisible Man* and Toni Morrison's *The Bluest Eye*."[103] Ramón Saldívar writes that the novel "imagines a new trajectory for narrative beyond the temporal imperative of the x-axis to something else—the finite-state verticality of UP/DOWN in the spatial dimension of the y-axis—figuring with it the brilliantly quirky conception of imperiled elevation as 'the boldest [*sic*] new racial allegory since Ralph Ellison's *Invisible Man* and Toni Morrison's *The Bluest Eye*.'"[104] Lauren Berlant reads Whitehead's elevator crash as symbolizing "the machinery of white supremacy at the heart not only of politics, corporate ideology, and the modernist city but . . . of its very engineering."[105] These readings are consonant with theorizations of upward trajectories as signifying modernity's promises, such as Jameson's "Hotel Bonaventure" reading, in which the elevator epitomizes postmodern spatial logic: "a transportation machine which becomes the allegorical signifier of that older promenade we are no longer allowed to conduct our own."[106] The skyscraper itself, Gordon Teskey argues, becomes a signal, uniquely American allegory for "the temporal narrative of human progress from Earth-bound primitivism to the highest stage of civilization, which touches the sky with its buildings."[107] In these examples, a linear trajectory is never quite itself. Instead, it is always obfuscating (while standing in for) a totalizing and no doubt sinister social-spatial order; the skyscraper and its elevators are vessels of material-semiotic entanglement in which each reinforces the other, vehicle and allegory in perfect alignment. But as the following pages suggest, it is not the totality but rather the instability of these entanglements that preoccupies *The Intuitionist*. In the American Third World, spatial disenfranchisement is the proving ground for revolution.

It is less obvious here than in *Mason & Dixon* that one of the novel's agendas is to expose its setting—in this case the modernist city—as an ongoing site of colonial-cum-racial capitalist violence. *The Intuitionist* is filled, however, with suggestions that the city as a material structure is built upon another world, which appears in this novel not as land, proper, but nonetheless as the ongoing domain of grounded normativity: an agentic and assertive material reality insisting upon itself against the idea of land that serves colonial authority. To dissect this fantasy of spatial control, and anticipating the spatial politics of Whitehead's *The*

Underground Railroad, the novel offers readers a history of the sky-scraper's, and particularly the elevator's, American origins in the context of how these infrastructures extend colonial allegories of westward expansion and progress into the vertical register. The first safety elevator, the novel tells us, was designed by Elisha Otis and unveiled at the 1853 World's Fair in New York. In its version of this origin story, *The Intuitionist* emphasizes that urban "verticality" was introduced alongside the spoils of colonial conquest, both entangled by the same complex of signification. Teskey notes that global expositions like the World's Fair were prime sites for the display of colonial allegories. Juxtaposing the wonders of the "primitive" world with the objects of Western scientific innovation and progress confirmed the colonial-capitalist state's inherent right to dominance. At Whitehead's World's Fair, "a stuffed Apache. Crimson fruit from Amazon vines and brown slivers of llama meat" are on display alongside Otis's elevator, which in turn appears alongside the American technologies of land theft: "reaping machines and threshers, still and elegant, like lithe animals stooping to lick moisture. The Bowie knives weep in the sunlight."[108] The full colonial-capitalist transaction is on display here, in which the wealth of the colonial peripheries—contained in the Indigenous bodies on display as literal commodities like the "stuffed Apache"—are exchanged for the steering light of reason that the imperial center offers, represented in all its implicit violence by Whitehead's catalog of licking, weeping machines.

This display of colonial curiosities takes place, moreover, in the Crystal Palace built for the occasion, which the novel frames as a "monstrous edifice . . . a replica of its namesake in London . . . Before they invented verticality, that was all there was to aspire to, glass and steel confection delivered by spyglass from overseas."[109] In the same breath, the novel points out that "to the west of the Crystal Palace is the fetid Croton reservoir; east is Sixth Avenue, a gargoyle of carriages and hooves."[110] In this passage, the repugnantly horizontal city not only houses the objects of conquest but is itself such an object, imported from an imperial motherland it pretends not to mimic while grasping after its palaces, frescoed temples (the Croton reservoir referenced a "truncated Egyptian pyramid"), and gothic architectural pretensions.[111] The Crystal Palace itself, however—its transparent plate glass structure a heavy-handed simile for the clarity and illumination that British (and now American)

Empire brings to the world's exotic peripheries—is an allegory that self-destructs. "The Crystal Palace will fall five years later in 1858," Lila Mae relates, "devoured by fire in fifteen minutes."[112] In this history, a building that functions as a figure for colonial-capitalist hegemony is burned to the ground. The symbolic light of reason fails to stand up to material contingency, which should convey important information to city planners about urban infrastructure's unstable ontological status. Instead, the Crystal Palace site becomes Times Square, itself a symbolic epicenter for a new phase of empire that will grow vertically rather than horizontally. As in other historical moments of urban infrastructural disaster, like the 1871 Great Chicago Fire, development does not slow its pace in response to disaster, instead redoubling its efforts.[113]

In the move from the horizontal city of carriages and World's Fairs to the city of skyscrapers, the force of colonial allegory proves difficult to immolate. As in the figure of the Mohawk skywalker, "the vertigo at the heart of urban modernity and the ephemerality ascribed to Indigenous peoples" map easily on to the vertical grid.[114] Colonial infrastructural logic is reproduced in the skyscraper's ambitious form, which recasts the colonial allegory of conquest into the postcolonial allegory of freedom without altering the fundamental structural operations of racial capitalism in the American city. This reading is consonant with Adrienne Brown's study of Black modernist authors, including Du Bois and Wallace Thurman, whose work explores the skyscraper's promise as a conduit to new modes of urban mobility.[115] For these authors, Brown writes, "The skyscraper serves as an instrumental site of rupture, cutting through the old, static horizontal infrastructure mired in patterns of segregation and colonialism, and offering a potential alternative to the spatial, and thus social status quo."[116] In the Black modernist imaginary that Brown traces, the skyscraper reverses the Line's doomed allegorical trajectory with vertical development that models different modes of social being and spatial belonging. But this potential never materializes, and instead reaffirms, as Brown argues, "the structure's singularly white ontology."[117] Another leap in technology, still mired in the colonial logic of the Line, does not ultimately translate into more equitable modes of being human.

Conversely, Whitehead's novel suggests that moments of intense technological progress become opportunities to simultaneously consolidate colonial-capitalist wealth while relegating colonial history to the status of metaphor. Brown's diagnosis of the skyscraper's "white ontology" is initially confirmed in *The Intuitionist* by the city's newest municipal building. In an attempt to manage an "increasingly vocal colored population," the building is named after Fanny Briggs, a slave inaugurated into official history—"the newer encyclopedias"—for teaching herself how to read.[118] In this municipal spirit, which favors a symbolic mode of reparation over economic and spatial redress, care of the building's elevators is given to Lila Mae.[119] A Black female elevator inspector paired with the building's conciliatory honorific symbolizes racial uplift and "distract[s] from the minuscule and cramped philosophy of what would transpire on the floors above."[120] Like the Crystal Palace, which contained empire's brutal history within a glass structure of clarity and light, Fanny Briggs's outward allegorical performance of social equality and the promise of upward mobility remains unrealized in its interior spaces.

In fact, the Fanny Briggs Building lobby confirms the skyscraper's role in the attempt to discursively frame colonial history as an allegory rather than an ongoing material condition. The massive lobby contains an unfinished mural of "cheerless Indians holding up a deerskin in front of a fire. . . . Two beaming Indians trading beads to a gang of white men . . . the first of many dubious transactions in the city's history. . . . The mural jumped to the Revolution then . . . skipped over a lot of stuff."[121] This mural is a textbook colonial allegory in which, Teskey writes, "All the happy bodies we see feel as if they are imprisoned. Such representations of the body are often governed by what . . . I called *capture* . . . Allegorical capture gives us the sense that a living body . . . has been confined to an alien structure of meaning, one in which the human person has been reduced to performing the function of a sign in a system of signs."[122] In the Fanny Briggs mural, capture can be traced through the movement from the "cheerless Indians" of the precontact moment, to the "beaming Indians" selling the island of Manhattan for a handful of shells. The full violence of the allegorical function, for which Teskey argues, materializes as the "Indians" in this scene personify the successful colonial capitalist transaction. Indigenous bodies are used to symbolically bolster colonial authority to the degree that they cease to produce meaning about human and environmental history.

Simultaneously, the "jump . . . to the Revolution" that "skipped over a lot of stuff" references the convolutions of history required to produce colonialism as a metaphor for American development. While the Indigenous body remains, in the Fanny Briggs lobby, a robust allegorical vehicle for colonial capitalism's development-as-progress narrative, the absent referent of slavery suggests that we are at a moment in history when Black slavery has become an unstable vehicle for celebrating such development. The Fanny Briggs Memorial Building itself operates as the new allegory for the history of slavery, which is now no longer contained by personification but by an abstract architectural form that signifies freedom and racial uplift relayed through the name of "a slave who taught herself how to read." By rendering slavery as isomorphic with emancipation, and emancipation as symbolized by vertical development, the history of slavery is absorbed into the broader American narrative of postcolonial self-actualization. The allegorical mural skips over slavery because the building itself is intended to reconstitute the allegory, to make it part of the story of a postcolonial nation that has freed itself from its colonial past through revolution. Much as the white settler is able to claim indigeneity through the successful colonial transaction that concludes with the Indigenous body disappearing into the landscape, slavery's history is recast as the history of freedom from enslavement in order to ballast that American narrative of postcolonial freedom and co-opt revolutionary Blackness into supporting Indigenous erasure. The symbolic work being done by the Fanny Briggs Building is thus part of what Jodi Byrd describes as "processes through which liberalism asserts freedom and forgets enslavement as the condition of possibility for what constitutes 'the human.'"[123] This conflation works to render illegible the colonial conditions that shape comparative racialization in the twentieth century: Indigenous claims to land and self-determination become increasingly difficult to assert in a nationalist narrative that conflates freedom from empire and freedom from slavery, thus rendering challenges to state power and property as implicitly anti-Black.

Antiracist Infrastructures in *The Intuitionist*

After establishing the slippage between infrastructural verticality and colonial allegories for progress, *The Intuitionist* asks if progress might instead look like an explosion. Just a few short years before 9/11 makes the enthusiasm for urban chaos taboo, the 1999 novel explores the potential generativity of a disaster that does not update a new set of allegorical operations but instead prompts "a renegotiation of our relationship to objects."[124] Martin Kevorkian compares *The Intuitionist*'s call for such a renegotiation to Latour's project, which "sets aside the subject-object pair in favor of a collective constituted on the relations of humans and nonhumans."[125] To take such a collective's political potential seriously requires embracing the idea that the physical environment does not conform to the colonial state's violent imposition of meaning and instead occasionally breaks out of this entanglement. Leanne Simpson suggests that one such breakout moment can come through rejecting the "artificial colonial division" between Indigenous land and (implicitly non-Indigenous) cities.[126] While Simpson is writing in terms of how this spatial division polices Indigenous mobility, in *The Intuitionist,* rejecting rural-urban divisions also makes it possible to see the force of grounded normativity in and through urban infrastructure in ways that can create spaces from which to resist anti-Blackness. When Whitehead's elevator enacts a breakout from the colonial relationship to objects, it allows him to write against the grain of the Black modernist literary tradition that makes the city's racializing social order one "from which there was no escape."[127] *The Intuitionist* posits instead that the modern city is precisely the place where colonial state power and its racial capitalist economy begin to fall apart.

By reframing urban modernity's vertical trajectory as potentially explosive rather than controlled and linear, Whitehead recasts the conditions of possibility determining the movements and futures accessible to Lila Mae as she moves through the city. In this sense, the novel is a kind of narrative of Black survivance not unlike Vizenor's definition of Indigenous survivance as "an active resistance and repudiation of dominance, obtrusive themes of tragedy, nihilism, and victimry."[128] While in Pynchon's novel, Mason and Dixon's scientific labor constrains their agency and mobility, Lila Mae's technological labor as an Intuitionist elevator inspector in a world dominated by Empiricist elevator inspectors opens up new possibilities for Black female agency and presence in the city. Intuitionists feel (rather than look) for mechanical problems in elevators. This approach challenges the Empiricists, who "stoop to check for tell-tale striations in the lift winch and seize upon oxidation scars on the compensating rope sheave."[129] An instance of the "onto-logical face-off" that Alexander Weheliye describes structuring relations between white colonial subjectivity and Black subjectivity, the Empiricist approach is obsessed with surfaces.[130] Within this terraformed surface world, there is no escape for Lila Mae from a "white people's reality . . . built on what things appear to be."[131] Intuitionists, conversely, work with the world that exists beneath the "skin of things" and thus express a professional desire to reconnect with an ontological order that is "post-rational, innate. Human," in short, what this project designates as the grounded normativity of the angry planet.[132] The oppositional ontol-ogy that Lila Mae represents through her labor asserts itself in the novel when Elevator Eleven in the Fanny Briggs Memorial Building crashes spectacularly. Through this disastrous event, an unruly material world that challenges subject-object boundaries bursts onto the scene.[133] When objects move in unexpected ways, as does Elevator Eleven, they send a message, Lila Mae thinks, "instructing the dull and plodding citizens of modernity that there is a power beyond rationality."[134] This power is the angry planet reasserting itself through the city's dense and contingent material infrastructures, a reassertion that in turn enables Lila Mae to disrupt the conditions of her own objectification.

In its focus on urban infrastructure, Whitehead's narrative ontology suggests the element of contingency, or what Vine Deloria Jr. calls "per-sonality" as a quality of grounded normativity that can emerge through city spaces. Deloria asserts that in many Indigenous ontologies, aware-ness and acceptance of change is gained through careful observation of the physical environment's "personality."[135] Wildcat interprets Deloria's concept of personality in terms of understanding concrete space as "the site where dynamic processes of interaction occur—where processes be-tween other living beings or other-than-human persons occur . . . Change is understood in a nonmechanistic relational- and process-dependent manner, with processes understood as changes in spatial relations and constellations of power."[136] While change is not the only facet of personal-ity, it encourages an understanding of physical environments as the loci of transformations that cannot be developed out of existence. This principle of grounded normativity thus anticipates a contiguity between aleatory materialism (an early iteration of new materialism) and an antiracist materialism rooted in asserting Black technological agency. Aleatory materialism, defined in the late work of Louis Althusser and in the revolutionary theory of Antonio Negri, approaches the city's density and complexity as the locus of a revolutionary potential that might emerge from the physical environment's "personality." "Disequilibrium and rupture," Negri writes, is "multiplied on the indefinite space of the metropolis . . . this is also where the multiplication of obstacles, borders, lines of fracture and walls can no longer be regarded as simply blocks dropped down by power or as swamps that one gets stuck in: they are interfaces that polarize relations."[137] These polarizing interfaces are produced by what Negri calls "the explosion of the aleatory," in which chance collisions among the city's objects—buildings, technologies, people—might produce conditions materially vulnerable to revolutionary change.[138]

As in Leslie Marmon Silko's *Almanac of the Dead* and Héctor Tobar's *The Tattooed Soldier,* which are the focus of a later chapter, *The Intuitionist* frames the city's potential for revolutionary change specifically in terms of an antiracist materialism that refuses to understand the physical environment as a servant to racial capitalism's social order. As Rayvon Fouché suggests in his investigation of techno-spatial innovators from Imamu Amiri Baraka to Grandmaster Flash, "Technology as material oppression is not the only way to consider African American technological experiences. As interesting as this mode of analysis can be for thinking about the technological control of African Americans, it strips Black people of technological agency."[139] To instead engage what Fouché calls "the ambivalence of artifacts" is to take seriously the technological object's "personality" as in excess of its creator's will and its concomitant openness to transformation and unofficial uses. This engagement links Whitehead's protagonist, Lila Mae, to a branch of the Black radical tradition that generates subversive modes of mobility and agency by repurposing architecture and technology.[140] By drawing out Black radical materialism's aleatory valences, Whitehead plots a modernist city in which the "catastrophic accident" that rationalist order "cannot account for" is privileged as a powerful locus of agency and revolutionary possibility.[141]

Without attending to the ontological face-off unfolding in *The Intuitionist,* it is easy to misrecognize the elevator crash as an allegory for racial uplift's failures. Lila Mae herself falls into this pattern of thinking.

She finds out that the elevator she just inspected went into "total free-fall," which is, she thinks, "a physical impossibility."[142] "The accident is impossible," she conjectures, and therefore, "it wasn't an accident."[143] The fall of Elevator Eleven is hypothetically coded and recoded by the novel's actors as the product of a variety of ideological contests. Lila Mae's supporters and detractors first posit the crash as a subversive political tactic arranged from within the struggle for control ongoing between the Elevator Guild's Empiricist and Intuitionist factions. When this theory loses popularity, suspicion moves on to interpreting the crash as the product of racially motivated and class-obsessed infighting among struggling Black urban professionals, a paradigm which leads Lila Mae to suspect Pompey—the city's first Black elevator inspector—of being so "eager . . . for a piece of the dream that [he] would do anything for massa," including sabotage her career.[144] However, this theory also falters once it becomes clear that it is reasoning along too-obvious ideological routes. The crash is then hypothesized as a strategic move orchestrated by Arbo and United, the elevator cartels that emerge as the secret engines behind the novel's superficial politicking: "Who's the better man—Intuitionism or Empiricism? No one really gives a crap about that. Arbo and United are the guys who make the things. That's what really matters."[145] Under these infrastructural conditions, elevators crash when humans tell them to crash. The city bends to serve its masters, and it does not really matter which of these theories turns out to be correct. No matter what a Black, female, Intuitionist elevator inspector accomplishes in this reality, she cannot escape "the machinery of white supremacy" that grinds away "at the heart," in Berlant's terms, of civic and social order.[146]

But the crash does not ultimately reveal, as Berlant suggests, "a secretly racialized map of twentieth-century capitalism, seen as a utopian technology gone haywire."[147] Rather, the crash reveals that what Lila Mae has never doubted is an *overtly* racist cityscape is in fact supported by "nothing," and a nothing, the novel argues, that is "telling the truth."[148] Near the end of *The Intuitionist,* Lila Mae exposes the true cause of the elevator accident as this "nothing. No telltale incision scar on an innocent inch of coaxial cable, no wires corkscrewing off the famously dependable antilocks. Nothing at all."[149] The truth of the accident is that there is no ideology or metaphysics entangled in the Fanny Briggs

Building's structural bones. The Pynchonian iteration of material conditions in which history is a whodunit search for which version of the white supremacist capitalist patriarchy is really running the show emerges as an assertion predicated on a belief in the stability and rationality of urban order. A fundamental ontological instability reveals itself instead: "The elevator pretended to be what it was not."[150] Lila Mae realizes that the unit somehow faked being a properly functioning piece of Arbo equipment, and this capacity for personality is a "message," from a place "without meaning."[151] As in the introduction's reading of Linda Hogan's *Solar Storms,* this place that sends messages "without meaning," or, at least, a "meaning not known to us" is the angry planet.[152] But what appears as anger here is more properly that quality of contingency within grounded normativity that reaches out through the caul of colonial terraforming, and reads like anger because it interferes violently with the mechanistic pretensions of racial capitalist order.

In one sense, this message from the unknowable tells us that there is precisely nothing to be learned about race in America from a catastrophic elevator crash. Rather than a fresh new allegory, Whitehead de-metaphorizes urban infrastructure to make the point that an elevator's motion does not symbolize or confirm a particular narrative trajectory dependent on one's race, class, gender, and location in history. Simultaneously, however, the novel's ontological proposition is that there *is* a message in this absence of meaning. The elevator's refusal to follow its path is also a refusal to conform to the allegory of freedom north of the Mason-Dixon Line and racial uplift performed by the Fanny Briggs Building. Locating new galaxies of meaning in the sudden absence of material-semiotic entanglement, Lila Mae realizes that the paranoiac practice of choosing between competing ideologically driven conspiracy theories is itself a concession to racial capitalist logic and the linear thinking that this logic naturalizes. The violence of such thinking, as *The Intuitionist* makes clear, is not only that it is inimical to change but that it points to material conditions as proof that change is not about to come. In urban race narratives that end in a reaffirmation of the allegorical and material entanglements produced by the color line, real political agency—real visibility and mobility for the Black female body—is always too risky and too unrealistic to be a narrative possibility. Conversely, a narrative in which the angry planet asserts its personality and ties that personality to a universe of meaning that has yet to be ontologically colonized by "Man," offers its Black female protagonist access to forms of bodily mobility and technological agency with revolutionary potential.

Revolutionary Agencies in *The Intuitionist*

By developing a narrative ontology in which the elevator crash is indeed caused by "nothing"—by that powerful agentic force exuded by the angry planet—Whitehead is able to repopulate his version of the modernist city with different conditions of possibility. *The Intuitionist* rewrites the narrative trajectories of Black urban modernity in much the same way that *Mason & Dixon* rewrites Pynchon's own allegories of linear oppression. However, while Pynchon's revision tracks the constitution of white male settler victimry as a way of claiming indigeneity, Whitehead's focus on Lila Mae's mobility rejects the emphasis on victimry that can come to overdetermine Black subject agency when narrating the afterlives of slavery. Drawing on an urban grounded normativity—what the city tells her, not what people say—Lila Mae is able to see herself as a mobile agent of that collectivity made up of all the humans and nonhumans invisible to those who are "slaves to what they could see."[153] From the novel's first pages Lila Mae is a revolutionary agent operating at the centers of social order. And unlike Mason and Dixon, who are cowed by the proliferative invisibilities that surround them, Lila Mae operates within colonial-capitalist infrastructure with an eye to destruction.

The Intuitionist models a kind of Black iteration of survivance in that it positions its protagonist as the inheritor of urban space. If "survivance means the right of succession or reversion of an estate, and in that sense," Vizenor writes, "the estate of native survivancy," then Whitehead imagines the white property wealth built on the legacy of slavery reverting to the estate of Black survivancy, a reversal of the colonial-capitalist transaction rooted in plantation slavery.[154] Lila Mae arrives in the city as an émigré from the American Third World, known in the early decades of the twentieth century as the Jim Crow South. She grew up in "colored town," while her father went to work as an elevator operator at a whites-only department store, and even her training as an elevator inspector takes place under segregated housing that forces her to sleep in a converted janitor's closet.[155] In some ways, then, her education allows her to leave the Third World behind, but Lila Mae brings with her a Third World revolutionary consciousness with which she works for the city and, also, *on* the city. Even before the elevator crash teaches Lila Mae to see herself as an agent of social-spatial transformation, she learns to work with the object world around her. Through Lila Mae's commitment to elevator inspection, Whitehead offers readers a narrative about a Black woman who is not forced into the labor of caring for white architecture. Rather, Lila Mae chooses her labor with the belief that she can play a role in reshaping the city. She approaches her profession with a battle tactician's strategic mind. Getting dressed in the morning, she thinks of herself as getting "armed"; mapping out her day entails "drawing plans for war."[156] Her body, like her living space, is ascetic. Corporate thugs who raid her apartment find "few possessions . . . the impression instead is that of slow moving-out, piece by piece."[157] She doesn't spend unnecessarily on clothes or food; instead, she chews tinned meat standing at her kitchen counter, going over strategy: "What's left of the animal when you have ground it up: a few stubborn pieces," she thinks, imagining herself as tough-to-remove gristle in the gleaming white teeth of the city: "She will not be so easily dislodged."[158] A soldier on a mission, Lila Mae carefully controls her object world because she sees its contingency too well. She uses her position's instability as a way station—precarious, certainly—but en route to a different future, "a slow moving-out" from one ontological order to the next.

Whitehead's attention to the physicality of Lila Mae's moving-out process emphasizes, as do Black studies scholars like Wynter and Weheliye, that race is made an ontological fact through the construction of physical environments that enforce and police "densely connected social separateness."[159] As Lila Mae gets to know the city, she learns from urban grounded normativity, her classroom being "long hours on trudging marches between the buildings."[160] These walks familiarize her with the terrain and the "anonymity" she can experience there. Nadine M. Knight reads these marches as Lila Mae's imprisonment. "She is entirely confined within the city," Knight writes, "forced to move covertly on its more marginal areas but never truly escaping."[161] This reading misses that Lila Mae does not want to escape the city. In the style of the Third World revolutionary, she wants to take it over. Her walks are about learning its shapes and how to align herself with them; her marginal position is tactical, a deliberate alignment with the city's object world. As Whitehead writes, "Her position is precarious everywhere she goes in this city . . . but she's trained dread to keep invisible in its ubiquity, like fire hydrants and gum trod into black sidewalk spackle."[162] The comparison evokes objectification and marginalization, but it also suggests a more complex set of relations between the human body and its object world. As a body that refuses to be processed on racial capitalism's terms, there is an affinity between Lila Mae and the city's everyday objects. These objects are urban algorithms, not unlike the "profoundly anticapitalist" moss algorithm that Leanne Simpson describes, offering Lila Mae cues for how to navigate the space around her.[163] Gum and fire hydrants are "invisible," but they also flag urban disorder's "ubiquity." The need for a fire hydrant on every corner identifies the persistent threat of fire that haunts the city's dense architecture.[164] The gum spackling the sidewalk evokes the endless tiny gestures made by individual subjects that mark the planned and ordered routes authorized for city travelers. Disaster's dramatic arcs as well as everyday motions signal to Lila Mae that movement through the city is punctuated by both risk and pliability. The Third World as a zone of possibility is here, too, and not left behind or delimited by colonially instituted geographic divisions of Southern-ness or ruralness. She remains entangled by the racialized division of labor but awaits that moment of urban disorder that will come like a call to action.

After the accident's message reveals itself as just such a call, Lila Mae ups her tactical game, becoming an infrastructural redesigner who develops modes of movement and trajectory for nonhuman objects that break linear boundaries: "the shining city" of the future that she imagines "will possess untold arms and a thousand eyes, mutability itself, constructed of yet-unconjured plastics. It will float, fly, fall, have no need of steel armature, have a liquid spine, no spine at all."[165] Just as Elevator Eleven breaks with its predetermined trajectory, the elevator of the future will break with trajectory thinking and its appeals to that "promenade we are no longer allowed to conduct on our own."[166] Revising urban infrastructure, Lila Mae positions herself not as the marginalized opponent of an ontologically fragile, unstable capitalist reality but as the inheritor of its full implications: radical contingency, heterogeneous mobility, a city where "all the people are gone," she thinks.[167] Rather than fighting colonial capitalist ontology's racializing function, struggling to be interpellated into the world of the human, Lila Mae imagines a future where the privileged humans currently gathered under the ontological category of "Man" will have to seek inclusion in a democratic field now populated by all the nonhumans and one-time subhumans that its hegemony is predicated on denying. In some ways, Lila Mae's vision is an Afrofuturist echo of George Manuel's description of the Fourth World as one "that reconstructs a tradition in which people can hold a common belief, and which uses all the benefits of a global technology" without "a belief in racial supremacy."[168] In a world where belief in human-nonhuman collectivity, rather than racial supremacy, structures material relations that develop out of subversive Afro and Indigenous futurist reconceptualizations of technology, "Man" and the racializing belief systems that consolidate its hegemony become the outsiders.

In the closing scene of the novel, Lila Mae "thinks about the accident and its message. Much of what happened would have happened anyway, but it warms her to know that the perfect elevator reached out to her and told her she was of its world. That she was a citizen of the city to come."[169] The accident's no-meaning message hails the Black female subject from the outer space that orbits beyond colonial capitalism's despotic linear infrastructures. The hailing of the human by the non-human—Althusserian interpellation turned on its head—destabilizes the line that defines fields of racial belonging and of subject-object binarism. Introduced to the ubiquity of nonhuman actors—the fire hydrant and sidewalk that assisted her as she "trained dread"; "traffic lights, the quintessential civil servants"; and, of course, the "elevator-citizen"—Lila Mae is inaugurated into a form of citizenship in which the agency of the citizen-subject does not require acknowledgment or authorization by institutional power.[170] Rather, she learns to deploy her own creative technological agency, becoming *of* the city without being subject to its ontologically dehumanized order. *The Intuitionist* proposes that to ontologize the human requires the resurgence of an ontological order in which race does not function as either a real or a realized category. The object's ontological status is crucial in this sense because how colonial capitalism instrumentalizes and exploits the object world is irreducibly entangled with its construction of the human subject, "Man," through the tactical exclusion of its racialized others. If nonhuman agency is made invisible, and the human body racialized through similar processes of violent exploitation and exclusion, then the way to ontologize humanity may be through the "renegotiation of our relationship to objects" that the novel proposes.

When Lila Mae begins to study the elevator crash, she uncovers an ontic instability that does not open on to the wilderness of capitalist terrors experienced by Pynchon's Mason and Dixon but rather onto a social protest staged by an infrastructural personality whose failure makes a statement about its own refusal to operate as a statement. This protest advocates for a revolutionary politics derived from the planet's own strategies for structuring relationality, and as such, precludes race as an ontologically real category. Significantly, this nonhuman social protest doesn't remind us that buildings are people, too. Rather, it reminds us that there is a quality to urban infrastructure that is a material register apart from the social structures that seem to define it. Whitehead's explosion of the figure of the line thus works in opposition to Pynchon's. While *Mason & Dixon* destabilizes linearity's power in order to reveal an entire world being devoured by colonial capitalism, *The Intuitionist*'s linear destabilizations reveal a rebellious world that can never be fully devoured, suppressed, or disappeared by colonial-capitalist terraforming. By effectively dehumanizing infrastructure, *The Intuitionist* claims the human as an ontological category that arrives when we begin to imagine futures beyond the growth of colonial capitalism.

The narrative ontology developed by Pynchon and Whitehead politicizes the work of ontological description, demonstrating that no physical environment is neutral, and narrates the rise of a specifically colonial-capitalist ontology as it is terraformed into the North American continent. Each novel presents the history of colonial development as a violence that produces racial difference and enforces the material investment of laboring bodies in (variously) maintaining or enforcing this difference. Thus, while *Mason & Dixon* and *The Intuitionist* make the argument that colonial capitalist terraforming may require the labor of material destruction to disentangle, they also suggest that this destruction defines a barrier to decolonial futurity consisting of the very racial cuts that are produced by the foundational ontological transaction of coloniality. For the white settler, already "disturbed by her own settler

status," decolonization requires taking a kind of responsibility that victimry narratives of a capitalist machine that wounds us all equally do
not prepare her to take on.[171] This is the relational responsibility man-
dated by grounded normativity—a close cousin to Vizenor's concept of
"natural reason"—in which "original, communal responsibility, greater
than the individual" creates no space for "nihility or victimry."[172] The
difficulty of rejecting white settler victimry narratives, particularly in
the context of possibilities for white allyship, generates those barriers to
decolonization that are not solely matters of understanding but of material conditions. Do these conditions make functional allyship impossible?
As Tuck and Yang assert, when we make the question of decolonization
one that places demands on all the subjects of colonial modernity, the
answers "may feel very unfriendly."[173] This is perhaps the case particularly as we move out of the realm of metaphor and into the material
stakes of the decolonial mandate. Narrative ontologies that explore just
how deep that "cut of property" Yusoff describes goes in the production of racial difference also point to why political imaginaries invested
in global visions of decolonial solidarity might turn to the agency of
the angry planet as a powerful cop-out. A belief in planetary agency can
become a way to step outside of history and the burden of colonial
responsibility. In this sense, planetary ecological disaster is like alien
invasion; it creates the conditions of possibility for a united front that
erases human history in the footprint of a more expansive planetary and
interplanetary "species-inclusive" historicity.[174] If, following Pynchon's
worst fears, the entanglements of race and space are too implanted in
the surface of the earth to be disentangled by human agency, then the
promise of an angry earth stepping in to assert its priority becomes
an ontological escape hatch: decolonization by environmental attrition.
These novels of "phases of objectification" in American history demonstrate how well the angry planet fiction of second chances and fresh
starts maps onto colonial narratives of New World redemption. In this
narrative, whenever the inheritance of possible futures is on the line, the
house wins. The angry planet, which promises to force the renegotiation of our relationship to objects, manages to shore up the settler desire
to be exculpated of all complicity. In a wave of destruction, the planet
generates the conditions of *terra nullius* that invite us to start the colonial transaction all over again.

2

FIRST WORLD PROBLEMS
JOHN EDGAR WIDEMAN'S
PHILADELPHIA FIRE AND KAREN TEI
YAMASHITA'S *TROPIC OF ORANGE*

IN 1986, one year after the city of Philadelphia bombed the rowhouse headquarters of the Black radical MOVE organization in the neighborhood of Cobb's Creek, director Louis Massiah and writer Toni Cade Bambara released the documentary *The Bombing of Osage Avenue*. The documentary is unique among visual records of the bombing because of its strategic narrative engagement with Cobb's Creek as "a wildlife preserve" and as a historical site of colonial violence. Bambara's narration of the documentary begins by linking these registers of exploitation: "The original people who blessed the land were the Lenni-Lenape or the Delawares, eldest nation of the Algonquin Confederacy. They called the area Karakung, 'place of the wild geese.' They called it home. Others would come to rename it . . . Cobb's Creek, would claim it with their guns and their plows and their dreams. Africans came, too, captive, but with dreams of their own."[1] Bambara's approach to the bombing forcibly reminds viewers of the histories of ecological domination and settler-colonial violence that shape Philadelphia. Her juxtaposition of "renam[ing]" and "claim[ing]" with guns and plows evokes the violent physical process of imposing the colonial idea of land on the continent and defamiliarizes the city by representing it as a form of infrastructural violence done to the land with which it remains, in the last decades of the twentieth century, at war.

Through her attention to the transformation of Cobb's Creek, Bambara emphasizes that colonial development defines the foundations of Philadelphia's urban order. Like many of the waterways and tributaries that flow from the Delaware River, Cobb's Creek was being terraformed by the agricultural and industrial agendas of Swedish, Dutch, and English settlers as early as 1634.[2] The twinned technologies of colonial settlement—population control ("their guns") and resource exploitation ("their plows")—drove the Lenape out of the area and policed the first Black Philadelphians brought to the East Coast by Dutch slavers. By the twentieth century, the Delaware watershed itself was forced, quite literally, underground, "incorporated into the city's 3000 mile sewer system."[3] Although this is a legacy of erasure, the scenes of the documentary that accompany Bambara's words—images of rustling foliage, flowing water, songbirds, and playing children—index the tenacity of hydrological systems and, as Bambara puts it, "the relation of a people to a place" that persist through the entangled histories of racial and ecological violence.[4] By making this link, Bambara also references MOVE's radicalism, which was rooted in a back-to-nature ethos focused on "stopping man's system from imposing on life . . . stop[ping] industry from poisoning the air, the water, the soil . . . put[ting] an end to enslavement of life—people, animals, any form of life."[5] The group's philosophy aligned with the Black radical intellectual tradition that, Camille Dungy writes, "investigate[s] the alignment between man and nature" even as that same nature is "steeped in a legacy of violence, forced labor, torture, and death."[6] Drawing attention to MOVE's tenacious refusal to be alienated by their physical environment, Bambara's approach to the MOVE bombing connects the processes of colonial violence and ecological exploitation, while also insisting on the irrepressible existence of the people and ecologies that these violent processes fail to erase entirely. Bambara's documentary stresses that it is this very refusal to be erased—and to erase their own relationship to the land and to its colonial history—that made MOVE such a threatening presence in mid-1980s Philadelphia.

This threat—of the presence of radical people-of-color organizing years after the civil rights era; of the potential for urban uprising—points to the deeply ambivalent relationship between American imperialist claims to the global superiority of First World liberal democracy and the presence of Third World struggles taking place at the heart of empire's urban citadels. In the civil rights era, as the introduction to *Angry Planet* elucidates, the concept of an American Third World evoked both uneven U.S. geographical development *and* the potential for anticolonial resistance emerging from the spatially disenfranchised populations inhabiting these zones. U.S. Third World social movements, like the Black Panthers and MOVE, provocatively and controversially framed their disenfranchisement in terms of what Cynthia A. Young describes as "the discourse of internal colonization" in which communities of color, often in urban contexts, were rhetorically positioned as colonized nations.[7] For some race-radical groups that advocated separatism, the Third World demand for sovereignty resonated more strongly than the emerging state accommodation strategies of social justice. Although these communities were non-Indigenous, their attempts to transform American Third World conditions through creating spaces—suburban properties, stretches of freeway—of economic and cultural autonomy align with that desire for sovereignty that is, in Indigenous struggle, so closely tied to questions of land use.

It is this desire for an autonomous relationship with the physical environment that emerges in the following chapter when Black and multicultural communities attempt to make claims to land and sovereignty that act much like the claims made by Indigenous groups. Tracking what angry planet fiction thinks of as the land-based processes of racial formation at work in such a context adds to what Jodi Byrd describes as "our understandings of how U.S. colonial policies targeting indigenous nations inform the assumptions of multicultural liberal democracy that now exemplify current U.S. preoccupations with race and diaspora and serve to deterritorialize indigenous prior claims."[8] In rejecting colonial state power and capitalist land exploitation through a Third World liberation framework, radical organizations like MOVE map social justice claims onto the framework of Indigenous land claims, "deterritorializ[ing] indigenous prior claims." However, the assimilation of these claims in multicultural contexts also exposes the colonial logic that defines the boundaries to liberal democracy in a settler state as being that of land use and property development. This chapter thus tracks where decolonial politics both meet across differing communities of interest and become impossible: when social justice claims ground themselves in a land-based decolonial mandate, they encounter the limit of the state's tolerance for dissent as a limit that develops out of the history of the settler state's relationship with its first nations. This in turn directs us to why Indigenous land claims are repeatedly defused in negotiation with the state into the dematerialized politics of recognition. What citizenship and democratic participation look and act like within the settler-state framework can be transformed; land use and development, on the other hand, are not up for negotiation. Claiming space from the settler state and attempting to reorganize land use in that space is the ultimate provocation to state violence.

When poor communities of color align themselves with the angry planet to disrupt urban space, the conditions of possibility for Third World hot zones erupt in the midst of First World power. Taiaiake Alfred suggests that "the state is determined to eliminate the intellectual threat posed by the idea of a politics beyond state sovereignty, and to that end is prepared to use terror."[9] While Alfred's focus is Indigenous sovereignty, his assertion holds true for many racialized communities in the American Third World that reject the givenness of urban order and acknowledge the ontological priority of the earth—what this project follows Glen Sean Coulthard in describing as grounded normativity. John Edgar Wideman's *Philadelphia Fire* (1990), about the 1985 MOVE bombing, and Karen Tei Yamashita's *Tropic of Orange* (1997), which imagines a similar eruption of direct state violence unfolding in 1990s Los Angeles, narrate precisely the deployment of terror Alfred describes as the response to Indigenous land claims. These novels represent U.S. cities as sites where global modernity forms a thin pretext for the conditions of ongoing colonial warfare that shape the city.[10] Both novels begin with the violence of racial and environmental entanglement that we saw being terraformed into the continent in *Mason & Dixon* and *The Intuitionist,* but each narrative's ontological force comes from describing how the angry planet, suppressed beneath the city, and its angry people, coloniality's racialized others, withdraw from these entanglements. When MOVE breaks up a concrete sidewalk to free the land underneath, or a homeless community occupies a freeway and makes its presence at the city center visible and undeniable, the angry land and the angry people work together to withdraw from colonial-capitalist spatial order. In doing so, they expose the smooth surfaces of global modernity as built on "a

colonial anti-black world . . . in which the non-ethics of war gradu-
ally becomes a constitutive part of an alleged normal world."[11] Both
Wideman and Yamashita identify the state's deployment of direct violence against its cities as a response to this refusal to play along with the
U.S. settler state's version of democratic order.

This chapter uses the term "withdrawal" in two senses. The first
is in the ontological sense proposed by Graham Harman who cribs the
term from Heidegger to refer to the ways in which the physical world
upsets, overturns, and troubles human systems of meaning-making. Harman's is "a strange world of autonomous, subterranean objects, receding
from all relations, always having an existence that perception or sheer
causation can never adequately measure."[12] In this ontological register,
the physical environments in *Philadelphia Fire* and *Tropic of Orange*
withdraw from relation to the colonial-capitalist state. Of particular
relevance to this definition of withdrawal is each author's description
of elemental forces—earth, air, fire, and water—that disentangle themselves from civic infrastructure. But withdrawal from specific sets of
relations—as opposed to "all relations"—is not quite what Harman
means, which evokes the second, more properly politicized sense in
which this chapter uses withdrawal. In *Philadelphia Fire* and *Tropic of
Orange,* withdrawing from the entanglements of colonial-capitalist state
power is also tactical in the sense suggested by William Melvin Kelley's
1962 novel, *A Different Drummer.* In Kelley's novel, the Black population of a small Southern town enacts a "STRATEGIC WITHDRAWAL"
from the environmental conditions of slavery that continue to structure
the postbellum South.[13] This second sense of withdrawal develops the
political valences of Harman's ontological drift to suggest that withdrawal from one ontological order can evoke the presence of other possible orders of being. Alfred also uses this sense of withdrawal to describe
the reconstruction of understandings of political and economic power
that need to occur in order for Indigenous communities to "negotiate a
withdrawal from the colonial relationship."[14] Withdrawal, as an onto-
political act, thus works to open up new spaces in which to rearticulate
power relations.

Withdrawal is modeled by the earth, angry planet fiction argues,
when an earthquake or flood disturbs the caul of colonial terraforming
across the continental surface. When these terrestrial motions interfere

with the operation of the colonial-capitalist state, they disturb its sense of ontological integrity and antecedently, political order, directing the planet's angry people to the ways in which withdrawing from bad relations can challenge state power. In *Philadelphia Fire* and *Tropic of Orange,* this politicized iteration of ontological withdrawal is effected, somewhat counterintuitively, through the material excesses that the angry planet and the angry people produce. The natural environment pushes its presence on the city in and through a destabilization of civic infrastructure, and the urban populations of the American Third World make their presence *too* felt, and *too* public in the heart of the city. This excessive material being makes up what Jodi Melamed designates as "threatening empirical surpluses."[15] These surpluses make the violence of racialization and environmental exploitation visible and unignorable in the First World city, and this shared visibility demystifies the objectifications of human life and of land that are coproduced in the management of colonial-capitalist state infrastructure. Intrusive material surpluses dredge up histories not easily repressed and realities not seamlessly managed by what Min Hyoung Song calls the 1990s "compensatory narratives" of official state multiculturalism and antiracism.[16] There is, then, an implicitly decolonial and antiracist component to ontological withdrawal in these novels. Wideman and Yamashita give narrative force to Melamed's definition of an antiracist materialism in which "multicultural terms of representation cannot seal off empirical complexity, the real histories of material violence, fragments of materiality, and empirically real experiences, all of which challenge, in their very existence, the forces that run the world."[17] Melamed describes the excesses produced by withdrawal as a political-ontological act. The angry people do not get up and leave town, as they do in Kelley's *A Different Drummer.* Instead, they—along with the angry planet—interfere with the strategies of neoliberal (read: neocolonial) urbanism that tolerate cultural difference only to the degree that it stimulates capital growth. As in Nancy Tuana's description of how Hurricane Katrina's "devastation gave witness to poverty and lingering racism, and to the power of ignorance," the excessive bodies and elemental forces in *Philadelphia Fire* and *Tropic of Orange* act as witnesses forcing the city to acknowledge its own underlying conditions of colonial violence.[18]

The decolonial ontology that I identify working across these novels builds on the materialist analyses literary scholars highlight in Wideman's and Yamashita's work. *Philadelphia Fire,* published in 1990 and looking back to the mid-1980s, attends, as do novels like Bambara's *Those Bones Are Not My Child* (1999), Ernesto Quiñonez's *Bodega Dreams* (2000), and Helena María Viramontes's *Their Dogs Came with Them* (2007), to the decades of the late twentieth century during which neoliberal policies were first being rolled out in U.S. cities and on the global stage.[19] James Kyung-Jin Lee and Madhu Dubey describe Wideman's attention to how the era's "rhetoric of growth (focused on downtown areas) and the rhetoric of crisis (focused on the 'underclass') seem to run along separate and parallel tracks, disabling recognition of how redevelopment policies themselves have contributed to urban immiseration."[20] In Lee's argument, these parallel processes directly foster intensified race-based inequality shaped in terms of "differential racialization," whereby "the political economy of 1980s Philadelphia produced . . . increasingly visible economic heterogeneity within Black communities."[21] *In Philadelphia Fire,* for the city's elite proselytizing uplift, and for its first Black mayor, W. Wilson Goode, MOVE activists "were embarrassing . . . mocking everything [Goode] was promising."[22] "Our work is to confront this system upfront," writes a group of incarcerated MOVE women, "to show people not only that they can fight this system and win, but to show them the urgent need to fight."[23] By refusing to allow the mechanics of differential racialization to take place invisibly, MOVE became a threatening surplus population that brought the city's social and spatial inequalities into stark relief.

Tropic of Orange was published in 1997 when cynicism regarding the promises of neoliberal multiculturalism at home and economic globalization abroad was at an all-time high. Yamashita's second novel, as Byrd suggests, is usually "discussed within a U.S. context [where] the emphasis is on the ethnic postmodern" or "placed into conversation with globalization" where the emphasis is on "the economic and the diasporic, the nation and the postnation."[24] Conversely, readings like Byrd's attend to neoliberalism's material shapes as they turn zones of racialized marginality like those of borderlands and internment camps into Agambenian states of exception, and extend the scope of Manifest

Destiny "within the larger forces of imperialism that attempt to continually consolidate U.S. control over Indian lands."[25] For Sarah D. Wald,
Yamashita's use of the freeway system is particularly germane to this
context of containment and control, "suggestive of the socioeconomic
mobility denied so many Angelenos despite the rhetoric of mobility and
freedom surrounding neoliberal globalization and free trade."[26] Similarly, Sherryl Vint writes that in *Tropic of Orange,* "freeways dominate
people, leading to a situation that is the literal embodiment of the alienation Marx describes in which the products of human labor return to us
as if from outside and dominate us."[27] These readings, like Dubey's and
Lee's, focus on how neoliberalism as a global phenomenon takes shape
in U.S. cities through the persistent dispossession of historically disenfranchised communities, which maintain the palimpsestic spatial status
of threatening Third World hot zone *and* Indigenous internment camp,
both, in the post–Cold War zenith of American exceptionalism.

My reading adds to these accounts a sense of how each novel
refuses the closure of this historical moment by shaping its narrative
around the motion of the angry planet, which ripples back from urban
order as if an ebb tide were expressing its disgust with the shoreline.
In Wideman's narrative ontology, we can see the presence of the Black
radical tradition's indebtedness to African animist epistemes, found in
the work of authors from Zora Neale Hurston to Toni Morrison, in
which the earth writhes in response to the violation of Black bodies and
communities. In *Tropic of Orange,* the planet comes alive to interfere
with the integrity of geopolitical borders, evoking the sense of an ani-
mated earth articulated by Gloria Anzaldúa's borderlands consciousness, which stresses the decolonial potential of "rooting ourselves in the
mythological soil and soul of this continent . . . to succor it [and] to be
nurtured by it."[28] In both novels, these approaches constitute a politicized ontological argument dedicated to shifting the terms of who and
what are legible as political actors on the stage of street-level geopolitical
conflict.

Colonial Violence in the Neoliberal City

Tropic of Orange and *Philadelphia Fire* pivot around moments of direct
state violence in which local government deploys military force against

the city. Wideman's novel concentrates on the MOVE bombing, a historical incident in which an armed standoff between the Black radical group MOVE and the Philadelphia Police Department leads to the PPD borrowing a state helicopter to drop FBI-supplied explosives on a rowhouse in Cobb's Creek, killing eleven people. *Philadelphia Fire* begins as Cudjoe, a Philadelphia writer who has been living in self-imposed exile on a Greek island, returns home, driven by the need to tell the story of the bombing. Cudjoe is a former Black Power radical who has embraced the capitalist comforts of the emergent Black professional class and sees his own failures to stay true to the revolution refracted back at him through the MOVE tragedy. As he researches the incident, Cudjoe uncovers a city whose order and politics of Black respectability conceal undercurrents of extreme poverty, brutal gentrification, environmental racism, and the systemic evisceration of the gains of the civil rights movement. In Philadelphia, these gains are reduced to "slogans and T-shirts and funny haircuts"—the trappings of official multiculturalism—while "they snatched back the car keys, the house keys," leaving the structural conditions of colonial-capitalist economic and juridical power intact.[29] What the bombing leaves behind, the novel slowly reveals, is a city that is still burning and one that can no longer conceal the neocolonial violence underpinning its appearance of First World democracy.[30]

In *Tropic of Orange,* direct state violence is the response to a coalitional rebellion staged by the Third World inhabitants of Los Angeles, and an angry planet that is on the move. Telling the story of seven days following the summer solstice, *Tropic of Orange* centers on a cast of ethnically and economically diverse characters who are by turns united and pulled apart as the Tropic of Cancer and the sun become locked together in the moment of Earth's maximum axial tilt. With the sun burning directly overhead, the Tropic begins to heave itself through terrestrial space, dragging the entire Global South north across the Mexico–U.S. border. As time and space are stretched by a summer solstice that will not end, the city's largest and most unpredictable structure, its freeway system, begins to interfere with the mobility of its privileged citizens, while offering new opportunities for mobility to spatially and economically disenfranchised residents. A massive pileup on the Harbor Freeway at Los Angeles's downtown interchange leads to the displacement of a homeless community that moves to occupy the snarl of vehicles abandoned at the crash site. Meanwhile, the Global South arrives in Los Angeles, anticipating a championship fight between two wrestling combatants known as *El Gran Mojado* (the great wetback) and SUPERNAFTA. Unable to manage the crowds seething around its blocked downtown interchange, the city's traffic system goes into total gridlock, and the state, at the limit of its tolerance for dissent, descends on the rebellious freeway community with tanks and helicopters.

Readings of the direct state violence in *Philadelphia Fire* and *Tropic of Orange* contextualize it within the 1980s and 1990s "international restructuring of industrial economy" in which "the problem of 'urban decay' cannot be understood in 'strictly American' terms."[31] Dubey argues that the shape of the neoliberalizing American city can best be understood "within a global economic order."[32] Conversely, to read with the motion of the seething North American continent stresses each novel's evocation of the profoundly colonial U.S. context in which this violence unfolds. *Philadelphia Fire* pulls Cold War–era neoimperial warfare off the global stage and forces it into U.S. city centers. In a metafictional break with his narrator, Cudjoe, Wideman and his wife watch coverage of the MOVE bombing on TV. When the images first appear onscreen, they are generalized, "burn[ing] on the screen. Any large city. Anywhere in America."[33] But no, the viewer thinks, not America. "It must be happening in another country. A war. A bombing raid. We're watching a Third World shantytown where there's no water, no machines to extinguish a fire."[34] Wideman's evocation of colonial violence forces the narrative from "Third World shantytown" back to a Philadelphia that is itself partitioned down First and Third World lines. Wideman and his wife are made to witness a terrible reality. "Philadelphia," the realization comes, and then again, offset in its own paragraph, "Philadelphia," and again, as a new paragraph, "West Philly. Osage Avenue."[35] The viewers are forced into awareness of the global contexts of Cold War hot zones and the unfinished histories of colonization that are not Third World imports but rather grown at home in the heart of U.S. cities.[36]

In *Tropic of Orange*'s final cataclysmic confrontation on Los Angeles's Harbor Freeway, a city as far away from colonial Philadelphia as is possible in the continental U.S. experiences another explosion of state violence. While *Tropic of Orange*'s confrontation is fiction, it is written in the shadow of the 1992 Los Angeles Riots, which Yamashita invokes in terms of a colonial administration at war against its subjugated population. "The most militaristic of nations looked down as it had in the past on tiny islands and puny countries the size of San Bernardino and descended in a single storm."[37] Those unfortunate enough to be trapped on the occupied freeway are slaughtered by "the coordinated might of the Army, Navy, Air Force, Marines, the Coast and National Guards, federal, state, and local police forces."[38] This litany of law enforcement organizations would border on the absurd if it did not find so much real precedent in incidents like the MOVE bombing in which racially motivated federal policy allowed for the integration of military and civilian policing. The scene recalls Los Angeles's long history of violent reprisals against citizen uprisings, from the 1965 Watts rebellion, to the 1970 Chicano Moratorium march, to the 1992 Los Angeles Riots. As historians of paramilitary violence suggest, the militarization of U.S. police forces occurred specifically in response to the Third World liberation movements of the 1960s and 1970s, and blossomed in the 1980s with the formally race-neutral War on Drugs helmed by the Reagan administration.[39] Yamashita's description of the massacre is banal and horrific: "The motley community of homeless and helpful and well-intentioned ran in terror, surrendered, vomited, cradled the dying."[40] The force of this scene lies in its insistence on the irreducible presence of colonial violence firmly at home in U.S. metropolitan centers. The helicopters strafing the freeway with automatic gunfire confirm "the utterly violent assumption underlying everything: that the homeless were expendable, that citizens had a right to protect their property with firearms."[41] Property ownership confers citizenship in juxtaposition to a condition of dispossession that confirms its opposite: not only an absence of citizenship but what Sylvia Wynter calls an institutionally defined "*Lack* of the human, the Conceptual Other to being North American," which identifies the occupation of the freeway by people experiencing homelessness as the proper target of state violence.[42]

By deliberately identifying their settings as terrains of colonial warfare, both novels carve out the historical and political conditions of Indigenous genocide that naturalize the U.S. city's militarization against its Third World archipelagoes. These settings suggest that cities struggling with the physical presence of political violence directed against communities of color are not the sites of make-live-and-let-die biopolitics, but rather, of what Achille Mbembe characterizes as the necropolitical order of a "sovereignty whose central project is . . . *the generalized instrumentalization of human existence and the material destruction of human bodies and populations.*"[43] Mbembe's emphasis on the necropolitical rather than the biopolitical links the reproduction of a necessarily brutal colonially terraformed order to the maintenance of the late twentieth-century neoliberal state's tenuous, constantly contested grasp on ontological authority. Rather than positing a Foucauldian social order managed by relays of power operating on all scales, from the infrastructural to the biological, these novels envision an order held in place by undercurrents of systemic violence always standing by to enforce colonial-capitalist property relations. Drawing out the shared material precarity of humans and nonhumans under these conditions allows these narratives to identify U.S. cities as sites of ongoing colonial occupation.

But Wideman and Yamashita do not stop at this analogy. Next, each novel asks what it is, specifically, about these already-precarious populations that presents such a threat to state power. Both authors propose that when the city's angry people form alliances with the ecological forces suppressed and instrumentalized within urban space, they become not only capital's surplus population but also a presence in the city that is, as Melamed puts it, a threatening ontological surplus. As they withdraw their support from a state formation that renders their existence illegible, the people and the planet become excessively present in the city. Marisol de la Cadena calls this "'unblinding' that spot [from which reality is enacted]" and thus offering "the possibility of questioning the ontological composition of modern politics."[44] When the city goes up in flames or into total gridlock, it is exposed, like *Mason & Dixon*'s Boundary Line and *The Intuitionist*'s crashing elevator, as a built environment that is not identical to itself, not the perfect expression of colonial administrative will but a terrain that is alive with other agencies and energies suppressed but not destroyed by colonial land use. In this way, both novels make the provocative suggestion that a U.S. city will bomb itself not only because that is how it has managed its dispossessed populations throughout its colonial history but because it perceives, rumbling within the Third World enclaves it created, a threat to its ontological order.

The Withdrawing World

As we saw in chapter 1 of *Angry Planet,* ontological entanglement does not just happen. There are material histories to how people, things, structures, and concepts become entangled and to the stability and durability of those entanglements. When entanglements do not evince the purity of physics, it becomes possible to track the political and material histories of ontological withdrawal, and why particular entanglements fail to hold or remain stable. In their study of road building in the Peruvian Andes, Penny Harvey and Hannah Knox describe how mineral aggregate from the mountainous terrain between Brazil and Peru is "mobilised and shifted, analysed and altered, manipulated and moved to turn crumbling tracks into an asphalted highway," which makes the highway itself the product of unstable entanglements among humans, technologies, soil, air, and spiritual beings.[45] Speaking from the knowledge that Indigenous stakeholders in this development share with them, Harvey and Knox stress that "the work to classify and separate land off as a substance whose autochthonous powers derive from its universal and inanimate properties, does not ultimately remove the ghosts from the soil."[46] Their argument draws out the inherent ontological instability of what Bruno Latour calls nature-culture hybrids, in which nature—in this case the former mountain terrain now synthesized into the highway construction project—persists in agitating against its new status as acculturated material. When the highway crumbles or disappears beneath a landslide, we can see the mountain withdrawing from its relationship to the highway construct. Marisol de la Cadena makes a similar point in her influential study of the relationship between Andean Quechua peasants and the mountains or "earth-beings" that the Quechua engage as agentic spiritual and political entities: "These entities forced the former president (against his will) to slow down the development of corporate mining in Peru."[47] From Cadena's position, however, earth-beings are in shifting, contingent, but permanent (as in *a*historical) relation with human life.[48] In the formulation that Harvey and Knox propose, conversely, rock and soil are haunted and therefore historied and historical; it is their histories of movement that model the capacity to withdraw relationality with human agendas. Latour's "Great Divide" of nature and culture *and* nature-culture hybridity appears as two polar but related moments of false security that allow the structural engineer to proceed with the fantasy of control over unruly terrestrial materials.

Four thousand miles north of the Andes, Wideman taps into a very similar sense of the planet's surface, trapped beneath but always about to burst asunder the infrastructural bones of the city, through his representation of MOVE, the Black radical organization whose immo-lation haunts *Philadelphia Fire.* In the 1970s and 1980s, MOVE led what might be called a lifestyle of strategic withdrawal. The organization believed that it was possible to disentangle human bodies and the natu-ral world from the material conditions that overdetermine social belong-ing and to access a reality expressed by the angry planet buried beneath the city. A letter from imprisoned MOVE members reads, in part, "As long as the city exists, to move to the country would be to divert from the problem and not to correct it."[49] Withdrawal, for MOVE, does not entail abandoning centers of colonial-capitalist power but rather carving out space in these centers for other ways of being-in-the-world. MOVE practiced a confrontationally back-to-nature lifestyle in the Philadelphia neighborhoods of Cobb's Creek and Powelton Village. Archival video shows properties filled with rescue animals, as well as the rats and insects that fed on the compost heaps in the backyards. "To us rats were just animals trying to survive like anything else," explains MOVE member Sharon Sims Cox, "Because life is important to us we didn't want to starve them."[50] In 1978, persistent complaints about the odor, noise, appear-ance, and function of the MOVE house in Powelton Village escalated into an armed standoff with police that ended in the death of an officer. This event led to nine MOVE members sentenced to life in prison.

Seven years later, another series of conflicts with neighbors and repeated violations of civic ordinances culminated in an attempt to forcibly evict MOVE from their rowhouse at 6221 Osage Avenue in Cobb's Creek. Frustrated by MOVE's heavy fortifications, on May 13, 1985, the city of Philadelphia bombed one of its own neighborhoods, dropping two pounds of water gel explosives onto a structure built on the rooftop of the MOVE rowhouse. Having failed to evict MOVE members with deluge guns, tear gas, smoke grenades, and over ten thou-sand rounds of fired ammunition, the city of Philadelphia's police com-missioner and fire commissioner, with the approval of Mayor W. Wilson Goode, allowed the fire created by the bombing to burn unchecked for an hour and six minutes. By the time the city decided to use the deluge guns already on scene to put out the fire, it was too late to stop its spread. The conflagration killed six adults and five children trapped inside the house, burned down sixty-five adjacent homes, and displaced over 250 neighborhood residents.

To research MOVE, as Wideman did, in the interest of writing about the bombing, is to identify the group as emerging conspicuously out of the urban landscape, deliberately challenging the limits of the state's tolerance for dissent. Approaching the houses they occupied as unceded territory in a sea of colonial-capitalist occupation, MOVE transformed those buildings to align them with an ontology that placed human bodies and the natural environment in a shared state of siege in U.S. cities. As neighbors complained and standoffs with police over zoning violations escalated, MOVE houses became compounds with high fences obstructing back lanes. Pictures and video show boarded-up windows, dismantled sidewalks, and surveillance platforms extending out from patios. At the rowhouse on Osage Avenue, the complex of bunkers that would be the target of the city's bombing looms over the edge of the rooftop. "Don't attempt to enter MOVE headquarters or harm MOVE people unless you want an international incident," warns a letter written to police by MOVE.[51] In their investigation of the events leading up to the bombing, Hizkias Assefa and Paul Wahrhaftig confirm that the conflict between MOVE and the city was so difficult to resolve because it was understood by many of the participants as a standoff between antithetical orders of knowledge, "a dispute between a rational party and an irrational party," framed in terms of "an international conflict."[52] Members sought to position their space in the city as sovereign territory and to isolate their borders against the onslaught of civic and corporate developmental pressures.

MOVE did not acknowledge the metaphysics of juridical process and strove to bring human life into sync with the reality dictated by the natural world and "natural law."[53] MOVE's philosophy dared to be radically egalitarian, as this quote from founder John Africa suggests: "All living beings, things that move, are equally important, whether they are human beings, dogs, birds, fish, trees, ants, weeds, rivers, wind or rain."[54] What MOVE demanded was a reexamination of what constitutes the nature of reality: "We refuse to compromise our belief because we know and can prove our belief is right," MOVE literature asserts.[55] In response, MOVE's ontological challenge was processed by the state as a foreign invasion, their presence in the city impossible to overlook or tolerate into nonexistence with political agendas preaching multicultural benevolence. By coding MOVE's ontological argument as a foreign threat to national stability, the city enforced the neoliberal multicultural era's strategic displacement of nonhegemonic truth claims into the register of identity politics. In this ideological sense, both parties agreed that they occupied separate territories. In a more physical, visceral sense, however, MOVE's existence jutted out into city space and into national time. The civil rights era had filled Philadelphia with Third World revolutionary collectives like the Black Panther Party. But as this political energy was suppressed by the conservatism of Frank Rizzo's 1970s and Ronald Reagan's 1980s, MOVE persisted. The organization became the awkward guest at the "celebration of the new Black middle class": less interested in demanding the right to representation than in seizing control of and transforming the basic material conditions under which this celebration was allowed to unfold.[56]

As a movement that saw itself dealing with questions ontologically prior to those of cultural identity, MOVE's influence can be seen in *Philadelphia Fire*'s preoccupation with aligning dispossessed humans and the angry planet together against the city. This coeval struggle emerges starkly in the novel's evocation of alienated youth taking over the city in the wake of the MOVE bombing. Wideman describes Philadelphia's Black children, disfranchised by age, poverty, and race, as part of "the cityscape nobody ever sees . . . unnoticed. Like dead trees, dead rivers, poisonous air, dying blocks of stone."[57] To these kids, the MOVE bombing is another manifestation of the gentrification processes leaving the city pockmarked with empty lots and the racially motivated civic neglect that keeps their neighborhoods decaying, polluted, and underserved. The civic erasure of their presence begs the question as to whether gentrification can be understood as a neocolonial reoccupation of space. As in *Tropic of Orange,* the city is explicitly framed as a site of colonial warfare, and the kids are ready to fight, "taking over downtown . . . you the blade, they the grass . . . swoop in like Apaches, like Vietcong."[58] In their identification with the colonial others of Third World hot zones, Philadelphia's children align themselves with the angry planet as their ally in the struggle against material conditions of systemic dispossession. They are not only "Apaches . . . Vietcong" but "the blade" to the grass of civic order, reversing the dynamics of subjugation by putting that order in the position of the controlled natural environment and casting their own bodies as the tools of violent social transformation.

Rather than eschewing colonial metaphorics, Wideman bends the relationship between tenor and vehicle to catachrestic breaking point, drawing out the profound ambivalence involved in turning the racial capitalist language of Black dehumanization against itself. Envisioning urban decay and environmental ruin as allies that teach dispossessed youth how to instrumentalize and even weaponize their own bodies, *Philadelphia Fire* also takes aim at one of the oldest tropes of colonial-capitalist logic: the use of the subject-object binary to dehumanize non-white bodies and to position Black bodies as always, in Camille Dungy's words, "accidentally or invisibly or dangerously or temporarily or inappropriately on/in the landscape."[59] *Philadelphia Fire* suggests—echoing Lucille Clifton's poetic claim, "what wants to be tree, / ought to be he can be it"—that decolonial action entails wresting control of the *thinking* of material conditions away from the purview of subject-object rationalism.[60] Children's bodies are not only blades and dead trees in *Philadelphia Fire*'s decolonial narrative, they are "a new crop . . . come up like grass," pushing toward the light from "under the sidewalk."[61] They are "tapped early and instead of oozing off the corners of the map . . . the geyser of their talent and potential explodes."[62] Wideman frames young Black bodies as moving freely through unrestricted registers of metaphoricity, upsetting associations of the objectified Black body as a unit of property or exploitable commodity. While MOVE itself rejected cities and technology outright, the ripple effect of their presence (and destruction) on the shape of the city suggests that the potential to glean knowledge about being-in-the-world from the earth, and to enter into diplomatic relations with nonhuman life, is not restricted to a privileged engagement with pristine natural environments.

In *Tropic of Orange,* the L.A. freeway system is a powerful representation of the politically and historically specific brand of nature-culture hybridity imposed by colonial-capitalist state power. Mbembe writes that colonial occupation "consists in seizing, delimiting, and asserting control over a physical geographical area—of writing on the ground a new set of social and spatial relations."[63] In these terms, freeway historian Eric Avila suggests, the development of the U.S. freeway system in the 1950s and 1960s, hailed as a triumph of good government, was a kind of study in internal neocolonial occupation. Freeway development projects in the United States, and Los Angeles, in particular, historically eviscerated "black commercial districts, Mexican barrios . . . Chinatowns and . . . land sacred to indigenous peoples."[64] In Yamashita's novel, Buzzworm, a resident of South Los Angeles (formerly and famously South-Central), supports this analysis when he refers to the freeway as "a giant bridge" that drivers can use to "just skip out over his house, his streets, his part of town."[65] Thinking of the freeway as a bridge, Buzzworm evokes its history and its purpose: to link white suburban enclaves to urban business centers by building over low-income urban neighborhoods, which are usually communities of color. The connected processes of white flight and the gentrification of city centers are the urban manifestations of the colonial-capitalist guise of neoliberal economic globalization that begins to take hold at street level as well as on a global scale in the 1970s.[66] These are the historically specific, racially coded entanglements of freeway infrastructure.

However, like Harvey and Knox, Yamashita also questions the freeway's status as colonial capitalism's evil avatar. Inspired by Octavia Butler's spatial poetics of the postapocalyptic freeway in the Parable series, which she quotes in one of her novel's epigraphs, Yamashita represents a freeway system whose status as a colonial object is challenged by the "complexity of layers . . . prehistoric . . . historic . . . natural and manmade . . . dynamic and stagnant" that make up its physical being.[67] These layers, rather than consolidating the force of the freeway, render it ideologically and physically unstable as a material expression of good relations between state power and transportation infrastructure. Mineral aggregate of stone, gravel, and sand makes up over 90 percent of the materials used to construct the National Highway network. "The vast system of roads and highways in the United States" is designed, in the words of U.S. Geological Surveyor Daniel E. Sullivan, to "provide a critical service to the country's economy and people" which includes "limited access" (for vehicles, not human bodies) and "a design to accommodate vehicle speeds of 50 to 70 miles per hour."[68] As Sullivan's catalog of this seemingly innocuous data suggests, infrastructure has particular historical, political, cultural, and affective valences associated with it that determine which bodies can access it, and how they are allowed to move upon its surfaces. But Yamashita's point is that the mineral aggregate that shapes the freeway is ontologically indifferent to these valences. Mineral aggregate does not become offended by improper use of its surfaces. It cannot be made to issue fines when its access limits are transgressed. It is not pro-U.S. economy or pro-petroculture. It is a historical but also a profoundly terrestrial entity, a kind of mutant earth-being produced by shattered grounded normativity, capable of supporting the weight of all objects, not only those that serve white privilege and global capital. The Harbor Freeway interchange that is the focus of Yamashita's narrative also allows the destruction of expensive vehicles and protects impoverished communities.[69] Yamashita focuses on the downtown interchange as if to ask, how much stuff—what life, what disasters, what threatening surpluses—might this stretch of concrete, gravel, and rebar support?

The beginning of an answer to this question, in *Tropic of Orange,* is a car accident. Two men in a red convertible Porsche eat an orange that, unbeknownst to them, international drug smugglers have loaded with a dangerous amount of cocaine. The driver overdoses, and the Porsche crashes into a semitruck transporting propane, causing an explosion and a chain reaction of collisions in which "hundreds of cars piled on to one another in an almost endless jam of shrieking notes."[70] A single wrecked car becomes hundreds; the freeway's burden already not "limited," but "endless." Next, a second semitruck crashes at the far end of the pileup and also explodes. "An entire mile of cars trapped between two dead semis," *NewsNow* producer Emi crows to reporter Gabriel Balboa, who is also on the scene, "not to mention two craters, fires, and the debris from the blasts."[71] Amid this litany of disasters, the interchange morphs into a primordial landscape, its concrete and steel body recalling its nonhuman origins in a clash of elemental forces—fire, natural gas, heaving metal bodies—that literalizes Levi Bryant's assertion that the object world, in its capacity to upset human expectation, harbors "volcanic potentials."[72]

Significantly, this revolt of the freeway's mineral aggregate-being— the ghosts in its concrete soil—does not restrict what weight it is capable of bearing. Like *The Intuitionist*'s unruly elevator, the destabilization of the freeway's state-sanctioned function reveals its true identity: a piece of the angry planet that is more sincerely itself the more it breaks down.[73] As drivers abandon their vehicles, the spreading fire forces people out of homeless encampments hidden in the overgrowth surrounding the interchange. They head down to the freeway and occupy the abandoned vehicles, flipping First and Third World race and class dynamics so that a space constructed to support the mobility of white privilege becomes the site of a multiethnic homeless community. The LAPD moves in, "lined up on either side of the Harbor Freeway readyin' up to catch any homeless wantin' to flee."[74] But tactical maneuvering down in the new homeless encampment, a ten-lane strip of freeway surrounded by off-ramps and skyscrapers, is difficult. Fires are burning on each end, fed by "a natural pocket of gas below the freeway," another ghost in the soil unleashed by the semitruck explosions.[75] This pocket of natural gas underscores the terrestrial origins of the materials used to build the freeway. The interchange is reconnected with its earthy, mineral roots, which reclaim it from its entanglement with colonial-capitalist terraforming.

Yamashita's interchange takeover describes the instrumentalized freeway system and its dispossessed human residents in full withdrawal from colonial-capitalist order. As the movement of the Tropic of Cancer stretches time and space, the homeless community settles in and grows, housekeeping in abandoned cars, turning shipping containers into businesses and co-ops, planting gardens, setting up medical services, and eventually taking over the airwaves of *NewsNow,* reporting on life in the "FreeZone" and demanding services and resources from the city.[76] The freeway rejects its special relationship to the state by "unblinding" its existence as a terrestrial entity. It became capitalist infrastructure when its materials were carved from the earth and shaped to serve urban development, but this status is transformed as the material burden that it bears changes and its capacity to support that burden remains intact. Its material ambivalence invites Third World citizens to repossess a visible and central location in the city, and to join it in modeling a political community asserting its autonomy and dream of sovereignty enacted on the edges of colonial modernity. In this scene, both instrumentalized nonhuman and dispossessed human reject their object status under colonial-capitalist state power. Claiming a collective subject agency that each might never fully access without the other, the freeway assemblage of humans, minerals, useless cars, and stranded commodities materially articulates an order of things that asserts its ontological priority over and against the logic and power of the state.

What happens on the Harbor Freeway reads like a great act of ontologically and politically strategic withdrawal, a massive infrastructural body throwing off its metaphysical status as the ultimate "domination of space" identified by Henri Lefebvre.[77] Despite the stranglehold that colonial capitalism seems to have over the freeway system, its material structures are not minions loyal to their overseers. In Yamashita's narrative ontology, the sheer size and complexity of the freeway manifests, as does the elevator in *The Intuitionist,* as a flat-out rebellion against the status of servant to "the country's economy and people."[78] Instead of an economy-driving, infrastructural thing, the freeway asserts its being as a mutant earth-being, minerally, stony, high ground in occupied territory, sincere in its commitment to terrestrial stability and open to the use of that stability as a base of operations for human acts of spatial rebellion. This rebellion models what a freeway stripped of the metaphysics of spatial domination might look like. Yamashita's freeway community enacts a set of social-spatial relations that is egalitarian, postcapitalist (a barter economy scavenging the ruins of capitalist excess), and committed to its own reproduction, even under conditions of extreme precarity.

Angry Planet Algorithms

So far, we have seen the angry planet in *Tropic of Orange* and *Philadelphia Fire* align itself with the struggles of American Third World liberation movements in ways that force the modern global city to reveal its violent colonial underpinnings. In both narratives, the ontological withdrawal of the natural world from human structures of order and control has generated material surpluses—burning skylines, exposed pockets of natural gas—producing physical evidence of the ongoing colonial conditions of racialization and the capitalist conditions of environmental exploitation that continue to structure urban modernity. *Tropic of Orange* and *Philadelphia Fire* go further, narratively drawing on forces and objects that operate on scales massively exceeding those of human agents. In these novels, two forceful objects, ashes and the planetary hydrological system, act as what Leanne Simpson calls *algorithms,* terrestrial problem-solving practices that model the capacity to restructure social-spatial relations.[79] These algorithms put pressure on the neoliberal order's capacity to produce "compensatory narratives" of 1990s U.S. global dominance that stress "cultural superiority, human progress and consumer desire."[80] Such compensatory narratives inculcate the belief that the internationalism of multicultural capitalism, along with the power of buying and owning, grant Americans a cosmopolitan citizenship that is the index of "an ever more egalitarian and fair society."[81] The empirical surpluses produced by the angry planet, conversely, intrude on these compensatory fictions. Elemental algorithms produce powerful counter-representations that force us to witness "why part of the richest country on earth looks like the Third World."[82]

Ashes

In *Philadelphia Fire,* ashes coat the earth, a surplus of the MOVE bombing that the city's compensatory fictions of multicultural uplift cannot erase. As part of his research, Cudjoe interviews Margaret Jones, a fictional MOVE member not in the house at the time of the attack.[83] Margaret's story avoids details related to the bombing, focusing, rather, on its aftermath, specifically on what is left behind by the fire:

> Those cinders they scraped out the basement of the house on Osage and stuffed in rubber bags . . . Those dogs carried out my brothers and sisters in bags. And got the nerve to strap those bags on stretchers . . . Lights on top the ambulances spinning like they in a hurry. Hurry for what? Those pitiful ashes ain't going nowhere . . . Why they treating ash like people now? Carrying it on stretchers . . . What they carried out was board ash and wall ash and roof ash and hallway-step ash and mattress ash and the ash of blankets and pillows . . . the pitiful house itself they carting away in ambulances.[84]

The intimate presence of the ashes in Margaret's story, and throughout *Philadelphia Fire,* speaks to their persistence as evidence that refuses to disappear. This refusal is significant in that the ash is a product of the city's efforts at erasure, indexed by "the nerve to strap those bags on stretchers." The ashes of the MOVE bombing are grisly chunks of materiality that cannot be talked around or shoved aside. They are empirical surpluses that are threatening because they are material evidence of the structural racism that continues to function in U.S. social spaces despite the era's official administrative rhetoric committed to race-neutral social policies. The ashes of Osage Avenue withdraw, in short, from the city's effort to make them mean otherwise.

Margaret's description evokes two iconic and disturbing moments from the documentary history of the bombing: first, the televised images of police and medical technicians transporting body bags, mostly flat, containing a few lumpy remains, into ambulances. Second, the fact reported throughout the literature on the bombing and in the findings of the Philadelphia Special Investigation Commitee (SIC) that, without a medical examiner present, "a crane with a bucket [was used] to dig up debris and bodies, result[ing] in dismemberment, commingling of body parts, and the destruction of important physical and medical evidence."[85] This documentary history indicates that the city of Philadelphia made an active effort to remove these ashes from the evidentiary economy surrounding the bombing. In cadaver bags, the remains of MOVE members were meant to register as bodies being absorbed into the shared public affect of respect for the dead. Margaret's demanding question: "Why they treating ash like people now?" evokes the macabre irony of humanizing the ash that is itself the product of a gross objectification of the human body.

As heavy equipment moved in to clean up in the aftermath of the bombing, the SIC report suggests that no effort was made to preserve physical evidence of the damage done to the bodies of MOVE members over the course of the twenty-hour siege.[86] By actively breaking down the difference between human bodies and "the pitiful house itself," the city attempts to conceal its own complicity in the specific brutalities inflicted on each individual body, physically blurring the difference between bodies and property. "All the evidence up in smoke," Cudjoe thinks, linking the bombing to the crematoria of holocaust death camps, "the dead were dead. What they possessed gone with them. On Osage Avenue bulldozers and cranes comb the ashes, sift, crush, spread them neat as a carpet over vacant lots."[87] In its attention to ash, the narrative performs a double move. The material composition and displacement of the ash indicates an absence of evidence, while the ashes' material presence in the narrative persists as an empirical surplus that carpets the city. The ash, by withdrawing from the city's performance of respect for

its victims, makes present the nonpresence of that which its own existence ostensibly indexes as absent.[88]

In this way, the ashes of Osage Avenue take shape as an evidentiary entity intruding on the city space of Philadelphia and its role as a
representative of state power. These objects possess such intrusive force
because they are not a metaphor for the state's dehumanization of the
Black body, or for the slippage, in U.S. history, of human body to nonhuman property. Rather, the ash and fragmented body parts comin-
gling with the ash and remains of the rowhouse are material evidence of
the nonmetaphorical, structural conditions that collapse Black bodies
into an inert and passive physical environment. Given its forced engagement with these documentary objects, the narrative cannot rest on, as
Madhu Dubey asserts, "an aborted modernist mission to shore up literary value against the ruins of the contemporary city."[89] Instead, the narrative labors on in the presence of ruins and finds that they cannot
be brought into the register of full aesthetic manipulation. Over and
over, *Philadelphia Fire* emphasizes that the ashes of Osage Avenue are
the product of an assault on bodies and infrastructure so comprehensive
as to take on the character of an environmental scandal. "Smoke, gas,
fire, bullets," this litany echoes throughout the novel, "bullets, bombs,
water, fire. Shot, blowed up, burnt, drowned."[90] The cataloging is an
apocalyptic inversion of the elemental quadrangle of earth, air, fire, and
water. This elemental register identifies colonial-capitalist ontology as
taking shape not only in bodies and infrastructure but through harness-
ing elements as natural resources, commodities, utilities, and weapons.
The ash from the bombing becomes a threatening ontological surplus
by calling the state to account for this elemental violence.

Hydrological Cycle

When Leanne Simpson writes about moss as "an algorithm, a practice
for solving a problem," she proposes that the algorithms of grounded
normativity "are profoundly anticapitalist at their core."[91] Many of the
terrestrial algorithms present in *Tropic of Orange* and *Philadelphia Fire*
also resist their status as good colonial-capitalist objects. However, in
both novels water takes on a more ambivalent status; it puts the violence
of global modernity on display not by misbehaving but by being an

obedient colonial avatar. Wideman and Yamashita tell stories about how the planetary hydrological cycle is aggressively instrumentalized by the colonial-capitalist state, a point that Bambara also stresses in her documentary engagement with Cobb's Creek. "The material history of water," urban historian Chris Otter writes, is "a history of the production of very primal forces of inequality."[92] Hydrological systems become threatening empirical surpluses in *Philadelphia Fire* and *Tropic of Orange* because they put this inequality on display, but as in Tuana's example of Hurricane Katrina, the kind of witnessing forced by these displays of inequality is no ally in the American Third World.

In *Tropic of Orange,* Yamashita mocks what Mike Davis calls the "humid fallacy," the idealist fantasy of perpetual California sunshine in which "imaginary 'norms' and 'averages' are constantly invoked, while the weather is ceaselessly berated for its perversity, as in 'We have had an unusually dry/wet season' or 'The weather isn't like it used to be.'"[93] It rains on the first day of the novel's seven-day plot, even though the forecast predicts sunshine. The downpour is another of those unsurprising surprises that, as Davis suggests, allow humans to indulge in the fantasy of a stable and predictable built environment. However, Yamashita complicates the banality of this event by pointing out that the rain does not fall equally on all L.A. residents. The storm washes away a camp of homeless trans folks along the L.A. River. "We get a wall of rain," reports Buzzworm. "And I mean a wall of rain. Flood conditions. Dumps a whole foot in five minutes . . . Shit floating down the river. Car parts, hypodermics, dead dogs, Neanderthal bones, props from the last movie shot down there, you name it."[94] The novel represents Los Angeles's concrete river, a locus of nature-culture agonism, as a site of extreme precarity when the weather doesn't "behave," and let's admit it, the narrative urges, the weather never does. Yamashita turns a regional joke about climate into a statement about the survival conditions endured by Los Angeles's spatially disenfranchised. In doing so, she makes the point that the humid fallacy is also a political strategy for ignoring the ways in which the angry planet draws attention to the gross material disparities among humans that are a daily reality along the California coastline.

Yamashita emphasizes that such grounded normative algorithms do not share knowledge gently. The hydrological cycle makes its point only by creating a violent juxtaposition between the city's absurd refuse and its homeless population. If a lesson about climate must be taught on the bodies of the dispossessed, it seems that there is little in terms of decolonial methodology to be gained from such an education. However, as quickly as it comes, the water disappears, "all gone. Concrete bed's dry . . . A flash-flood-L.A.-river-transvestite-drowning story with a happy ending."[95] No one dies, and through this reprieve, the narrative is able to pin the problem of political and ontological belonging on the city. Colonial unknowing has to work hard here to misrecognize the evidence presented by the angry planet. Gabriel, in his capacity as the novel's intrepid reporter, can't drum up much enthusiasm for the story, and resists publishing it. Overlooked, underrepresented, the strange menace and equally strange clemency of the hydrological event vanishes. The novel suggests that the error here is one of modes of understanding. If we fail to attend to the planet's algorithmic data, if we fail to report on this data and instead silence its evidentiary quality, we cannot learn, cannot change, and we certainly cannot save ourselves.[96]

Philadelphia Fire considers the logic of the deluge guns used to fight the MOVE organization in the standoff leading up to the 1985 bombing as an entry point for thinking about water as a resource weaponized across the city as a whole. What understandings of space and elemental force can be drawn from an event in which these weapons are used to pound a rowhouse with millions of gallons of water, and conversely, sit unused while that same house burns down with a dozen people inside? To answer this question, the novel draws the reader's attention to Philadelphia's monumental architecture, particularly public fountains, in which water plays a similarly selective role. Philadelphia's fountains run by day as a symbol of abundance and peace, creating a space in which the city's children can play and bathe on hot summer days.[97] By night, however, this architecture bolsters the "iron will [that] has imposed itself on the shape of the city" by being withheld from undesirable users like homeless bathers, vandals, and marginalized youth.[98] This day to night schedule, which lends the First and Third World partitioning of the city a temporal dimension, yields representations of civic violence as the subtext of a shared public commons. In one of the novel's penultimate scenes, a homeless man is burned alive because a fountain in Independence Square only flows during the daylight hours of bustling civic activity. Waking up to the smell of gasoline and his own burning clothing, the man makes a run for the fountain although "he knows as he pumps his legs and pumps his heart and pumps his scorched lungs and clutches with his fingers for white flutes of spray, by this time of night the water's been turned off for hours."[99] In this scene, Philadelphia's monumental architecture is incapable of managing its role as the material articulation of First World power and progress. The city's own political decision to strategically withdraw the flow of water from its residents becomes an ontological scandal. The body in the fountain is evidence of the absence of social and juridical order. The fountain is not a public and symbolic commons but a real material site of living and dying, a locus for the ongoing struggle to survive experienced by so many dispossessed city dwellers as neocolonial processes of urban renewal sweep U.S. cities in the 1980s and 1990s.

In the face of this spatial violence, Wideman and Yamashita do not narrate a decolonial ontological order into being so much as identify the limit to its realization as that of land, land and resource use, and land development; limits that are foundational to the settler state's relationship with Indigenous demands for land-based sovereignty. The focus on the reoccupation of land demanded by the witness of Black radical environmentalists and by people experiencing homelessness may participate in practices of Indigenous erasure that occur through competing land claims. However, simultaneously, these communities, by basing their challenges to the settler state in land use, find themselves exposed to the same practices of colonial violence perfected by what Taiaiake Alfred calls the "perpetual relations of force" normalized by the settler state in its domination of first nations.[100] While there is minimal Indigenous presence in these novels, then, their narratives of resistance are welded to dynamics of state violence forged in the historical conditions of Indigenous genocide. While the differing claims of resistance communities may make coalitional practices as uneasy as is allyship with the angry earth, these novels suggest that from the perspective of the settler state, any challenges to land use can be processed with the same force used to decimate the original inhabitants of the continent. In Leslie Marmon Silko's *Almanac of the Dead,* one of the major texts studied in the next chapter, Silko points to incidents like "the blocks of rowhouses fire-bombed by the Philadelphia police" as "proof" that "the U.S. government would not hesitate to firebomb . . . hundreds of city blocks" to crush a threat to its sovereignty.[101] And it is just these efforts to claim alternative spaces of sovereignty that draw the violence of state terror in these novels.

Despite their powerful evocations of ontological withdrawal as a political, decolonial act, Wideman and Yamashita's narrative ontologies conclude by identifying the bloody ends to American Third World revolution, rather than its realization. While *Tropic of Orange* leads us up to the moment when an ontological threat is met by direct state violence, and *Philadelphia Fire* explores its aftermath, both conclude in fragmentation and abstraction, an incomplete withdrawal that leaves each narrative stuck in an uncomfortable threshold space. Cudjoe never manages to write his account of the MOVE bombing and redeem the political promise of the Third World, and is left at the end of the novel disoriented and adrift at a sparsely attended memorial to the MOVE dead, turning "to face whatever it is rumbling over the stones of Independence Square."[102] *Tropic of Orange* ends with Los Angeles in total gridlock and mass social confusion, the Tropic itself held together by one struggling human body on the brink of being ripped apart; "That's it," goes the novel's last line.[103] While Wideman and Yamashita tend to move easily across time and space in their prose, both novels freeze in conclusion before the monolithic figure of settler-state power reconsolidating its ontological order and the idea of land that supports this order. Both Third World revolutionary action and Fourth World land claims can be and are defused in a hail of military-issue bullets. Through the different types of human-nonhuman coalitional action that unfold in *Tropic of Orange* and *Philadelphia Fire,* it is possible to see a decolonial coalitional politics that takes shape as shifting and contingent—a surprise of associations that variously run through the co-implicated registers of the environmental, the infrastructural, and the bodily. But allyship with the angry earth emerges as complicated by the limits of what it can offer human beings. The planet's surplus motion and intrusive algorithms force us to witness the everyday operations of colonial-capitalist spatial violence but also to admit the price of using that witness to threaten the state's monopoly on violence whose spatialized character itself signifies a form of property wealth appreciated from the foundational colonial transaction explored in chapter 1. To demand a transformation of material conditions at the level of urban infrastructure and property development is to become the object of state violence, and a truly land-centric decolonial mandate in post–Cold War neoliberal America confronts this violence and the limit of the planet's capacity to defend against it. In this chapter, the angry planet models resistance as onto-political withdrawal from the colonial-capitalist relation, but it cannot realize revolution. In the next chapter, the angry planet will need to do more than produce evidence in the form of empirical surpluses of colonial-capitalist violence. As threatening as this evidence may be in *Philadelphia Fire* and *Tropic of Orange,* it is just enough to ensure the state's ongoing reproduction of its relations of force.

3

THIRD WORLD LIBERATION
LESLIE MARMON SILKO'S *ALMANAC OF THE DEAD* AND HÉCTOR TOBAR'S *THE TATTOOED SOLDIER*

IN SEPTEMBER 1992, seven years after the bombing of the MOVE house in Philadelphia, John Edgar Wideman published an op-ed in *Esquire* reflecting on the Los Angeles Riots.[1] The title page of Wideman's piece reads "Dead Black Men and Other Fallout from the American Dream." The black block lettering, bordered by sharp black chevrons, is set against a canary yellow background, referencing roadwork signs that advertise both Caution—Dangerous Road Ahead, and Caution—Men at Work. The dual connotations of this design evoke the irony of road signage. These signs warn us about a seemingly temporary state of infrastructural exception in which the risk to human bodies is heightened and the rules that keep streets civil and orderly do not apply; however, the ubiquity of these signs also flags the everyday disastrousness of infrastructure. It is always dangerous. The rules of the road are contingent, situational, and specific to subject positions. Rules that are delineated by infrastructural arrangements can protect one genre of human subject—as we saw in the previous chapter—and condemn another to political obscurity, bodily precarity, and death.

The article's road sign title page directs us to one of Wideman's points, which is that the rioting, however chaotic, was also an important reorientation: a reminder, like the permanent disasters of road work, of the paradox of modernity built on the foundations of a colonial world. As in Yamashita's *Tropic of Orange*, Los Angeles is both a smooth hub of global modernity and what Mike Davis calls a zone of "low-intensity warfare."[2] These conflicting conditions—of modernity and of its persistent colonial subtext—define a present in which, as Nelson Maldonado-Torres puts it, "a colonial anti-black world"—and implicitly, an anti-Indigenous, anti-Latinx, anti-diasporic Asian world—has become "a constitutive part of an alleged normal world."[3] In the American Third World, privilege and precarity exist side by side across uneven terrains of development and disaster, and the only thing that seems to be on permanent decline, Wideman writes, "is the possibility that change, the change that's gonna come, will occur in my lifetime. Or the lifetime of the U.S.A."[4] For all the work done since the 1960s to restructure conditions of poverty and inequality, we arrive again and again, Wideman laments, back in the burning city, among the crumbling infrastructure, wondering how the new world order always amounts to the same dead black and brown bodies.

Connecting the events in Los Angeles to the MOVE bombing in Philadelphia, Wideman observes that during the rioting, he was never afraid of the rioters and looters, the structure fires, or the car wrecks. Instead, he writes, "Scared arrived and carved out a dwelling place . . . the day Mayor Bradley lifted curfew and the city resumed its normal face. . . . What was this 'normal,' anyway, for whose return people prayed? For whites, normal meant not having to worry about the violence and desperation endemic to areas of the city like South-Central. For residents of such areas, normal meant hunkering down again and accepting again the degrading portion of life in South-Central allotted them."[5] As Wideman suggests, for racialized communities living in the American Third World, the normal of modernity is a permanent state of psychological terror and physical danger. Ruth Wilson Gilmore adds nuance to this assertion to stress that resistance within the structures of racialization can reinforce these conditions: "The very capacities we struggle to turn to other purposes *make* races by making some people, and their biological and fictive kin, vulnerable to forces that make premature death likely and in some ways distinctive . . . renewing the racial order of the U.S. polity as normal, even as it changes."[6] In the wake of a crisis like the L.A. riots, when order is restored, viewers who have been glued to television sets return to what Thomas Dumm calls "normalized communities" circumscribed by "white, suburban, middle-class, male, straight, and law-abiding" cul-de-sac neighborhoods.[7] In the whiteness-privileging First World, crisis retreats to its status as the lurking but ultimately distant subtext of everyday experience. For those economically and spatially disenfranchised people of color who return to "hunkering down," crisis dominates, enfolding communities like South-Central in the insidious rhythms of environmental and infrastructural violence.

Héctor Tobar, reflecting on his own experience as a young reporter covering the Riots, writes that "the city will not be consumed in flames again soon, but like other troubled parts of the United States, it burns a little every day. It smolders with seething resentments. The people there know they deserve better, but their most common act of resistance is simply to work hard, plant gardens and watch them grow."[8] Tobar is describing the paradigm and contradiction of the American Third World; it smolders and seethes, existing as both the constant reproduction of the ruins of modernity's promises and the seat of resistance. Those South L.A. gardens evoke the plot system that Sylvia Wynter describes as "a source of cultural guerilla resistance to the plantation system" whose spatial logic persists in the city's anti-Black and anti-brown police violence as well as the invasive monocultured farmland and orchards, worked by all-but-slave labor, that surround the city.[9] But a garden plot by itself is a revolutionary force that speaks of resistance in isolation, and the defense of a small square of property eked out against the landed wealth of state power based on that foundational colonial act of violent expropriation from which racial making and mattering achieves its force. With each reconsolidation of First World normal, as Wideman argues, the possibility of change seems more and more distant.

The problem with normal in 1992 Los Angeles is why Rodney King's plea to "all get along" becomes both a mantra and a punch line in the aftermath of the protesting that erupted in response to the "not guilty" verdict in the trial of the police officers who were filmed brutally beating King. Robert Gooding-Williams notes that a less-quoted part of King's speech asserts that the reason we've all got to "get along" is because "we're all stuck here for a while." Being stuck, Gooding-Williams writes, "identified a condition that is at once ontological and social" in which spatial fixity (being "stuck here") demands social civility (that we "get along"). In his own way, Gooding-Williams writes, King was "calling our attention to the facticity of being stuck" and thus affirming the impossibility of social (let alone ontological) change.[10] But what if being "stuck" is an ontologically untenable condition? The endemic desperation inherent in accepting the ontological fixity of conditions like racial violence and spatial stuckness is precisely what prevents the communities to which King directs his plea from "getting along" within whiteness-privileging social-spatial conditions that are impossible to get along *with*.

The obverse of the terrifying return to normal that Wideman describes is that uprisings like the L.A. riots can, in the spirit of radical Third World social movements, direct us to the possibility of different social-spatial conditions in which racialized bodies do *not* register as what Sylvia Wynter, writing on the Riots, describes as "the *Lack* of the human."[11] The possibility of a shift in physical order ties the effects of social uprising to one of the tenets of object-oriented ontology, which asserts that the smooth normalcy of the everyday—morning coffee, freeway commute, glass and concrete office building—is more phenomenological effect than ontological fact. Timothy Morton uses the example of "travel to a strange country" as an experience in which this effect lifts and—jetlagged, fumbling through unfamiliar hotel rooms—we see the object world around us weirdly naked, stripped of its semiotic entanglements. And this is not because we are somewhere strange, but because the world around us, "your regular house on your regular street," is always secretly strange, not "stuck," smooth, or normal, but instead concealing different possible surfaces that suddenly "lurch toward you with . . . clown-like weirdness."[12] Wideman's analysis draws out the political stakes of this ontological claim. Crises like riots or earthquakes can have a defamiliarizing effect similar to that of long-distance travel, allowing us to glimpse the possibility of different material conditions. The L.A. riots were not a time for getting along but for becoming unstuck; and the aftermath, for many, marked a disturbing return to the terror of the normalized community.[13]

Angry planet fiction embraces crisis and disorder as potentially generative events. The novels in this chapter describe the impossibility of accepting the normal and tell stories about social subjects who are not "narratively condemned."[14] In Leslie Marmon Silko's *Almanac of the Dead* (1991) and Héctor Tobar's *The Tattooed Soldier* (1998), the subtext of colonial warfare bubbles to the surface of modernity so that the normal of colonial-capitalist state power becomes visible as the locus of terror, and crisis becomes the site of revolutionary potential. Revolution itself, understood as sudden political change and as the rotation and reorientation of physical bodies, emerges in this chapter as an expression of that particular face of grounded normativity that Leanne Simpson suggestively describes as "shattered."[15] Both authors develop this narrative ontology—in which a decolonial ontological framework allows for a revolution in the conditions of narrative possibility—by enlisting terrestrial motion as an agent of generative chaos. In *Almanac of the Dead,* Silko maps out a near future in which earthquakes, droughts, volcanic eruptions, and landslides operate as a global call to action, prompting the earth's Third World populations to "realize they must rise up" on a global scale.[16] In *The Tattooed Soldier,* more subtle terrestrial motions do this work. Tobar describes a Los Angeles in which "there were plenty of crumbling walls . . . and thus no shortage of ammunition," framing urban decay as a form of terrestrial motion that, through the algorithm of erosion, destabilizes civic order.[17]

By developing a narrative ontology in which the earth is an agent of disorder, Silko and Tobar engage the intelligence of shattered grounded normativity. This ontological framework offers human subjects lessons that are less generative of, as Glen Sean Coulthard puts it, "living our lives in relation to one another and our surroundings in a respectful, nondominating and nonexploitative way" than they are contingent and exigent lessons in decolonial revolution.[18] Shattered grounded normativity, in these novels, plots modes of agency and mobility for social subjects who might otherwise be narratively legible only as "stuck" in the material conditions and histories defining their lives. Both authors push beyond the limits arrived at by Wideman and Yamashita, in which planetary forces produce evidence of colonial-capitalist violence without identifying points of egress out of these conditions. Instead, as will Amitav Ghosh in *The Great Derangement* (2016), Silko and Tobar recognize representations of catastrophism as both a means of identifying the ontological crises produced by colonial-capitalist social order and of imagining the conditions of its overturning.[19] In both novels, the angry planet moves in ways that upset the stability and rational order of colonial-capitalist state power, and dispossessed communities of color follow that motion, taking landslides and urban decay as models for strategies of what Walter Mignolo calls "delinking," separating people and planet "from the colonial matrix of power."[20] For scholars in the Latin American modernity/coloniality/decoloniality project, delinking means to detach or escape from "ways of thinking, languages, ways of life and being in the world that the rhetoric of modernity disavowed and the logic of coloniality implement," Mignolo writes.[21] While decolonial revolution is described by Mignolo in largely epistemic terms, delinking for the angry planet is a profoundly material process, entailing shifts in the earth's crust and human populations on the move around the planet. In *Almanac of the Dead* and *The Tattooed Soldier,* delinking emerges as a physically aggressive activity, in which the land actively decouples from the infrastructures of state power, and human subjects access new modes of agency and mobility in its wake.

Silko and Tobar present these acts of rebellion not as anomalous but as political projects disengaging from the normalized experiences of violent racism and economic precarity faced by dispossessed communities of color in the 1990s. A range of late twentieth-century U.S. novels, including Chuck Palahniuk's *Fight Club* (1996) and Paul Beatty's *The White Boy Shuffle* (1996), share an interest in the revolutionary potential of chaos and disorder. But as a representational politics, the defense of chaos runs counter to twenty-first-century theories of crisis, which thoroughly cede its transformative potential to neoliberal capital accumulation. Naomi Klein's articulation of shock doctrine capitalism explains how both environmental and political disasters serve to consolidate the control of neoliberal economic policies on the global stage.[22] Similarly, David Harvey's histories of urban crises demonstrate that uprisings in the United States have served as opportunities for "the re-engineering of inner cities," gentrification projects that have widened spatial and economic gaps between the rich and poor.[23] These critics argue that times of massive social and environmental upheaval strengthen and accelerate capital development and U.S.-led global imperialism. But why then is literary production leading up to the millennium so narratively invested in the ontologically transformative power of crisis?

Rather than ceding all political power to capital development, these novels represent chaos and disorder as what Gilmore calls "the raw material of profound social change."[24] In *Almanac of the Dead* and

The Tattooed Soldier, anyone with the resources to do so can seize upon and take advantage of catastrophic destabilizations of social order. Of course, this approach parallels that of Klein's neoliberal economists, who await (or generate) the disaster or crisis that will provide them with "a clean slate on which to build a reengineered model society."[25] But Gilmore's point is to challenge us to see disorder as "raw material" ripe for social change, rather than as the ontologically cooked materials of ever-greater social inequality. In the wake of the L.A. riots, she asks how we might "push and pull the current tendency of crisis away from a national resolution in fascism."[26] If crisis tilts toward benefiting those with the capital to take advantage of it, it might seem that any riot, rebellion, or natural disaster can but feed colonial-capitalist power. But to hand a monopoly on crisis over to the state is also to condemn American Third World citizens—the immigrants and refugees, homeless and struggling poor, Indigenous, Black, Latinx, and Asian Americans that move through *Almanac of the Dead*'s and *The Tattooed Soldier*'s pages—to permanent and inescapable economic and spatial disenfranchisement. This might be the lesson of history, but it is also, as Gerald Vizenor argues, a key characteristic of "the literature of dominance" in which "the sense that nature is precarious" and "the realities of chance, fate, and tragic wisdom [are] denied."[27] Vizenor's point is that narratives of crisis in which the house always wins map smoothly onto colonial storytelling in which Black and Indigenous people of color are inevitably the victims of history. And for authors interested in representing these communities, this is not a tenable condition under which to exist or to craft a narrative.

The untenable ontology of the normal drives Silko and Tobar to narratively enlist the angry planet as a powerful counter-resource to that of capital and as the grounds for "a new logic to tell the story" of modernity.[28] The human actors in these novels develop their everyday relations to the angry planet in ways that prepare them to seize the moment of disorder and to follow the planet's lead in decolonizing the terrestrial surface. This approach can easily register as naïve. Silko's vision of revolution has come under fire for being, as Rebecca Tillett puts it, "virulently violent and hopelessly optimistic in its portrayal of the ability of the dispossessed to end their own exploitation."[29] But my reading of these novels emphasizes that positioning the planet as a furious and powerful ally is a strategic decolonial and anticapitalist representational practice that emerges out of a long-standing solidarity with Third World social movements. Silko's and Tobar's representations of the angry planet resist the pressures of a historical moment in which, as Min Hyoung Song notes, there is "little optimism about the future, a general sense of futility about the possibility for positive change, and, as such, a *vulnerability* to arguments for greater state repression."[30] Refusing to reproduce the narrative conditions schematized by colonial literatures of dominance, Silko and Tobar take a chance on the planet as an entity with the force to counter colonial-capitalist state power.

Both novels also pursue the possibility that if planetary motion rebels against the violence of colonial terraforming, this rebellion has the potential to unite disparate communities struggling against the legacies of colonial land expropriation, plantation slavery, and immigration-based labor exploitation. Rather than succumbing to the vulnerability Song describes, in *Almanac of the Dead,* Silko writes from a perspective that sees environmental devastation, the poverty and disenfranchisement of Indigenous peoples, and the breakdown of civil society in the Americas as reaching "a kind of breaking point."[31] Like the Maya codices that she draws on as inspiration for her novel's almanac-like structure, in Silko's narrative ontology, history is cyclical. Just as Maya civilizations morphed alongside "overpopulation, reduced food production from depleted environments, warfare, and periodic droughts [that] brought famine, disease, [and] violence," *Almanac of the Dead* predicts the downfall of colonial-capitalist power based on a conjunction of catastrophic forces.[32] Similarly, in Tobar's *The Tattooed Soldier,* the lack of state support for Central American refugees in California, the statewide recession and housing crisis that was at its peak in 1992, and the everyday brutality of the LAPD, are portrayed as the precursors to a city-wide rebellion that is the direct product of the city's history of colonial racial violence and capitalist environmental excess. By representing colonial-capitalist order as having a breaking point where angry people and angry planet meet, both novels rewrite the linear, progressive temporality of modernity and insist that development can be reversed and transformed—and that no empire can expand infinitely.

These authors do not identify crises as guaranteeing a better future. Rather, through representing Third World conditions and communities in the United States as the seat of revolutionary energy and potential,

Silko and Tobar pursue temporal and spatial alternatives to being stuck in the normal. The following chapter identifies the physical spaces in each novel where the angry planet rules and social actors become unstuck. Through earthquakes and rioting, deserts and decaying infrastructure, freeways, golf courses, and micro-sites of contingent material destabilization produced from shattered grounded normativity, this chapter tracks how the narrative representation of a damaged and unpredictable object world creates different conditions of narrative possibility for social actors. A world defined by chaos and contingency delineates the different moral universe that operates from within what Maldonado-Torres defines as colonial modernity's *"non-ethics of war."*[33] Within this reversed moral universe, both novels suggest, the catastrophic event does not inevitably punish poverty and difference and reward First World exceptionalism. Silko and Tobar develop a new logic to tell the story of global modernity, and in doing so, dismantle the state's monopoly both on crisis capitalism and on what counts as ethical and political belonging. The alternative, as Song argues, is to succumb in despair to an imaginary that charts the rise of an increasingly fascist and repressive capitalist state.

Earthquakes and Riots

In *Almanac of the Dead* and *The Tattooed Soldier,* Silko and Tobar make comparisons between earthquakes and riots, suggesting that both are similar types of crises that break down the infrastructural foundations of social order. "What the Hopi talks about is the day all the walls fall down," a follower of one of the revolutionary leaders in *Almanac of the Dead* explains, "Ask him if he means earthquakes or riots and the Hopi smiles and says, 'Both.'"[34] The neoliberal economists in Klein's *The Shock Doctrine* make the same move; to them, any "great rupture—a flood, a war, a terrorist attack" contains the same opportunity to create a "clean slate" upon which to vent surplus capital through new developmental agendas and hence to restructure social order around more profitable, more efficient circuits of capital accumulation.[35] Although thinking along very different lines, Silko's Hopi revolutionary and Klein's economist both recognize disasters and riots as material reconfigurations of the very basic structural foundations of colonized land. And while for neoliberal developers this means the chance to build a bigger, bolder capitalist order, for

Silko's and Tobar's revolutionaries, a disaster that destabilizes infrastructure means that the terraformed roots of colonial violence and capitalist power are vulnerable. As in the rain and earthquake that work together to rupture the dam in Thomas King's *Green Grass, Running Water,* the planet intimates to would-be revolutionaries that political hegemony, like terrestrial stability, is always a contingent assemblage of materials.

Written in the years leading up to the Columbus quincentennial, *Almanac of the Dead* presents one of angry planet fiction's clearest articulations of planetary motion as decolonial action. "The earth's outrage and the trembling that will not stop" drives *Almanac of the Dead'*s story of how angry people and an angry planet might come together against the everyday repressive violence of state power.[36] Silko explores the potential of "conjunctions and convergences of global proportions" to coalesce into a revolution that will overthrow the colonial-capitalist state and return the damaged and exploited land to Indigenous people.[37] The earth's "outrage and . . . trembling" becomes a call to action for dispossessed communities who begin preparing to quit capitalism. The homeless population of Tucson is organized by Vietnam vets Rambo and Clinton into a sleeper strike force. Along the U.S.-Mexico border, Yaqui and *mestizo* drug smugglers Calabazas and Zeta begin to hoard arms and forge alliances with the Barefoot Hopi, who is coordinating a worldwide prison abolition movement. In the mountains near the Mexico-Guatemala border, an all-tribal people's army led by Angelita La Escapía, and twin brothers El Feo and Tacho, gathers and begins to walk, in a movement much like the march of the Global South in Yamashita's *Tropic of Orange,* toward the Mexico-U.S. border. These movements build in response to tectonic motion, directly connecting the decolonization process to the earth's delinking of its body from colonial-capitalist exploitation. In this sense, for Indigenous people to take back their lands is not to insist on a fixed relationship between body and soil that entitles some and not others to dwelling on a particular piece of earth. Instead, this revolution is about transforming the human relationship to land to reflect a nondominating, nonexploitative ontological order based in and modeled after the grounded normativity that these revolutionaries hope to restore to the center of the planet's ontological order.[38]

While that ontological order is shattered, however, human movement takes its cues from the planet's disorderly conduct to develop a revolutionary politics. If the earth can be said to have an agenda in this novel, it is to delink from structural relations with the colonial-capitalist state. As the moment of uprising approaches in the novel, signs of this delinking include "days at a time" in which "the ground had not been still in northern California; dozens of volcanos had erupted along the Aleutian chain"; "all the southwestern states" are about to "run out of drinking water"; and weather systems are "in chaos; the rain clouds had disappeared while terrible winds and freezing had followed burning, dry summers."[39] These ecological catastrophes signal to the novel's revolutionaries that a time of physical and social transformation is at hand. The "raw materials" that Gilmore invokes create "just the occasion for . . . uprising," as several of *Almanac of the Dead*'s prophetic characters assert.[40] The novel's revolutionary leaders believe that following and modeling the earth's disastrous motions can amplify the agency of previously politically illegible subjects.

A terrestrial politics based in shattered grounded normativity is markedly different from contemporary models of human-planet relationality, like that of the Anthropocene, that interpret planetary motion as anthropogenic side effects. *Almanac of the Dead*'s revolutionaries understand volcanic eruptions, droughts, and chaotic weather not primarily as the extensions of human activity but rather as the earth's responses to human activity. This is not only a semantic reframing but an ontological deprioritizing of the human as the central agency of ecological planetary crisis. In Silko's novel, the earth is in control and humans (or at least human revolutionaries) follow its lead. As Angelita La Escapía thinks, "No human, individuals or corporations, no cartel of nations, could 'own' the earth; it was the earth who possessed the humans and it was the earth who disposed of them."[41] In her reading of the novel, Heather Houser calls this "the geophysical theory of revolution," and points to the potential limitations of this thinking.[42] "By making planetary forces the instigators of social, political, and ecological changes," Houser writes, "*Almanac* posits revolution as independent of *both* identity as history *and* history as class struggle."[43] While this reading works with both historical and cultural materialist analysis, envisioning a revolution that unfolds independent of the human frameworks of identity politics and class struggle is precisely Silko's difficult and contentious point. "Land first," El Feo tells his followers, "talk and ideology later."[44]

This statement articulates the decolonial mandate in a way that positions the planet—"Land first"—at the top of a hierarchy of being that takes priority away from colonial systems of meaning making. The only way out of the conditions of the present, Silko insists, is for humans to model a terrestrial politics that takes ontological priority over all anthropogenic categories of culturally and economically determined action.

Decolonization of the earth's terrestrial body requires, in the terms that Angelita suggests, an absolutely radical reconfiguration of the ontological assumptions that underlie a belief in politics, identity, and history as the products of individual actions *or* of class consciousness. Walter Benn Michaels accuses Silko of positing an Indigenous revolutionary ethos that, in demanding redress for historical wrongs, becomes reducible to a "straightforward ethnonationalism" in which decolonization means reversing the terms of racial belonging so that precontact North American populations are the only humans with political and land rights.[45] But the kind of history that Angelita evokes, which defines belonging as beginning with the earth's own terms of possession, is more geological and less geopolitical than Michaels allows. As Silko frames the issue elsewhere, decolonization does not require that "the European people themselves will disappear, only their customs."[46] In a novel that repeatedly appeals to readers to attend to "the spirit forces of wind, fire, water, and mountain"—those "earth beings" described in Marisol de la Cadena's research—central among these colonial customs is the assumption of human ontological priority in effecting political change, as well as its antecedent logic, ventriloquized by Michaels, of interpreting all non-Eurowestern intellectual production as cultural ideology rather than realpolitik.[47] *Almanac of the Dead* demonstrates that the colonial grounding of these customs has been effected through the idea of land that authorizes human domination of the physical environment and the strategic disregard of grounded normativity. In this sense, Silko and her revolutionary characters anticipate the contemporary Land Back movement, which, as Hayden King asserts, "is not merely a matter of justice, rights or 'reconciliation'; Indigenous jurisdiction can indeed help mitigate the loss of biodiversity and climate crisis."[48] To be directed by Indigenous ontology in returning terrestrial agendas and demands to geopolitical center stage is a decolonial action centered on reversing the relations of ontological privilege that prioritize human agency and instrumentalize the planet.

It is because they are, in effect, quitting colonial capitalism that the all-tribal people's army marches north in *Almanac of the Dead* without vehicles or guns. On foot, they can cross over "the landslides which the mountains had shaken down in previous weeks."[49] Conversely, the police and military vehicles tailing them become trapped by these terrestrially generated blockades. Walking, as a form of revolutionary motion, explicitly stresses a collective withdrawal of support from patterns of capitalist consumption, particularly petro-imperialism. Collective motion models the terrestrial politics of the landslide, which occupies space with implacable force without relying on a targeted command and control logic: "If the people kept walking, if the people carried no weapons, then the old prophecies would come to pass, and all the dispossessed and the homeless would have land."[50] What Silko describes here is a delinking from circuits of consumption and violence that deplete land and destabilize human community. The prophecies that her characters follow anticipate the end of colonial rule in the Americas, but they also recall the fall of Maya civilizations during which people fled war-torn and resource-exhausted areas to resettle and to reorganize social order.[51] A terrestrial politics dedicated to moving one's own body without the aid of machines or weapons is not one that assumes the earth will take care of itself and therefore abdicates human responsibility. Instead, these revolutionaries physically model an amplified political responsibility in which human actors attend to the earth's orders, demands, and claims to "possess" and "dispose" of us. Despite Michaels's charge of depoliticized essentialism, there are no limitations on who can follow this lead; limitations to political belonging are instead determined by *how* we follow.

A terrestrial political agency defined by nonproductive, non-petroconsumptive motion follows the cues of the planet, stressing collectivity rather than individual action, and a mobility that models terrestrial algorithms rather than class-based alignment. Distinctions between human and natural disasters collapse. El Feo thinks of the people operating not as an organized army but as a leaderless force that "moved as a mob or swarm," that "follows instinct, then suddenly disperses."[52] El Feo emphasizes not the fury of the mob or swarm but its spontaneity and the nonhierarchical identity conferred by this capacity to move without militarized organization. He envisions the sheer numbers of those who have been designated the "despised outcasts of the earth"—Fanon's *damnés*—as coming together with a force akin to that of a storm or an insect cloud.[53] Clinton, one of the leaders of the homeless army in Tucson, thinks about this convergence of forces not in terms of a simultaneous event but a cascade. He references the success of the 1791 Haitian slave revolt as based on a cascading algorithm, in which "storm winds and floods had struck a terrible blow to the Europeans and gave the slaves advantages they sorely needed to launch their revolution."[54] As an alternative to the political agency of the white, liberal, humanist subject, *Almanac of the Dead's* collective human agent moves like a landslide, wants not to develop but to destroy, and defines subjectivity not as consumer choice and productive agency but as a being-with-the-earth. The swarm patterns its political agenda after the mountains that are "shaking the earth and would not stop until the white man's cities were destroyed."[55] Again, tectonic motion is the primary actor here, while human agency rides its tailwinds.

Acting as a kind of landslide in miniature, the crumbling infrastructure of Tobar's *The Tattooed Soldier* creates the conditions for the landslide of human rebellion in 1992 Los Angeles. Tobar's Los Angeles is, as Caren Irr puts it, "a collapsing structure, one that fails to maintain the balance between country and city, citizens and peasants. Hence, it releases a vengeful starving peasantry rather than buying them off with limited privileges and the promise of upward mobility and legal status."[56] Irr's reading goes against the grain of critically engaging *The Tattooed Soldier's* "geopolitical aesthetics" in order to stress the novel's feudal spatial aesthetics.[57] Taking Irr's attention to the failed promises of urban modernity in the collapsing city quite literally, the practice of reading for the angry planet identifies Tobar's city as in a state of actual and physical collapse through the geophysical algorithm of erosion. Erosion is an ontological quality present in the life cycle of rock and stone that cannot be developed out of existence. In a concrete city like Los Angeles, this decomposition is visible everywhere: discarded wood from temporary building materials, concrete and brick that are returning to their primordial states of rock, gravel, and dust, and layer upon layer of evidence pointing to previous ages of boom and bust.

Against this terrain of urban decomposition, Tobar tells the story of Antonio Bernal, one of thousands of Guatemalan immigrants and refugees who fled the Guatemalan Civil War to California and to Los Angeles, in particular. Haunted by the state-ordered executions of his wife and son, Antonio fails to maintain his refugee status and steady employment and joins the city's massive homeless population. While Antonio has escaped outright civil warfare, he finds himself at the mercy of the same racializing state form that criminalized indigeneity in Guatemala.[58] Antonio sinks into a depressive stupor, stunned by the geopolitical contingencies that have transformed his circumstances, before an accidental encounter in MacArthur Park with Guillermo Longoria, the army sergeant and death squad leader who murdered his family. In a reversal of that first traumatic meeting, his second run-in with Longoria allows Antonio to reconstitute his identity and political agency, sending him on a crusade for vengeance that culminates in his brutal murder of Longoria at the height of the L.A. riots, or what the novel calls "the municipal day of vendettas."[59] Tobar's narrative framework parallels the racialization that Antonio experiences as an undocumented refugee with his experience of urban space. Both race and space appear in *The Tattooed Soldier* as structures of state violence that resist their own integrity—that resist, in short, staying normal, whole, and coherent.

As each form of colonial-capitalist structural violence crumbles, the city's homeless and economically destitute populations and its infrastructures form unexpected alliances. In *The Tattooed Soldier,* the first grumblings of urban unrest come with "the sound of a window breaking."[60] This auditory warning identifies infrastructure as the interface through which an angry but illegible population communicates with the repressive state. In the wake of a police shooting that occurs only days before the Rodney King verdict, a young Latinx man lies dead outside of Guillermo Longoria's apartment building in Westlake. The crowd that gathers to watch "as the ambulance crew performed a ritual of shaking heads over the body" finds an outlet for its rage in the detritus on the streets.[61] They begin to hurl "rocks, bricks, and bottles," whatever objects are at hand, at the police on the scene.[62] Like the people's army that follows the landslide in *Almanac of the Dead,* the crowd's rock-throwing reproduces the crumbling motion of urban decay. A brick that falls off an apartment block's façade is already a projectile.

The crowd's actions repurpose that Heideggerian assertion that we only notice a tool—his example is a hammer—is not quite the object we thought it was when it breaks. Caroline Levine extends this assertion to infrastructural systems. "We are likely to notice them," Levine writes, "only when they disintegrate or fail."[63] Levine wants us to take notice of the daily privileges that North Americans enjoy via invisible infrastructures. Conversely, in this scene the city's disintegration and failure suddenly appear as useful and usable—what Heidegger calls "ready-to-hand"—to the angry Central American immigrant community of West-lake. Instead of the coldly distant avatar of "substantial public investment as well as wealth and privilege," civic infrastructure appears as richly accessible in its tool-being when it fails.[64] As pieces of the city's crumbling buildings are taken up by angry hands, Tobar's narrative adds the political valence of the angry planet to Heidegger's ontological analysis: depending on the relative privilege or precarity of our material existence, the hammer's difference from its human purpose does not appear only when it breaks. We might notice it all the time, as something that we do not have access to; we also notice when its qualities as a tool suddenly show themselves to be the qualities of a weapon. Although the first day of the L.A. riots is still a few days away, the first "chunk of concrete that sailed over the top of the crowd and landed beyond the police tape next to one of the officers" signals the beginning of a rebellion that will use the detritus of modernity as a powerful weapon against infrastructural violence and its leering appearance of the state's "substantial public investment."[65] For the rest of the novel, rioters weaponize the city's "rocks" against its concrete body and its human enforcers. Through this infrastructural interface, the city's institutionally illegible populations force their way toward political visibility.

What Longoria then thinks of as "the explosiveness of the city, the correlation of forces on the street" is an aggregate of human frustration and rage that follows in the wake of the parts of the physical environment that have already delinked from dominant structures of social order.[66] "Young men with rocks were roaming the streets," Antonio thinks. "Where did the rocks come from? How did they get rocks in the middle of the city? Antonio looked closer and saw they were just chunks of concrete and brick, pieces of crumbling walls. There were plenty of crumbling walls in this neighborhood and thus no shortage of ammunition."[67] The angry citizens that turn the city's decaying infrastructure against it demonstrate the instability inherent in the physical expression of civic order. As L.A. infrastructure historian Nathan Masters writes, "The progress concrete once embodied seems today as brittle as some of its aging structures."[68] Concrete, Masters observes, appeared to modern developers to be a building material of control—mastering nature by funneling its unpredictable network of flatland creeks into the L.A. River canal; conquering distance by piping water 242 miles from the Colorado River; solving engineering problems by turning on-the-ground traffic congestion into the largest urban freeway system in the world. As the twentieth century aged, however, concrete began to demonstrate a tendency to revert to its aggregate forms of sand, gravel, and stone. The more than one billion tons of stone quarried to make up Los Angeles's concrete body took thousands of years to move from the San Gabriel mountains to where the river of the same name flattens out in the gravel industry city of Irwindale, itself now a "wasteland of old mining craters."[69] It took less than the span of the twentieth century for Los Angeles's infrastructure to begin to shed rocks and gravel. These weirdly rebellious terrestrial materials (speaking, as they do, to the decaying promises of modernity) lead the city's dispossessed social actors into that "beautiful disorder" that Antonio will think of, in the aftermath of the Riots, as "a fleeting storm gone out to sea."[70]

As in *Almanac of the Dead*, *The Tattooed Soldier'*s narrative elides rioter and "fleeting storm" to elucidate how collectivities of humans and nonhumans might disrupt the smooth operations of state power. While there is certainly an idealism to Silko's vision of mountains and Indigenous peoples marching north together as a collective landslide, before which "the police . . . soon realized they were greatly outnumbered and they had withdrawn," this is just what unfolds during the L.A. riots.[71] In *The Tattooed Soldier*, Longoria describes a scene in which he is disgusted by the LAPD "surrendering the field to an unarmed mob, scared off by a few rocks."[72] This scene evokes the LAPD's pivotal abandonment of the Florence and Normandie intersection in South-Central Los Angeles to rioters with rocks and two-by-fours. Many analysts see this moment as decisive in allowing an isolated outbreak of mob violence to take over the city.[73] This historically and materially realist moment in *The Tattooed Soldier* offers a sense of how the larger-scale, tectonic planetary motion that Silko envisions could indeed be taken up by a dispossessed population as a conduit to more dramatic and sustained urban rebellion. It also points to how acts of colonial delinking might themselves prompt the state to pull out of sites that are overtaken by an ontological insurgency. By characterizing the Riots as authorized and empowered by the crumbling city that speaks in the voice of rack and ruin, Tobar draws out the potential of earthly motion—in this case, the erosion of the mineral aggregate used to build the city—to act as an ally in becoming unstuck from the normalized community based on rational order and stability. Silko's "swarm" and Tobar's "fleeting storm" propose that dispossessed communities of color might operate transformatively, not because these communities have the money or weapons or politicians in place to take advantage of a moment of crisis but because the earth itself can operate as such a resource. For these people's armies, the earth serves as capital, weapon, ally, and investor in change. The earth's objects in motion—from the macro-force of mountains to the small and subtle algorithm of erosion—evince solidarity with the oppressed populations of modernity because they signal that the ontological order of things is not fixed; that one's body is not "stuck here," as Rodney King put it. This sense of solidarity with the angry planet becomes necessary, Silko and Tobar suggest, in the face of the impossibility of surviving the colonial-capitalist version of normal.

Deserts and Detritus

In *Almanac of the Dead* and *The Tattooed Soldier*'s narrative ontology, it is not only proliferative destruction that interferes with colonial modernity's version of normal. Silko and Tobar also explore those parts of the physical environment that are threateningly nonproductive and that delink, by virtue of their very uselessness, from circuits of capital value production. In *Almanac of the Dead,* the Sonoran Desert that stretches across the Mexico-U.S. border operates as such a threateningly nonproductive space. It is not that the desert is empty or devoid of life, but that it is not fertile ground for the capitalist logic of property rights or for the criminalization of raced bodies. *Almanac of the Dead*'s Zeta and Calabazas model this terrestrial nonproductivity, which refuses to yield well-defined property lines and well-managed racialized borderlands, in their cross-border drug trade whose "impunity," T.V. Reed remarks, "represent[s] a kind of transnationalism that preceded colonization and continued despite colonization; it also presages a truly postcolonial reality."[74] By recalling a seemingly vanished past and presaging a decolonized future, the desert operates as a nonhuman business partner to Calabazas and Zeta, offering them what is effectively a decolonial temporality in which to do business. Their drug mules cross the border undetected by working with the subtle complexities of the desert. The smugglers find a host of nonhuman allies in "not just the differences in the terrain that gave the desert traveler critical information about traces of water or grass for his animals, but the sheer varieties of plants and bugs and animals."[75] Calabazas takes his employees out to the desert to learn to "read" its rocks, noticing the subtle differences in basalt formations that will keep them oriented to "desert trails and secret border-crossing routes."[76] As in the case of the landslide, the terrestrial politics that Silko posits here is shaped by a cascade algorithm. Human actors gain in agency and mobility through following the contours of the land.

Where the colonial capitalist sees an unproductive wasteland, the Indigenous businessperson sees a rich resource for the development of alternative economic orders. "White men were terrified of the desert's stark, chalk plains that seem to glitter with the ashes of planets and worlds yet to come," Calabazas relates, emphasizing the desert's unsettling generativity.[77] As in *Mason & Dixon,* colonialists experience the anxiety of encountering a terrain already engaged in its own developmental processes. These pre- and postcapitalist relations of production are those evoked by George Manuel's description of the Fourth World economy where wealth is based on "an accurate reflection of the environment."[78] This terrain does not invite development so much as demand recognition and respect from its human inhabitants. Caren Irr argues that an important part of *Almanac of the Dead*'s revolutionary ethos is its appeal to time scales and cycles that deconstruct "the metaphysics of Eurocentric temporality."[79] While this Eurocentric temporality privileges a linear, progressive *telos,* the desert's "stark, chalk plains that seem to glitter with the ashes of planets and worlds yet to come" evoke cycles in which old empires fall and new orders gestate suggestively. Instead of a divinely ordained, capital-fueled expansion of empire without end, this cyclical temporality represents an ontological order expressed by the desert's own motion of transformative erosion and temporal scales beyond human lifespans. This motion does not terrify human subjects that draw their sense of ontological and political belonging from grounded normativity. It does, conversely, intimidate humans in search of territory upon which to impose a developmentalist agenda. The desert prophecies an end to empire that the colonialist refuses to countenance.

Silko's Southwest is one in which colonial warfare appears dramatically through modernity's failure to adhere to surfaces of sand and rock. In *The Tattooed Soldier,* it is not only these mineral materials but wood—the temporary and ad hoc scaffolding of construction sites and undeveloped lots—that fails to remain a stable material expression of state power and its racial capitalist agendas. Thrown out of their tenement apartment at the beginning of the novel, Antonio and his friend José Juan join a homeless community on Crown Hill, a small rise in the center of Los Angeles overlooking the financial district to the south and the massive stack interchange connecting the Harbor, Hollywood, and Pasadena freeways to the east. Antonio and José find the hill covered in crumbling buildings and occupied by a homeless encampment, "some sort of geographic anomaly, a lush knoll of wild plants and grasses in the middle of the city."[80] As the new arrivals explore Crown Hill, they find beneath the tents and shacks "the ruins of a lost community, a forgotten neighborhood built with brick and cement."[81] Antonio thinks about the hill's previous inhabitants, "What sins did their parents commit, he wondered, to bring such destruction upon themselves?"[82] The ruins remind Antonio of the burning cornfields and demolished bridges he saw in Guatemala before his departure. They also call to mind Maya ruins in Guatemala City, "a vast empire," he thinks, now "little more than a series of earthen mounds covered with wild grasses."[83] Like Silko's Sonora Desert, Crown Hill exudes a cyclical temporality that interferes with the linear-progressive narrative of modernity. What happened on Crown Hill, however, was not civil war or the end of empire so much as the normalized "low-intensity warfare" that defines the history of Los Angeles property development.[84]

Tobar selects Crown Hill for his narrative because it is part of the Westlake area that fills with Central American immigrants from Guatemala and El Salvador in the 1970s and 1980s.[85] This choice of setting connects Westlake's role as a gathering place for this community of refugees and immigrants to the hill's history of colonial occupation and reoccupation. The history of Crown Hill itself is one in which, as Arturo Arias puts it, "mobile, deterritorialized transnationalist polyglot communities are, willingly or not, connected to the territorializing forces of colonialism."[86] Before Antonio and José arrive in the spring of 1992, Crown Hill has been the site of multiple phases of colonial terraforming. Originally the home of the Kizh (Gabrielino-Tongva) people, the hill was part of vast tracts of land that became open to development after the federal government mismanaged treaty documents in 1852.[87] By the 1880s, the area had become an upscale residential district, but this first wave of intensive development was curtailed in 1892 when speculators struck oil on the hillside.[88] Readers of Upton Sinclair's *Oil!* (1926) can imagine how this boom transformed the topography of the hill into a soupy morass of mud and crude.[89] As the boom years faded in the early twentieth century, a wave of redevelopment brought residential housing and a large public high school to the hilltop. Post–World War II city planning, on the other hand, cut short urban residential growth in Los Angeles and brought in the nearby freeway stack exchange to export middle-class white families to cul-de-sac neighborhoods outside the city center. Over the postwar decades, now populated by "senior citizens and immigrant families," Crown Hill began to "suffer from an aging infrastructure, widespread neglect, and private disinvestment."[90] Efforts to revitalize the area during the 1980s real estate boom led to the demolition of small, aging apartment complexes, and then to a building moratorium, which halted further development of Crown Hill until the early 2000s.[91] Beginning with a foundational act of Indigenous expropriation, Crown Hill's is a history of how the terraforming imperative of coloniality returns again and again to exploit land and dispossess communities of color in the interest of capital development and white Anglo (re)settlement. It is this developmentalist logic that makes 1990s Los Angeles what Min Hyoung Song calls "a patchwork of negative and rationalized spaces," offering a sunny suburban ideal to a white middle class, and obscurity, poverty, and social-spatial stuck-ness to the city's racialized others.[92]

This terrain, shaped by decades of exploiting and asserting control over the hill's topography, appears as a site of "disaster" and "destruction" to Antonio and José. But despite this history, Tobar suggests that the very cyclical temporality of Crown Hill escapes spatial stuck-ness and resists operating as the obedient avatar of the city's "'cultural logic' of hygiene, rationalization, and control."[93] The subtle terrestrial motion of erosion eats away at the "forgotten neighborhood built with brick and cement" and like *Almanac of the Dead*'s desert, the very nonproductivity of these forgotten spaces produces other forms of flourishing.[94] *The Tattooed Soldier*'s narrative presents a mode of conceptualizing the generative possibilities of marginal spaces that responds to a critical problem Madhu Dubey identifies in what she calls "the romance of the residual."[95] "How exactly," Dubey asks, "are the material sites of racial oppression transformed into spaces of resistance?"[96] Dubey is critical of spatial theorists who attempt to salvage sites of oppression by reinterpreting them as heterotopias of creative cultural resistance, but Tobar's narrative ontology posits that survival may unfold in these sites through their very material contingency. In the city's abandoned lots, the agentic force of the earth produces material goods such as discarded wood that make marginal spaces survivable. It is via this weird harvest that the hill offers "kinship" to Antonio and its other homeless residents.

Crown Hill's history of disaster yields tools and objects that become ready-to-hand for those humans who cannot buy their way into the circuits of capitalist production. The hill provides Antonio and José with the materials they need to build a shelter and fuel for cooking fires. They erect a roof "with six rotting two-by-fours José Juan had rescued from an alley on Alvarado . . . braced them upright with bricks and chunks of concrete."[97] They find "sheets of plywood" in abandoned lots, and "when the rains began . . . the water did not seep through."[98] "In this city of asphalt and concrete it was surprising how much wood you could find lying around," Antonio thinks, experiencing the same sense of disorientation he expresses when he wonders where the rioters get their rock projectiles.[99] This unexpected wealth of wood is the surplus of urban development and its temporary structures. Previously employed to block off construction sites and underdeveloped private property, the wood is the remains of scaffolding and temporary fencing left behind as the valueless excess of building "this city of asphalt and concrete." The urban lumber employed as temporary scaffolding for the city's real architecture falls out of the circuits of value production and lies fallow. By registering as valueless, the wood delinks from its job as a value-creating commodity and returns to the earth, reverting back to its status as what Marx calls the "materials of nature."[100] The wood reinhabits the physical environment, recalling its existence as a not-yet-commoditized tree form.

Like the desert rocks in *Almanac of the Dead,* the decommoditized wood is a reminder of object worlds that escape capitalist commodity circuits and their production of racialized stuck-ness. In her work on the relationship between object worlds and racial belonging, Sara Ahmed notes that "the commodity might be one moment in the 'life history' or career of an object."[101] A piece of wood might fall in and out of existence as a commodity, and even serve use values, as it does for Antonio and José, that defy the circuits of capital. Ahmed wants us to think about what it means for racial belonging when objects fail to do what they are intended to do. In Tobar's narrative, this framework applies particularly well to the object that fails to "do" for the reproduction of colonial order. "Failure, which is about the loss of the capacity to perform an action for which the object was intended is not a property of an object," Ahmed writes, "but rather of the failure of an object to extend a body."[102] Like a natural disaster that is only disastrous because it interferes with human control over the environment, an object becomes a failure only when it fails to meet human expectations, and in this case, the expectations of some humans more than others.[103] As Antonio and José harvest the city's discarded wood, the wood fails to extend the body of capital, failing in its assigned work of delineating property lines and excluding racialized bodies. Instead, discarded wood extends the bodies of homeless immigrants who have not paid for it or invested in it as a means of production.

Not only, then, does this new phase in wood's career fail to serve the state's developmentalist agenda, it fails to bolster the racializing project of benign neglect whereby Antonio and José would ideally die of exposure, illness, or violence, random or targeted by state terror. In this chapter's understanding of the city as a site of ongoing colonial warfare, to be homeless and undocumented is not to be a surplus population waiting in the wings of biopolitical order but to inhabit what Achille Mbembe describes as the "peculiar carceral space" of necropolitical state power, "in which people deemed surplus, unwanted, or illegal are governed through abdication of any responsibility for their lives and their welfare."[104] By failing to work for this state power and moving closer to its original ontological status as "materials of nature," wood expresses the earth's own failure to consistently reproduce the colonial-capitalist relations of production that not only make surplus but make death out of illegible human bodies. The city's projects of strategic neglect fail to keep its racial others stuck unto death. In an antithetical sense, then, Tobar imagines urban neglect and racial exclusion working together by not working for the city and surviving together by delinking from the normalized community. If being a good employee of modernity means participating in its ontology of development and control, civic infrastructure delinks through a strategic nonproductivity that tells modernity, in the American tradition stretching from Bartleby to the Dead Kennedys, to take this job and shove it.

Freeways, Golf Courses, and Other Disasters

In a narrative ontology in which the planetary surface quits colonial capitalism, tiny accidents abound. Every surface is slippery and uncertain; every confident step forward is an act of hubris that human social actors can only hope will keep them on the safe side of the cracks snaking beneath their feet. When Antonio and José first arrive on Crown Hill, they visit with the homeless camp's leaders, Frank and the Mayor, sitting on an old couch positioned on the edge of a cliff "providing a panoramic view of the Harbor Freeway, the Financial District, and City Hall."[105] What the homeless men like about the view, they explain, is "watching accidents" on the Harbor Freeway, "the most dangerous stretch of freeway in California."[106] "People switching lanes so much they can't help but run into each other," Frank explains. "Trying to get over to the Santa Ana, the Pasadena, the Hollywood. Sideswiping each other and shit. It's the funniest thing I ever seen."[107] Frank's description of Los Angeles's Four Level Interchange evokes the sense, also central to *The Intuitionist,* that colonial-capitalist modernity, and especially its cities, are such dense accretions of complex systems, always in motion, always at high speeds, that accidents become a kind of inevitable part of spatial order.[108]

Their devastating consequences make such encounters disastrous, rather than, say, serendipitous. Frank describes "fender-benders, sideswipes, flip-overs" that radically transform their material settings, costing money, ending and altering lives, setting off ripples of cause-and-effect that may never return those involved to a state of normalcy.[109] What makes these disasters "the funniest thing . . . ever" from Frank's perspective is that they contravene the driver's belief that, secure in his vehicle, secure on the freeway whose very material composition seems to speak Lefebvrian "domination of space" by capitalist order, he cannot possibly be the victim of a disastrous accidental encounter.[110] That such encounters do occur—that they "can't help but run into each other"—is a gleeful experience for the observer experiencing homelessness because, like an earthquake or a riot, it puts the lie to the stability of capitalist order in which only society's uninsured and undocumented members are at risk of being the victims of an accident's disastrous consequences.[111] It also reveals the ways in which the urban environment is not so clearly separated from the rhythms of the earth and that "sense that nature is precarious," as Vizenor writes of the grounded normative knowledge imparted by "natural reason."[112] In such a narrative ontology, the accident, like the crisis, does not prey only on the already disenfranchised. Whether on the freeway or navigating the global flows of capital, no amount of wealth, privilege, or power can save you from an angry planet in motion.

While the above sections of this chapter focus on terrestrial motions that delink from colonial-capitalist order by failing to serve the state, Frank's freeway tableaux evoke the Lucretian clinamen, a material quality not of detachment or escape but of collision, in which a small and unpredictable swerve diverges from the smooth order of matter in motion with the potential to generate a cascade of devastating consequences. Louis Althusser's late work on what he calls "the underground current of the materialism of the encounter" speaks to how sites of capitalist domination create conditions that tend toward the accidental collision. Althusser's argument begins with Epicurus and Lucretius, who describe the primordial state of matter as "an infinity of atoms . . . falling parallel to each other in the void . . . then the clinamen supervenes . . . and, breaking the parallelism in an almost negligible way at one point, induce *an encounter* with the atom next to it, and, from encounter to encounter, a pile-up and the birth of a world."[113] What Frank sees in every pile-up on the stack exchange is the generativity of the *swerve,* a different possible world peering out from behind the leering mask of the freeway's domination of space. Althusser uses Epicurus to make the point that the rise and dominance of capitalist state power is historically contingent. The problem with a strong historical materialist analysis, Althusser argues, is that it ascribes a retroactive inevitability to capitalist order that makes it seem stable when it is, in fact, "haunted by a *radical instability*."[114] To see a crash on the Harbor Freeway, then, is to see the hegemonic narrative of historically determined social trajectories as ontologically unstable. It is to see the swerve in action as an expression of the angry planet, in which the sideswipe and flip-over that shatter capitalist fantasy signal the possibility of a different future for those living the capitalist reality.

An aleatory event can reach out to pluck the usually mobile capitalist from the stream of securely flowing commodity circuits. Silko, with particular deliberation, uses her narrative ontology to set up loci of colonial-capitalist security—the geological survey, the golf course, the insurance company, the "bombproof, bulletproof, fireproof" vault—only to explode that fantasy of security.[115] *Almanac of the Dead*'s capitalists are consistently (and for many readers, disturbingly) figurative types who are disabused of their fantasies of control by the angry planet.[116] In a motion that is the ontological obverse to the clinamen crash, Zeta and Lecha's father, a geologist hired by their family's silver mining company, becomes the victim of the encounter that accidentally fails to occur. The geologist's job is to predict the location of silver veins and deposits. He is a representative of scientific colonialism, the branch of colonial capitalism employed, as in *Mason & Dixon,* to gain control over not only the surface but subsurface of the earth. "The inscription of geological principles in the founding narrative of the colonial state, in terms of the colonization of both resources and racialized belonging," Kathryn Yusoff writes, "encodes the brutal calculative logic of inhuman materiality" while nonetheless relying on "the fixity of geologic description to facilitate exchange."[117] By this, Yusoff identifies an aporia in scientific reasoning based in the colonial idea of land: that the seemingly neutral geology that enables mineral extraction feeds the colonial logic of racialized dehumanization *and* "remains stubbornly resilient" to questioning the social ontology inflecting its mineralogical discourse.[118] To put it bluntly: science cannot be racist and accurate at the same time. *Almanac of the Dead* illustrates this aporia when the geologist fails in his task unto his own dissolution. His predictions do not yield ore. "While the mining engineer could still name the formations and the ore-bearing stones and rocks . . . his calculations on the maps for known deposits and veins had been wrong; he had directed the miners to nothing."[119] Other geologists "could find no fault with his work. They could not account for the absence of ore in the depths and areas he had designated."[120] Silko presses on the absence of "fault" here to emphasize that the colonial violence of mining and the geological science that supports it as a rationalist enterprise cannot fully predict, understand, or know the earth's secrets. In *Almanac of the Dead,* the failure of mining ventures such as these is proof not only of the scientific but the profoundly ontological error that comes from mixing human and inhuman materiality.

The veins of ore that evade entanglement with the geologist's predictions have profound implications for the construction of racialized belonging. *Almanac of the Dead's* unpredictable sites of capital accumulation model the spatial order that Thomas Pynchon's Charles Mason fears at the end of *Mason & Dixon.* On his deathbed, Mason anxiously intuits a future in which capital as a ravenous, space-and-time-consuming engine has so subsumed the North American continent that human subjects—and in particular, for Mason, the white male bourgeois subject—become nothing more than automatons, figures playing their role in the perpetuation of the capitalist machine. In *Almanac of the Dead,* Mason's grim prediction is realized when the earth's delinking from capitalist meaning-making also destabilizes the identity of its meaning makers. Zeta and Lecha's father is nameless, known in the novel only as "the failed geologist." He is, as Mason feared, not a recognizable subject with a name but an automatic function that fails to create value for capital circulation. Following this failure, the geologist withers away until he dies a husk of his former self. The punch line here that would surely have *The Tattooed Soldier's* Frank laughing is that the geologist dies from his investment in being a white male bourgeois professional. He can neither admit that he is a cog in a system *nor* emancipate himself from that system by admitting that the earth might be more complex than "the fixity of geological description" allows. Ironically, by insisting that he is to blame for the miners' failure to strike silver, by choosing to remain stuck in a logic of racialized belonging in which the subjectivity of what Yusoff calls "White Geology" is infallible, he dissolves into nonexistence.

This failed encounter, the missed opportunity to operate as a realized human subject within colonial-capitalist ontology, reverberates through *Almanac of the Dead* as some of the novel's most confident capitalists meet their deaths in spectacular accidents. Menardo is a Chiapas man who is ashamed of his Indigenous identity and conceals it in order to succeed in the business world. His success makes him a ruthless capitalist, an insurance salesman whose company, Universal Insurance, protects wealthy businessmen against "acts of God, mutinies, war, and revolution."[121] Like any good neoliberal capitalist, Menardo knows that both earthquakes and riots present the same type of risk to business investments—destruction of property, destabilization of the market, production slowdown—and so he builds an entire career around securing investment capital against the aleatory event. In other words, Menardo provides insurance for the exact type of encounter—also a focus of *The Intuitionist,* in which the founder of Intuitionist elevator inspection is a Black man passing as white—that he fears will expose him as a racialized subject. The problem with passing, as Menardo experiences with some acuity, is that the one passing lives on the constant edge of exposure. But while, in a colonial-capitalist ontology, the secretly raced subject is always about to be exposed by a racist environment that moves to reify capitalism's integrity, in a decolonial ontology, what is instead on the edge of exposure is the contingency of that integrity.

His desperate need to guard against the possibilities of the aleatory event leads Menardo to become obsessed with a bulletproof vest, "a modern miracle of high technology, the wonder fiber was neither bulky nor heavy but possessed a unique density that stopped knives and bullets."[122] Menardo wears the vest everywhere, even to bed at night, where he sleeps cocooned both in the vest and with the brochures describing the vest's miracle properties, which he pores over repeatedly. His maid "often found the color brochure about the vest in the bedcovers, evidence Menardo fell asleep reading about the vest."[123] Wrapped in these layers of protection—material, discursive, ideological—Menardo's obsession becomes a parody of material-semiotic entanglement; if he can wrap himself tightly enough in the vest and its promises, his body will be transmuted, untouchable. But Menardo's engagement with the commodity's use value cannot rest on security, and he decides that he must try the vest himself. "He wanted to witness the superiority of man-made fibers that stopped bullets and steel and cheated death."[124] Silko has Menardo stage his test of the vest's power on the ninth hole of the country club golf course where he and other key Chiapas politicos and businessmen go to shoot guns, get drunk, and do deals. The golf course is an ur-site of colonial excess and capitalist venality, emphasized by the group's enthusiasm for using "the back of the mound" at the ninth hole as "their private pistol range."[125] Golf courses are often built on the sites of tribal earthworks, mounds that to the course developer's eye seem ideal additions to the undulating terrain of a challenging course.[126] As if the massive resource drain and class privilege built into the physical environment by the country club were not brutal enough, the gun club actually shoots their weapons at the traces of expropriated Indigenous societies, "the mound," left in the land.

Part of the perverse parody of Menardo's test is that his body replaces the mound as the target, unwittingly evoking his own concealed Indigeneity in the very moment that he directs his driver, Tacho, to fire a 9mm automatic at his chest. This is also the moment that the vest reveals its secret identity as a bad object, a piece of the angry planet in disguise. The vest malfunctions, and the bullet hits Menardo directly in the chest. "A freak accident! How tragic! Microscopic imperfections in the fabric's quilting," police explain, "a bare millimeter's difference and the bullet would safely have been stopped."[127] Menardo dies on the golf course, puzzled as to why he feels "a warm puddle under himself. Why had the waiters poured soup over him?"[128] This last thought, steeped in befuddled class privilege, sustains Menardo's fantasy that he is still ensconced in that warm circle of commoditized security that he built for himself. This is "How Capitalists Die," as Silko explains in her title for the scene.[129] Menardo "falls for the worst con of all: he believes in his own con; he trusts in a technology of violence that is itself a con."[130] Menardo's life as a rapacious capitalist, predicated as it is on concealing his identity and insuring against accidents, is ended by the very type of aleatory event that he builds his empire to safeguard against. And in refusing both his Indigenous identity and the power of the aleatory, he condemns himself to a death in which he is made, through a grisly substitution, into the Indigenous earthworks that he has participated in subjugating.

Guillermo Longoria's death at the end of *The Tattooed Soldier* recalls Menardo's in the sense that it could not be a more obscure, undignified, muddy conclusion to a life spent fighting to get out of the dirt. Like Menardo, Longoria is an agent of colonial-capitalist violence, a soldier trained by the U.S. military to quell peasant insurgency in Guatemala. Also like Menardo, Longoria has Indigenous roots. He is a K'iche' peasant who works a plot of land with his mother before being forcibly recruited into the army, where he learns to see peasants like himself as a "cancer" or "virus" whose communist sympathies "threaten Guatemala's sovereignty."[131] Julie Minich points out that this origin story complicates Longoria's characterization as a brutal death squad leader. He and Antonio are both "victims *and* agents within a violent national project predicated on mestizaje."[132] But *The Tattooed Soldier* stresses Longoria's agency above his victimhood. He comes to the United States not as a refugee like Antonio but as a retired soldier eager to return to a "country where order and cleanliness reigned supreme."[133] And so it seems to be with deliberation that Tobar sets Longoria's death at novel's end in a muddy tunnel, a subterranean obverse to the freeways the soldier admires when he visits the United States for training at Fort Bragg. Like Menardo, Longoria dies in a puddle, which in both novels flags death as a melding with the earth that refuses the dignity of what Heather Houser defines as the environmentalist trope of planetary "merging" that "presents body and land as conduits to healing."[134] Instead, going "back to the land" for Menardo and Longoria confers ignominy, obscurity, and dissolution.

Taking the narrative quite literally underground, Tobar sets Longoria's death in the Belmont Tunnel and Toluca Yard at the foot of Crown Hill. This space takes on an active role in *The Tattooed Soldier*'s plot when bulldozers chase the homeless community off Crown Hill and they escape to the dark, abandoned tunnel. Tunnels are thus flagged in the novel as refuges from modernity. The city's subterranean spaces authorize modes of agency and mobility that are foreclosed in the world above. The Belmont Tunnel has a history as fraught by the vicissitudes of colonial-capitalist development as is Crown Hill. Built by Pacific Electric in 1925 to house the city's first subway line, the tunnel and station yard were active for a few short decades before the rise of the freeway system in Los Angeles signaled the city's decision to invest in the highways of personal mobility over the subways of public transportation. After a final run with the banner "To Oblivion" hung across its front car, the line closed in 1955 and the tunnel was abandoned. In subsequent decades, the concrete yard surrounding the tunnel became a nerve center for L.A. graffiti, offering West Coast artists a way to connect spatially with the train yard and subway car graffiti scene developing in New York in the 1970s and 1980s.[135] In these same decades, the Toluca Yard's floor, cement giving way to grassy field, became a meeting place for Central Americans looking for space to play *terasca*, an Olmec ball game.[136] The tunnel was eventually blocked off at one end by the construction of the foundations to the Bonaventure Hotel.[137] The remaining tunnel was used over the decades for storage, raves, and as a homeless refuge, as it is in *The Tattooed Soldier*. While the Belmont Tunnel has today been developed into the same class-conscious condos that carpet Crown Hill, in the early 1990s it was still one of those "negative spaces" of uneven redevelopment characteristic of Los Angeles.[138]

In Tobar's description, the Belmont Tunnel is an urban zone of neglect and decay where the planet reclaims its terrestrial body and shapes environments that authorize extra-legal activities officially condemned by the state. Long unmaintained, the tunnel's concrete construction materials delink from social order, reverting back to an organic state. Stripped of tracks when the subway line closed, the tunnel has a "muddy floor" pocked with "puddles of brownish water."[139] Its ceiling is "a broad arch of crumbling concrete the texture of sandstone" punctuated by "stalactite glistening ice white."[140] Frank, who shows Antonio the tunnel, explains that the puddles and the stalactite come from the same place, "all that rain that falls on the stockbrokers. That water has minerals and it leaves that shit right here."[141] Abandoned by capital investment, the tunnel engages in its own processes of growth and development, working with rain and minerals to become what Antonio characterizes repeatedly as "a cave."[142] Frank's description emphasizes that this is not a metaphor. Cave-ness is a geological quality that the tunnel grows toward as it delinks from civic order.

The Belmont Tunnel's concrete infrastructure reaches toward its earthy origins, delinking from the everyday violence of the dominant social-spatial order and becoming the site of a violence more clearly associated with the terrains of guerilla warfare that Antonio and Longoria believe they have left behind in Guatemala. After Antonio shoots him and leaves him for dead, Longoria, staggering from blood loss, follows

Antonio back to the tunnel. This slow pursuit tracks the novel's motion from the clean spaces of modernity to the violence of colonial warfare. The two men move "into a barren area of the city, a place with fewer and fewer buildings, fenced off fields of green . . . empty land . . . a green mountain."[143] As he bleeds out and "the concrete floor beneath him yields to mud," Longoria wonders, "are they still in the city?"[144] A good question, because Antonio is leading him, in a sense, out of the city and into the angry earth. After demanding if the soldier remembers his wife and son and getting no response—Longoria "doesn't remember. There were so many villages, so many people"—Antonio lets the dark and slimy indifference of the tunnel finish the job for him.[145]

Bleeding to death alone in the tunnel, Longoria's memories are "swallowed by the muddy floor," taking him back to the cornfields he worked as a young boy.[146] "Stalks rise from the black mud and push against the cement walls" and the soldier's last vision is of his mother; he joins her at her work "smil[ing] at his dirty toes, mud caked in the nails" while she calls him *Balam* (jaguar), like the tattoo he has to represent the jaguar battalion he fights for in Guatemala.[147] Longoria's final thoughts of a return to the land are activated by the tunnel's muddy floor, and the hallucinatory memory takes him from fear and grief to a sensation "strange and happy."[148] From the perspective of a terrestrial politics, the salient point here is that there is an absence of ethical judgment in this final moment. There is an account settled—Antonio gets his revenge—but there is not a reckoning. Longoria is never forced to face the contradictions of his life. Instead, the muddy floor offers a fantasy of reconciliation. Longoria's smiling mother is much like Menardo's annoyance that a waiter has poured soup on him. Just as Menardo remains imbricated in his capitalist fantasy world, Longoria remains deep within his own fantasy of triumphal colonial violence. Like Menardo, Longoria never faces the consequences of his actions, and his final moments are "strange and happy" because his split identities as "agent and victim" merge in the moment that his mother welcomes him home by the name *Balam* that he has learned to take pride in as a soldier.

Despite this final vision of return, however, Longoria's days of mobility are over. His lifetime as an agent of "disorder" and "chaos personified" confers on him only the illusion of mobility in death.[149] And unlike the global networkers that Fredric Jameson describes traveling programmatically on "people movers" (elevators and escalators) through the Hotel Bonaventure above, Longoria's body is well and truly stuck in place.[150] He will rot in the tunnel that operates as a limit point to the fantasies of globalization as flow, connectivity, and mobility. The muddy floor of the Belmont Tunnel thus authorizes Longoria's murder while refusing to make it mean something. The mud does not force him to see the global entanglements that connect the horror and contradictions of his history. Mud refuses to punish Longoria in the sense that it offers the material basis for a hallucinatory return home. But it gives Antonio his revenge by providing the material circumstances for Longoria's death. Dirt and obscurity make up the punch line of globalization and the angry planet both. You're not going anywhere.

Disorder and Delinking

Almanac of the Dead and *The Tattooed Soldier* conclude at points where disorder seems to have overtaken the normalized community. *Almanac of the Dead* with the planet on the brink of revolution, and "that safe old world that had never really existed" dissolving.[151] *The Tattooed Soldier* in the immediate aftermath of the L.A. riots, in a moment "nostalgic for the running crowds, for the sense of power, for the world turned upside down and the supermarkets where everything was free."[152] While these conclusions rest on opposite ends of the revolutionary moment, both stop immediately before the state steps in to reassert order. Unlike Wideman's *Philadelphia Fire* and Yamashita's *Tropic of Orange*, Silko and Tobar avoid aesthetically engaging the moment of direct state violence, but each also shies away from crossing the threshold into decolonial futurity. In *Almanac of the Dead*, revolutionaries are on the march before "the immense casualties" that will surely come when "the government would firebomb the crowds of angry citizens."[153] *The Tattooed Soldier* ends in the moment of possibility between the rioting and its aftermath, when state funds and policy will be directed toward increased policing and surveillance rather than community reconstruction.[154] These conclusions suggest that Silko and Tobar reach the limits of their narrative ontology at the threshold of positing how people and planet might cross over into a future that comes after the fall of the colonial-capitalist state. There is no possibility of the state offering disaster relief, social welfare,

or climate justice within this ontology, and it seems equally unimagi-
nable that the revolution will succeed in a way that allows for something
other than cataclysmic violence.

To be clear, the decolonial mandate that emerges from reading
with shattered grounded normativity is apocalyptic. Heaving fault lines,
crumbling concrete, cars careening off freeways, and sucking mud make
planetary motion a revolutionary ally only insofar as it is an alternative—and in these novels, oppositional—force to state power. It is only
in the absence of the state as a benevolent actor aligned with the interests of its citizens that destruction and violence become available as
the recuperative narrative framework that Tobar names "beautiful disorder."[155] And it is only within this same colonial-capitalist ontology that
extra-legal economies and abandoned infrastructures can be sources of
alternative social order and something akin to if not identical with justice. These are the forms of political belonging that an angry planet has
to offer its angry residents. Not entirely human, and not necessarily or
entirely survivable. But *Almanac of the Dead* and *The Tattooed Soldier*
make the point that these are the types of community and economy that
humans seek out in an American Third World shaped by the absence of
political or institutional recognition, by histories of trauma that limit
access to legible and survivable modes of citizenship, and by the total
failure of the colonial-capitalist state to protect or secure the welfare of
its people, or to offer redress in response to its own direct, infrastructural, and environmental violence.

What we arrive at, under these conditions, are possibilities for
decolonized spaces that are not automatically or necessarily habitable
by human communities. There are individuals in these spaces, but not
conditions for the return of communal life. While the world marches in
the novel's extradiegetic spaces, *Almanac of the Dead*'s narrative frame
closes with a grassy valley to which herds of buffalo are returning, and
an abandoned mine where a stone snake effigy, *Ma ah shra true ee,* rears
its head. Sterling, the novel's only Laguna Pueblo protagonist, gazes out
across the valley but remains a solitary human figure in this decolonizing
space, returned home, but in violation of an exile ordered by the Laguna
government. *The Tattooed Soldier* ends with the street after the Riots,
"the fields of broken glass" and "the soggy ashes that covered the sidewalks."[156] Antonio walks these streets alone, wishing for the return of

chaos and reluctant to join in the post-riot cleanup often invoked as a shining moment of solidarity in the L.A. riots' divisive history. These conclusions share a sense of space from which the state has absented itself and of a people more inclined to negotiate with the ground beneath their feet than with each other. If both novels celebrate the forms of solidarity that take shape within revolutionary struggle, they are less optimistic about maintaining and extending human community when the storm subsides. The solitary figures of Sterling and Antonio, moving through fields of animal life and mythic reason, broken glass and soggy ashes, suggest that after the lessons of shattered grounded normativity, applying the grounded normative demand to rebalance relations among humans is a different kind of challenge. Even a "land first" decolonial mandate imagines a future with humans still populating the earth. However, these novels conclude with the problem that launches the final chapter of *Angry Planet:* it may be easier to learn to live with the angry earth than to learn to live with each other.

4

THE FOURTH WORLD RESURGENT

GERALD VIZENOR'S *BEARHEART* AND OCTAVIA BUTLER'S *PARABLE OF THE SOWER*

I GREW UP ON TREATY ONE TERRITORY, in the Canadian city of Winnipeg, which is built at the confluence of two unmanageable rivers: the Red and the Assiniboine. These rivers are the reason for Winnipeg's location in what First Nations call "the Heart of Turtle Island."[1] It is not exactly prime real estate by colonial modernity's standards, but it is at the center of the continent. The pulse of life created by the rivers' intersection has resulted in the area functioning as a major transportation hub for thousands of years. And yet, these rivers have never been easy to live with. They are fast flowing, wide, deep, and thick with silt and debris. When the snow that blankets this part of the continent melts in the spring, the land floods, destroying riverfront property. Civic infrastructure suffers, too. Even in years without flooding, the rivers eat away at the city; parking lots along riverbanks erode, and hunks of asphalt spill into the water, exposing rusting rebar foundations. In 1962, the province built a floodway to keep the Red's annually rising waters from submerging the city. Still, in 1997, the house I lived in was almost destroyed by a flood that inundated the Red River Valley, a transnational disaster affecting towns and cities in North Dakota and in Manitoba. Although it cuts the state line between Minnesota and North Dakota, the Red does not have a great deal of respect for borders. The Red and Assiniboine are much like the unruly rivers in Thomas King's *Green Grass, Running Water,* and Linda Hogan's *Solar Storms.* These rivers look like good business propositions, but the environmental economies that they foster have a real problem with human administrative authority.

Despite a history of bad behavior, in 1989, when many midsized North American urban areas were struggling to make themselves over as world cities, Winnipeg developed a major tourist attraction dubbed "the Forks" at the V-shaped cut of land created by the Red and the Assiniboine. The Forks includes parks, markets, museums, hotels, and preserved historic sites. It is promoted as "a vibrant downtown Winnipeg public space where people gather for celebrations, recreation and, much like the early Aboriginals, to meet one another."[2] This reference to "the early Aboriginals" evokes the Forks' three-thousand-year history as "a meeting and trading point" for Assiniboine, Ojibwa, Cree, and Dakota First Nations, who used the area as "an intermittent seasonal camp."[3] But unlike these seasonal dwellers, Canadian settlers are determined to use the Forks as "a year-round attraction."[4] The problem with this colonial-capitalist fantasy is that every spring, the rivers swallow the Forks, covering the docks and fishing jetties and creeping over the riverside walkways, absorbing public art installations, benches, and lampposts. Water laps at the steps leading up to the main arcade and flows over the restaurant patio decks that tier the sloping banks. When the rivers recede in early summer, they leave behind a carpet of reeking mud, riverweeds, and debris: all good for what was once the rivers' floodplain but bad for the vibrant downtown public space. The thick clay deposits take the budget-conscious city weeks to clean up, and some years the river path is submerged until fall.[5] Every flood prompts debate over what can be done about the city's problem, but few speak from the position of grounded normativity to point out that the fork of the Red and the Assiniboine is not amenable to permanent settlement.

The floodplain that surrounds the fork of these rivers describes a long-standing struggle for spatial dominance between land as an expression of what George Manuel calls the Fourth World, and the instrumentalized land of the settler city. The persistence of the Fourth World is often most visible at sites where colonial spatial logic has failed to completely control and instrumentalize the physical environment. And in this case, the failure is a direct historical result of refusing to learn from the land or its original inhabitants, who respected a seasonal and contingent relationship to the rivers' confluence. Instead, at the heart of Turtle Island, the colonial developer digs in. Settlers built trading posts and stables, then railway yards, and then the Forks complex itself. These structures express a fantasy of colonial administrative power built on refusing to acknowledge the rivers' Fourth World agency, which becomes terrible when pitted in struggle against human life. It is terrible in the sense that it expresses the fury of a planet that is ontologically indifferent to who suffers the consequences of its wrath. It is not unusual for the bodies of the city's most vulnerable residents—Indigenous women and street kids—to be pulled from these rivers, their deaths explained away as the results of dangerous sex work and drug abuse.[6] As the novels discussed in this project demonstrate, when the subject of the planet's angry motion is the state, this motion can provocatively model an emancipatory terrestrial politics. This emancipatory potential cannot, however, be divorced from the supreme indifference of elemental fury. The appearance of this fury is, as angry planet fiction argues, the result of what Leanne Simpson calls "shattered grounded normativity," in which a damaged relationship between humans and land renders the material terms of knowledge production painful and often devastating.[7] The river's energy, its potency, and its imperatives express what this chapter designates as a form of sovereignty—the planet's own, terrestrially expressed right to self-determine social and spatial order on its surface. While the colonial-capitalist state works hard to erase the land's terrible agency, the novels discussed in this chapter ask what it looks like when the planet finally, furiously, refuses to be ignored.

The rumblings and landslides that we have seen from the angry planet in previous chapters subsume the North American continent in Gerald Vizenor's *Bearheart: The Heirship Chronicles* (1978 [1990]) and Octavia Butler's *Parable of the Sower* (1993). The two novels have parallel apocalyptic plot structures. In both, civil order in the United States collapses due to a combination of economic crises and environmental and geological disasters. Pushed to its limit, the planet rejects the entanglements of colonial terraforming, generating terrestrial conditions that are instead shaped by lightning-scorched earth, wildfires, oil and water shortages, collapsing coastlines, and swarms of earthquakes. If, as Achille

Mbembe suggests, colonial power is realized through "writing a new set of social and spatial relations on the ground," the land in *Bearheart* and *Parable of the Sower* moves to rewrite these social and spatial relations on its own terms.[8] As the state crumbles, changing material conditions force people out of their homes and onto the vehicle-abandoned freeway systems of Vizenor's Midwest and Butler's West Coast. Bands of travelers collect around charismatic leaders—Proude Cedarfair in *Bearheart* and Lauren Olamina in *Parable of the Sower*—and search for new spaces of belonging. These cross-country journeys rescript the Trail of Tears and the Underground Railroad, narratively marking histories of racial exploitation and colonial expropriation that ask readers to question the colonial spatial logic upon which the nation is founded. This time, rather than colonial soldiers or slave catchers, the sovereign planet drives these journeys, destabilizing the racializing operations of this logic, reversing the trajectory of frontier expansion, and welcoming different forms of human community into the newly resurgent terrains of Turtle Island. What this chapter designates as *terrestrial resurgence* occurs when the land delinks from the colonial-capitalist state and generates new conditions of possibility for being human in the process.

Resurgence, in the context of angry planet fiction, is the next step on the path to a decolonial future after delinking from colonial order, and it is a step that moves us from the American Third World into Manuel's Fourth World, a transition that is also evoked by Vizenor in *Bearheart*.[9] I use the term *resurgence* to connect the planet's motion in *Bearheart* and *Parable of the Sower* to the decolonial concept of resurgence that, more vibrant than ever as the twenty-first century progresses, first became central to Native American political mobilizations in the 1970s. Jeff Corntassel describes resurgence today as engaging Indigenous communities in daily practices that "reclaim and regenerate one's relational, place-based existence by challenging the ongoing, destructive forces of colonization."[10] Simpson stresses the importance of practicing what she calls "radical resurgence," which cuts through limited state-sanctioned modes of cultural and political resurgence to prioritize "an extensive, rigorous, and profound reorganization of things."[11] And as things are reorganized, so too is the category of the human. Radical resurgence identifies Indigenous "mobility imbued with agency" as "a flight path out of settler colonialism."[12] Simpson's radical resurgence thus centers on reconfiguring the relationship between land and human bodies through grounded normativity as the pathway to decolonization. Not dissimilarly, Vizenor and Butler describe the physical terrain of the continent as possessing this potential to reclaim and regenerate land-human relations and to challenge colonial orders of being. But in the following chapter, this potential becomes visible through the forced mobilities generated by terrain in apocalyptic upheaval. This is not quite the Indigenous model of reconnecting to land by getting out to the bush or the desert and relearning the earth's subtle algorithms. If capitalism grounded in colonial land theft has acted as "a kind of malware released into our ecological system," as Land Back activists posit, this is what happens when the system crashes and reboots, and humans are left with no choice but to acknowledge the land's own capacity to produce change that makes demands on human life.[13] Daniel Heath Justice offers a way into understanding these demands when he writes about the kinetic, bodily work of decolonization: "agents of change exist in relationship to one another and demonstrate by those interactions their ability to both influence others and to be self-determining."[14] Justice's point here is that in a politics of resurgence, social agents operate relationally while also respecting the radical autonomy of individual beings, including the land itself. This "relational, place-based" Indigenous praxis reconfigures the human relationship to land *and* recognizes the earth's often-terrifying capacity to disentangle itself from this relationship. The planet not only decolonizes its surface by demolishing state infrastructures. As these novels propose, it also puts forward its own set of social and spatial relations to model an alternative to global capitalism rooted in Fourth World land-based systems of governance and sociality. Resurgence unfolds in *Bearheart* and *Parable of the Sower* as unruly terrestrial motion translates into a demand that humans recognize land as an entity ontologically distinct from and with priority over property relations and resource extraction schemes.

For Vizenor in the late 1970s, the energy crises wracking the United States are ample proof of the planet's own nonanthropogenic agendas. When he first publishes *Bearheart* as *Darkness in St. Louis Bearheart* in 1978, the relationship between oil shortages—a reference to the oil shocks of the 1970s—and the collapse of colonial-capitalist society is direct. "White culture is refined from oil," the novel's introduction states, "No oil, no laws, no shame, no guilt, no more culture to hold people down together."[15] When the novel is republished in 1990, these lines are excised from its opening pages, and the plot focuses on a more generalized global environmental crisis in which "first the fish died, the oceans turned sour, and then birds dropped in flight over cities."[16] Oil shortages are, in *Bearheart's* republication, not an isolated issue but instead an expression of the earth asserting its existence as something other than a support system for white petroculture and what Reza Negarestani calls the "epic narratives" petroculture proliferates.[17] For Butler, global warming is a similarly noisy interlocutor. "I was aware of [global warming] back in the 1980s," she says in an interview, "and a lot of people were seeing it as politics, as something very iffy, as something they could ignore because nothing was going to come of it tomorrow."[18] As in *Bearheart,* Butler's representations of resource and climate catastrophe are not an attempt to point out bad environmental politics but to address a state of ontological crisis that is already beyond the scope of partisan politics in the 1970s and 1980s.

Like other writers of angry planet fiction, Vizenor and Butler track the entanglements of racialization and environmental exploitation back to their origin point in colonial capitalism. Readers often approach Vizenor's and Butler's work as narratively challenging dominant constructions of textuality and identity.[19] More recently, Lee Rozelle, John Gamber, and Lee Schweninger have produced persuasive accounts of each author's materialist and environmentalist imaginations.[20] This chapter adds to these assessments an account of how Vizenor's and Butler's imaginaries share a complicated decolonial agenda in their representations of the resurgence of terrestrial sovereignty. Butler's oeuvre, in particular, troubles any straightforward designation of the author as a decolonial thinker. Her enthusiasm for space travel can appear to "counsel a new colonialism."[21] And *Parable of the Sower* is marked by Lauren Olamina's efforts to learn survival strategies by reading books about "California Indians, the plants they used, and how they used them."[22] This is the kind of fascination with Indigenous epistemologies that Vizenor might call "manifest manners," in which "the tragic wisdom [of tribal others] that was once denied is now a new invention."[23] At the same time, Lauren's commitment to imagining and building a world after racial capitalism and its colonial foundations is suggested by her understanding of the world around her as governed by "Change." Lisa Brooks proposes that the right to change is a characteristic of terrestrial sovereignty. Before colonial conquest, Brooks writes, Turtle Island was defined by "a network of relations and waterways containing many different groups of people as well as animal, plant, and rock beings that was sustained through the constant transformative 'being' of its inhabitants."[24] As the world around her is thrown into physical upheaval, Lauren identifies the land's constant transformative quality as constitutive of its grounded normativity. The fact of change, and the right to change, also shapes what Vizenor calls the "*sui generis* sovereignty" of "transmotion, that sense of native motion and an active presence" that asserts the unceded Indigenous right to move across and with the land.[25] In stressing the sovereignty of agentic motion, Vizenor rejects the colonial mindset that views Indigenous bodies and cultures as fixed in history and in space. And despite the property-centrism that inflects her narrative ontology, Butler's emphasis on transformation and motion does similar decolonial spatial work, proposing that human life cannot survive under structural conditions that trap racialized bodies in place and time.

The following argument tracks the resurgence of terrestrial sovereignty—in other words, the emergence of the Fourth World as a terrestrial revolutionary agency—in *Bearheart* and *Parable of the Sower*. In the first part of the argument, I look at how the transformative motion of the angry planet dismantles state sovereignty and its property-protective function. In the next section, I detail how the sovereign planet restructures the terrestrial surface on its own terms and consider how this act of decolonial resurgence unfolds through each novel as both painful and emancipatory for human actors that must now engage modes of agency and mobility that operate in the absence of state power. In the final section, I consider how the human, as an ontological category that we have seen compromised into a hierarchy of racial ciphers throughout angry planet fiction, finds the conditions for Fourth World resurgence in each novel's apocalyptic landscape. However, it is also at this point that an adherence to property and to thinking a land-based identity *as* property delineates each novel's arrival at a barrier to decolonial futurity. What George Lipsitz names "the possessive investment in whiteness," wherein white wealth and privilege thrive through the colonial history of "expressly discriminatory and racist land use practices," is stripped of its racializing force in these novels by the angry planet.[26] However, this does not stop the emergence of a new kind of land grab defined by survivors claiming a unique relationship to the earth. Proude Cedarfair and Lauren Olamina's privileged understanding of their relationship to the angry planet, I argue, reproduces spatial patterns of ownership that are deeply rooted in the same notions of property that produce the foundational colonial alienation of human life from land. If becoming human, in angry planet fiction, is an aspiration and a struggle, it becomes a kind of contest of pointing out who is failing the earth's test in these apocalyptic terrains. Unlike post-9/11 apocalypse novels—Cormac McCarthy's *The Road* (2006) for example—there is no agenda in these novels of preserving something like the human spirit in hopes of reconsolidating old orders of being. *Bearheart* and *Parable of the Sower* are interested in what new modes of being human emerge through the destruction of the old spatial forms of anthropocentric privilege, but this commitment to claiming new territory ultimately complicates each novel's decolonial mandate.

Resurgence

Vizenor and Butler's narrative ontology begins with the angry planet transforming the colonial-capitalist organization of space. Both novels describe the Fourth World that comes after the planetary revolution imagined in Silko's *Almanac of the Dead*. The planet's major target for revision is what Beth A. McCoy, writing on *Parable of the Sower,* calls the "property-protective foundation of the American state."[27] Each novel's starting point is a specific site of property development where American First and Third Worlds exist in the uneasy tension of racialized partition: the Native American reservation in *Bearheart,* and the southern Californian gated community in *Parable of the Sower. Bearheart* begins in a tiny, self-proclaimed sovereign nation situated within the Red Cedar Indian Reservation in Minnesota. The cedar circus, an isolated corner of the larger Red Cedar Reservation, is organized around a circle of cedar trees near the headwaters of the *Misisibi* River. The trees are "celebrated" and "defended" by four generations of Proude Cedarfairs, who define the cedar's space as sovereign in contrast to the "grim reservation" and the political machinations of federal and tribal officials.[28] The Cedarfairs recognize, as Kathryn Hume puts it, that the cedars have "the same status, rights, and rites as humans," and reject the settler-colonial idea that federal or tribal governance can define the uses of the cedars within the space created by their presence.[29] In the novel's recognition of non-human sovereignty, I see an important facet of grounded normativity, which is the relationship between the interconnectedness of all beings and the radical autonomy of individual beings. "While the land herself is of central concern to most indigenous epistemologies," Justice writes, "we don't know her outside of our relationship(s) to her."[30] Recognizing this autonomy places constraints on colonial-capitalist modes of relationality. If the cedars cannot be fully known or understood, then to exploit or instrumentalize them without limit can have unpredictable consequences.

Of course, colonial-capitalist logic denies any such premise. When the fuel-short federal government demands half the timber from Red Cedar, it threatens the ring of ancient trees. Proude recognizes that Jordan Coward, the Red Cedar tribal president who hates and resents the Cedarfairs' rejection of reservation politics, is using the trees as political fodder. Rather than adhering to what Vizenor calls a "terminal creed," an inflexible ideology that would require Proude to take on the role of the tragic Indian, sacrificing his life—and the life of the cedars—in service to a perceived special relationship to the land, the Cedarfairs decide to leave the cedar nation. "If we are gone [Coward] will have no use for these trees," Proude explains, "to defend the trees now we must not defend them again."[31] By leaving the reservation, Proude hopes to delink the trees from the focal register of human "word wars," Vizenor's term for discursive contests that attempt to replace reality with the force of representations.[32] Proude and Rosina are already on the road when government agents arrive at the cedar circus. Furious at their disappearance, the agents burn down the Cedarfair house, distracted, as Proude hoped, from taking the trees. While this act of destruction is punishing, it seems to prove Proude's point: it is a human dwelling, rather than the trees, that absorbs the "crazed mongrel" Coward's "evil energies."[33] By allowing the trees their autonomy, Proude extricates them from the colonial entanglements that condemn them to a fate determined by human representational politics.

This opening scene describes a relationship between humans and land that is explicitly decolonial in its rejection of the politics of property rights and of ethnic or cultural belonging as tied to territorial rights. While Proude is deeply connected to the red cedars, he denies that this connection can be understood through the colonial logic of property ownership. Instead, the Cedarfairs model an ontological understanding of, in the words of Glen Sean Coulthard, "what the land *as system of reciprocal relations and obligations* can teach us about living our lives in relation to one another and the natural world in nondominating and nonexploitative terms."[34] Coulthard's emphasis on *reciprocal relations and obligations*, just like Proude's position in this scene, stresses that a decolonized relationship to land is one of "transmotion": mobile, flexible, adaptable interactions between people and place with none of the territorial fixity enforced by federal policies that circumscribe tribal groups and Indigenous identities. Transmotion in *Bearheart* models Mishuana R. Goeman's call for "a recuperation of the mobile Native subject" as a means of disrupting "the logics of [settler] grammar."[35] While it is not easy for Proude and Rosina to leave the cedars, they take with them the "relations and obligations" that they have with the space that the trees create. The transmotion modeled in this scene theorizes grounded normativity in a way that asserts the Indigenous right to land by refusing to be delimited by the borders of a reservation or authorized by the violent ethno-culturist equivalence of blood and soil.

Robledo, the gated community in which Lauren lives with her family at the beginning of *Parable of the Sower,* is a kind of refraction of the reservation's spatial logic. Colonial-capitalist state power is reproduced in the gated community by spatial borders that misrecognize land as private property. The multiracial families behind Robledo's walls attempt to survive the privations of the collapsing state by adopting a semiagrarian lifestyle, cultivating the land they have, and sharing resources communally. However, the strength of this communal world is rendered insupportable by its spatial form. As Jerry Phillips suggests, "Privatopia, the walled or gated community, is, at bottom, a fantasy of escape, that one can be in the world without having to live through the sharp contradictions that the world presents. Lauren sees that a community based on such bad faith has little hope of averting eventual catastrophe."[36] The novel's restriction of its vision of multiracial cooperative solidarity to this "fantasy" space evokes the gated neighborhood's "historically vexed relationship" to racial belonging.[37] Such spaces are generally white or ethnically homogenous and tend to magnify and expel racial difference; they are also physically designed to profile and police belonging, even when their racial makeup is shifting.[38] Robledo's communal ethos does little to mitigate the class privilege structuring its borders, as is enforced by Lauren's insistence that her neighborhood's "supposed wealth and privilege" is only such in comparison to extreme poverty.[39] Her phrasing voices the middle-class lament for the suburban absence of 'real' wealth, power, and cultural prestige.[40] The pervasive sense of being made insecure by security is endemic to the socially pathologizing, spatially racializing function of private property ownership.

While the plot trajectory of *Parable of the Sower* drives toward a new type of community and of community belonging, the forms of land misrecognition generated by property ownership qualify the novel's ideal of communally shared space. When well-defended multinational corporate enclaves start to spring up around the country, Lauren's family disdains those willing to buy protection in exchange for what amounts to "debt slavery."[41] "'Your mother says all you'll have is an apartment,'" Lauren says to a friend whose family is buying in. "'No yard. No garden. You'll have less money, but you'll have to use more of it to buy food.'"[42] This scene is often read as the Olamina family's bold refusal to be co-opted by neoliberal economic products—in this case, a privatized city that reproduces the spatial order of industrial-era labor camps and share-cropper economies.[43] Butler certainly intends this reading, as she links the American export of neoliberal spatial logic directly to the legacy of slavery and debt bondage in U.S. history.[44] However, as an illustration of the felt link between property ownership and freedom, Lauren's reaction, specifically couched in terms of apartment living, also evokes the First World horror at urban population density and shared space that justified white flight and fed the development of land-consuming suburban enclaves in the post–World War II period. This refusal to give up on a privileged relationship to property will haunt Lauren's attempts to build the new community of Acorn in the isolated hills of Humboldt County. On terrain ruled by the angry planet, all privatopias are doomed to fail.

Although emerging from a distinct history of property development, the spatial logic of Butler's gated community resembles that of Vizenor's Red Cedar Reservation. The same racial capitalist developmentalism that went into the internment of Indigenous nations on reservations, often at dramatic removes from both ancestral tribal lands and resource-rich bioregions, is also used to develop gated enclaves.[45] The spatial logic structuring both assumes that once territorial borders are defined, a community formation can operate as a placeless anyplace. In *Almanac of the Dead,* Silko makes this point through a description of the real estate boom that hit Arizona in the 1980s, when efforts to fill the southwest desert with lagoon-like gated developments spatially dramatized the connections between the area's history of racial violence and, as Heather Houser puts it, the "bio- and ecotechnological violence" required to construct deregionalized pleasure palaces for the leisure class.[46] Under the ostensible heading of protecting and defining an ethnically homogenous community, both the reservation and the gated neighborhood are predicated on the refusal to acknowledge that the outside world continues to shape—and be shaped by—bordered spaces. In the case of the reservation, these borders isolate and disenfranchise even as they claim to allow for Indigenous self-determination; in the case of the gated community, the privilege of property owners is ostensibly protected from an unsavory heterogeneous outside even as it is made the target of that outside's hostility and left to the dubious mercies of its own homogenously constituted victimhood. By plotting terrain that cannot sustain the contradictions of these spatial divisions, *Bearheart* and *Parable* demonstrate how easy it is for terrestrial upheaval to interfere with spatial fantasies of privilege and containment.

In *Bearheart,* terrestrial upheaval comes in the form of the planet's failure to yield the resources required to support the colonial state's terraformed surface. "National supplies of crude oil had dribbled to nothing," Vizenor writes, and "the cities were gasless and dark."[47] Vizenor's emphasis on "national supplies" hints at the OPEC embargoes that drove global oil prices up in the 1970s. However, it also evokes U.S. struggles with managing its own peak oil production. It is not that the planet has been sucked dry in *Bearheart* but that the nation can no longer access the crude oil it needs to sustain its epic narrative of global dominance.[48] Crude oil is, in effect, withdrawing from its relationship to the national economy. Vizenor connects the fuel shortage to the failure of the city as a form of spatial organization. Now "gasless and dark," the cities that have profited from exploiting ecologically rich rural peripheries are abandoned, and disenfranchised rural communities themselves become withdrawn, "hostile toward those from the cities who had consumed all the fuel and resources with electrical devices."[49] To build a city that requires so much fuel to survive, Vizenor suggests, is precisely the kind of ideological fantasy that collapses without a fuel-driven economy. As oil withdraws its support from the colonial-capitalist state, it also forces a reconfiguration of the state's exploitative center-periphery resource model.

In *Parable of the Sower*, economic collapse is driven by water shortages, extreme weather events, and seismic activity: a confluence of "failing economies and tortured ecologies" brought on by global warming.[50] Butler describes the town of Olivar as paradigmatic of these conditions. An L.A. beach suburb constructed on the privileged capitalist relation between economic wealth and prime coastal real estate, Olivar is "unstable . . . parts of it sometimes crumble into the ocean."[51] As in *Bearheart*, cities become unsustainable models of spatial organization. When refugees stream out of an imploding L.A. area, Olivar finds itself caught between "an influx of salt water from one direction and desperate poor people from the other."[52] A cascading motion that is the obverse to *Bearheart*'s shrinking oil reserves and hostile rural spaces, this sudden influx of ocean water and human need is the same kind of material excess that interferes with colonial-capitalist order in *Philadelphia Fire* and *Tropic of Orange*. The angry elements, and the angry people, refuse to stay in their state-allocated places. The ocean no longer plays the role of domesticated preserver of class advantage, offering beachfront luxury to a privileged few.

What Amitav Ghosh calls "the unpredictable furies of the ocean" expose the unsustainability of the settler relationship to coastlines.[53] Ghosh identifies this relationship as stemming from "a colonial vision of the world, in which proximity to the water represents power and security, mastery and conquest . . . now incorporated into the very foundations of middle-class patterns of living across the globe."[54] The irony and danger of this vision, Butler makes clear, is that as a pattern of living, it "can't protect itself from the encroaching sea, the crumbling earth, the crumbling economy, or the desperate refugees."[55] The strategies that colonial order has used to confer classed and raced forms of privilege are not only environmentally and infrastructurally violent; they mark, as Ghosh argues, a "bourgeois belief in the regularity of the world" that has "been carried to the point of derangement."[56] And as the increasing instability of coastlines and climate systems bring this deranged belief to light, they also put the lie to the rationalism and stability of colonial-capitalist modernity. Refusing to stay in place or to yield without limit, the oceanic and terrestrial forces in *Bearheart* and *Parable of the Sower* devalue and reorganize the colonial mantles of "property" and "resource."

Terrestrial Sovereignty

The assertion of terrestrial sovereignty is the unshattering of grounded normativity. As is characteristic of angry planet fiction, borders that do not hold and ecologies that refuse to be instrumentalized or partitioned are expressions of the planet rejecting the colonial-capitalist state's "totalizing control of the historical forces that might undo it."[57] As an unshattering, planetary movement is not a purely destructive force in either novel. The resurgent earth that Vizenor and Butler describe also delineates new modes of social-spatial organization based on its ontologically sovereign being. This revolutionary imaginary resonates with Third World–inspired American social movements, like the 1969–71 Indigenous occupation of Alcatraz that planned to turn the former prison into an "all-Indian university," identifying the reorganization of space as the precondition for reconceptualizing sociality.[58] *Bearheart* provides the most direct articulation of the new spatial logic dictated by terrestrial sovereignty when officials arrive at Proude and Rosina's house with an executive order claiming the trees of the cedar nation for the new federal timber plan. The officials read the order out loud to Proude, emphasizing that resistance would not be in line with "the meaning of being a citizen."[59] Proude responds by stating that the signifying function of the executive order is defused within the space of the cedar nation: "These trees were the first to grow here, the first to speak of living on this earth . . . These trees are sovereign," he explains. "We are cedar and we are not your citizens . . . Can you see and feel how we shun your indifference to our lives."[60] I read this appeal as invoking not only an arboreal but specifically terrestrial sovereignty in that Proude frames the cedars as indivisible from the broader community of beings—"we are cedar"— out of which they "grow" and "speak."

In this short passage, Proude makes several ontological assertions that propose grounded normative alternatives to the extractive and exploitative function of colonial-capitalist spatial order. He states that the cedar trees possess sovereignty that is ontologically prior—"first to grow"—to the dictates of state jurisdiction. This assertion modifies Hume's claim that "for Vizenor . . . sovereignty represents a state to which we might all aspire."[61] Sovereignty is, rather, an ontic quality of being that human and nonhuman agents occupy through their relationship to each other. In these terms, the sovereignty of being, which is expressed through the "ability to both influence others and to be self-determining" is sacrificed when we allow the state to operate as the locus of sovereignty, and understand citizenship as the only conduit to an individual being's relationship to sovereignty.[62] By asserting the terrestrial sovereignty of the cedars, Proude locates sovereignty beyond the framework of state politics. *Bearheart* thus follows Taiaiake Alfred's call to "create a meaning for 'sovereignty' that respects the understanding of power in indigenous cultures" in which "power flows from respect for nature and the natural order."[63] This sense of respect for natural order is described by Proude when he argues that by being "first to speak," the cedars' existence materially expresses a set of social-spatial relations among beings that precedes and supersedes "those phrases [the government officials] were reading from the green paper."[64] Proude's rejection of anthropogenic "word wars" and "terminal creeds" demands that the state recognize nonhuman acts of spatial production and the order that these acts articulate. Finally, Proude asserts that this ontological priority has a political valence: he and the other members of the cedar nation cannot be understood as engaging in "the meaning of being a citizen" as it is defined by the federal government, its language, and its sense of political authority. This authority does not hold under the premise of the radical (in the sense of "from the root") sovereignty of the cedars.

Proude claims that, given the persistent and irrevocable sovereignty of the cedars, colonial capitalism has never mastered the nonhuman world in the sense that its extractive economic practices assume. Moreover, from within this nonhuman sovereignty, "we," a community including the bones of ancestors, birds, bears, and trees, among others, "shun your indifference to our lives." In this context, the act of shunning is a collective rejection of colonial-capitalist entanglements; an act of delinking that makes the nation-state the outsider, transgressor of natural order, now exiled from the sovereign object world. For Proude, the sovereignty possessed by the trees expresses the reality of planetary geology at the limit of its capacity to feed colonial-capitalist order. Although

Proude and Rosina leave the cedar circus, the resurgence of this sovereignty plots the narrative of their journey in ways very different from those assumed by colonial-capitalist order. The pilgrims move more freely across the apocalyptic continent than they ever did in the circumscribed spaces of state power.

The political term "sovereignty" does not appear in *Parable of the Sower,* but the novel's descriptions of unruly terrestrial movement make a similar claim, which Lauren articulates as the central tenet of the ontology that she names Earthseed: "God is Change." Lauren develops Earthseed as an alternative to the ideological allegiances that she sees destroying the world. Although Lauren defines Earthseed using the rhetorical strategies of monotheism, she maintains that it is not a religion but an attempt to access and express a truth that exists beyond the spatial and temporal specificity of a given ideological system or philosophy.[65] "Earthseed deals with ongoing reality," she explains, "not with supernatural authority figures."[66] Lauren emphasizes that her use of this language is largely practical, an attempt to convey the importance of change as a sovereign force: "'People forget ideas. They're more likely to remember God—especially when they're scared or desperate.'"[67] For Lauren, "God" is a convenient signifier for the less familiar concept of change as an ontologically incontrovertible force. The need for this placeholder is itself an expression of the failure of language to offer access to a reality that by definition cannot be tapped by human meaning making. Lauren, like contemporary new materialist and decolonial thinkers, works with a set of inadequate laws governing language, discourse, and juridical process—themselves exposed in the novel as reifying set functions for white privilege and environmental exploitation—even as she attempts to articulate the reality operating beyond those laws.[68]

I read Earthseed as ontologically akin to the Anishinaabe ontology articulated by Proude in *Bearheart.* The sentences "these trees are sovereign" and "God is Change" make a closely related ontological point: the earth possesses a privilege of determination in the material shape of social-spatial relations. "Trees," in these terms, are synecdochically representative of land, which possesses a spatial privilege juridically expressed as "sovereignty." Similarly, "Change" is metonymically representative of the shared transformational quality of all material being—"whether you're a human being, an insect, a microbe, or a stone," as Lauren puts it—

which possesses a privilege of spatial determination metaphysically expressed as "God."[69] In *Bearheart,* the centrality of transmotion in the fight to keep the government from cutting down the cedars links to *Parable of the Sower* through their shared stress on transformative motion.[70] The sovereignty of the land is predicated on its capacity to shape social being and spatial belonging through its own motion of resurgence. *Bearheart* and *Parable of the Sower* have such similar plot structures precisely because Vizenor and Butler work from the same narrative ontology. Bringing together the concepts of sovereignty and change—the sovereignty of instability; the material force of change—defines a natural order that is always on the move and therefore ontologically resistant to the constraints of terminal creeds.

In *Bearheart,* Vizenor's pilgrims encounter the new spatial relations dictated by the sovereign planet in Oklahoma's Antelope Hills, "dark blue and blazing with lightning."[71] Lightning strikes seventeen times a minute here, creating "perfect balance" between earth and sky.[72] The terrain is in balanced relation with itself, and the pilgrims have to learn to respect this relation in order to survive. The pilgrims must "feel the water and listen to the streamers" in order to cross the hills without being struck by lightning.[73] "Lightning is no worse than the old automobile traffic on the interstates," explains the Master Stranger, a hermit who lives among "the harmonies of earth and lightning" much like homeless populations and itinerant merchants live amidst freeway traffic in *Tropic of Orange* and *The Tattooed Soldier.*[74] The Master Stranger's point interprets the message of the lightning hills by using a human analogy: this terrain has its own spatial order, he suggests, but the pilgrims, like good freeway travelers, might survive by respecting the restrictions that it places on human movement. The analogy evokes now-dated anthropocentric modes of spatial production—the freeway networks of late capitalism—while replacing them with Anishinaabe modes of spatial production in which laws, as legal scholar John Borrows puts it, "are sourced in the thunder and lightning."[75] This assertion of the land as a kind of legal archive carries the juridical force of the Fourth World that precedes and, in the novel's present, postdates colonial administrative authority.

As Vizenor's Master Stranger suggests, this terrain demands that humans recognize its autonomy from systems of meaning-making based

in anthropocentric privilege. Unlike the historical settler-colonial pilgrims' spiritual regeneration through capitalist expansion, genuflecting
to a given ideological dominant is no guarantee of social agency or spatial mobility here.[76] One pilgrim, Bishop Omax Parasimo, allows his fear
of the lightning to overwhelm his capacity for recognizing its autonomy.
His "tension and fear" are magnified by an ethical transgression: he's
been caught trying to short the Master Stranger on payment for guiding
the pilgrims through the hills.[77] Vizenor's characterization evokes the
history of bad faith deals made with First Nations by the proselytizers
of European settler colonialism. The bishop, imbricated in the Roman
Catholic ideational economy of guilt and atonement, cannot perceive
the fierce independence of the world around him. Guilty and panicked,
he runs "howling" across the hills and into the path of the lightning.[78]
The bishop pays with his life for misrecognizing the relationship between
land and lightning as something that is shaped by human ideological
investments. Lightning and hills together assert that continuing to think
of material relations as shaped by anthropocentric concerns is now inimical to human survival.

The resurgent terrains of Butler's *Parable of the Sower* similarly
rewrite the human claim on the production of space. The shifting tectonic plates along the San Andreas Fault transform the California coastline while freeways crumble and fires engulf ill-placed infrastructure. The
novel's band of survivors, led by Lauren, walk into this volatile terrain
while traveling up Highway 101 toward Salinas. They see earth and fire
devour a town built along the highway and watch as other travelers
"flood . . . down into the small community to steal."[79] "It's odd," Lauren
records in her journal, "but I don't think anyone on the road would
have thought of attacking that community en masse like that if the
earthquake—or something—had not started a fire."[80] This scene is an
inversion of the incident in *Bearheart*'s Antelope Hills. Starving, desperate, the travelers on Butler's 101 are learning to recognize the signals
being transmitted by the planet's unruly motions. The scavengers get
the "odd . . . thought of attacking" from the earthquake and the fires it
generates. These nonhuman forces signal that human law is no longer the
determinant of social-spatial order, and travelers at the limits of privation
react to these signals in order to develop their own ways of belonging in
the new spatial order.

The overrun town dramatizes the point that these new ways of belonging do not fall along the lines of old moral economies of good property owners and bad thieves. "The quake had set the mood," Lauren writes, taking for granted that the physical environment generates what Lauren Berlant calls "the emotional weather, the atmosphere, the public discussion of causality and consequences."[81] Unlike Berlant's, however, this emotional weather is not generated in the atmosphere of the national-historical but rather by a poststatist public that counts the angry planet among its influential social actors. The members of the burning community play the role of Vizenor's hapless Bishop. "They should have hidden their homes away in the mountains," Lauren thinks, envisioning a series of defensive scenarios: "They should have set up overwhelming defenses . . . they should have grabbed their money and their kids and run like crazy . . . they should have had hiding places already prepared."[82] Instead, the community's ideological investment in the persistence of property relations sanctified within the space of the colonial-capitalist state is as dangerous as the Bishop's investment in a Judeo-Christian spiritual economy. Humans depending on the property-protective function of the state to shelter them, rather than recognizing the land's authority, are unlikely to survive under the sovereign reign of the angry planet.

In *Bearheart* and *Parable of the Sower,* the freeway system crumbles in response to the collapsing fuel economy and to infrastructure-toppling seismic activity. Vizenor and Butler's similar dry sense of humor can be seen in their shared assertion that when Americans cannot afford to drive cars anymore, the end is upon us. "People get killed on freeways all the time," says Zahra, one of *Parable of the Sower's* band of survivors heading north along the interstate.[83] She is referring to the danger of traveling by foot down major thoroughfares, now empty of vehicular traffic but shared by other desperate travelers and seismic activity. Rather than being a physical structure that enforces processes of racialization, however, now "the freeway crowd is a heterogeneous mass—black and white, Asian and Latin, whole families are on the move with babies on backs or perched atop loads in carts, wagons or bicycle baskets."[84] On an interstate no longer governed by the state, old spatial rules delineating racial belonging do not apply. Butler's "heterogeneous" walkers deconstruct the romanticization of the open road and car culture that is, from *The Great Gatsby* (1925) to *Fear and Loathing in Las Vegas* (1971), such a handy placeholder for the mutually reinforcing paradigms of white privilege and white tragedy in U.S. literary production. As in Silko's *Almanac of the Dead,* walking in a group becomes a profoundly decolonial and anticapitalist activity capable of generating new modes of being human. While there is still danger on these roads, that danger is not determined by the state's production of threatening racial otherness. It is as if the sovereign planet demands postracial social organization but with no guarantees that an end to racial violence can put an end to the dangers of being human.[85]

Vizenor's pilgrims travel down a similarly self-destructing interstate system. "Pools of brume flowed across the road near the marshes. Since the end of gasoline, weeds were growing over the asphalt roads. Tough flowers crept over the unused shoulders of the road and sprouted from cracks and potholes. . . . In time trees would take root and turn the cement and asphalt to dust again."[86] In this passage, cement and asphalt are eager to reunite with the earth—to be reabsorbed and materially decolonized. The plant life that grows out of and over the cement testifies to the traces of living, always-moving earth and rock that persist in the most oppressive development projects. Even as the terrestrial surface is made to work for settler-state interests, an impetus toward resurgence remains in the soil and takes quick advantage of opportunities to reassert its autonomy.

Vizenor proposes that this expression of autonomy also becomes the conduit to a resurgence of Indigenous models of community and of communication:

> From the ruins of personal properties some walkers stopped walking to live in wickiup shelves and berths tied together and covered with flapping plastic or swatches of carpet. The wickiup people offered various services from their transient berths on the meridians. . . . Oral traditions were honored. Families welcomed the good tellers of stories, the wandering historians of follies and tragedies. . . . Facts and the need for facts had died with newspapers and politics. Nonfacts were more believable. . . . Stories were told about fools and tricksters and human animals. Myths became the center of meaning again.[87]

In this passage, the interstate that crumbles back toward earth produces new spaces of dwelling and exchange. The "transient berths" that Vizenor describes are a temporary form of housing that does not privilege property rights. The mode of exchange is "barter," emphasizing reciprocity over capitalist value creation.[88] The "new meaning of families" allows for forms of expression and belonging that are not determined or authorized in the registers of political and official state discourses. While Vizenor's "nonfacts" might ring differently to twenty-first-century audiences rhetorically stunned by the Trump presidency, his point is that a transformed physical environment allows for knowledge production and exchange based in storytelling and mythic reason rather than in the rationalist frameworks—namely, "facts and the need for facts"—normalized by scientific colonialism. This does not mean that truth is arbitrary but that it requires the scaffolding of a meaningful and plausible narrative (rather than, say, a series of disjointed tweets) in order to cohere. In the postinterstate world that Vizenor and Butler describe, terrestrial sovereignty, rather than state politics, becomes this source of coherence.

A similar attention to the relations between plant life and terrestrial materials that intrude on the state and its epic narratives inspires Lauren's development of Earthseed. She writes that she "found the name" Earthseed "while I was weeding the back garden and thinking about the way plants seed themselves, windborne, animalborne, waterborne. . . . They have no ability at all to travel great distances under their own power, and yet, they do travel."[89] This description evokes the creative instability inherent in the material conditions generated by terrestrial spatial production. The agency created by the encounter of seeds and air currents, as well as the seeds' ability to take root in unexpected places and to piggyback on the movement of others, suggests—much like Vizenor's transmotion—that terrestrial sovereignty is oriented toward upheaval and dispersal but also toward a material persistence that, while long suppressed by colonial terraforming, returns to disrupt the presumption of First World colonial-capitalist spatial hegemony.

The new social-spatial order described in *Bearheart* and *Parable of the Sower* delineates what a political community defined by grounded normativity might look like. It would be anticapitalist, with an economy that is nonexploitative and "an accurate reflection of the environment."[90] It would be respectful of difference and of the right to self-determination in that this latter right would necessarily balance the demands made by humans, land, trees, and the host of other entities clamoring for inclusion. This vision has emancipatory potential, linking Third World political imaginaries to contemporary decolonial thought like that of Justice, Alfred, Coulthard, and the Land Back movement, which argues that decolonization and Indigenous resurgence have a great deal to offer a North American social order plagued by toxic environments and racial violence.[91] But as the following section stresses, there is nothing utopian, or even particularly hopeful, about either novel's representation of how humans will respond to these reconfigured material conditions. While dated categories of being associated with property ownership and racial identity might be crumbling, both novels suggest that new forms of privileged identification and belonging will be quick to take their place. In the space between the revolutionary knowledge of shattered grounded normativity, and the "nondominating and non-exploitative terms" of life in the Fourth World, a new kind of land grab unfolds around the terms of the journey to decolonial futurity.[92] In both novels, the threshold to the Fourth World is policed along the line of those humans who cannot change fast enough to survive and those who are eager to estrange themselves from this bad old iteration of humanity.

Strange Humans

Chapter 1 of this project cites a line from Colson Whitehead's *The Intuitionist* that resonates with angry planet fiction. One of the novel's characters suggests that in order to understand an elevator—its functions as well as its catastrophic malfunctions—we must engage in a "renegotiation of our relationship to objects."[93] In that chapter, and throughout this book, I argue that in angry planet fiction, this renegotiation is ultimately about renegotiating our relationship to being human. This need for a renegotiation, as something that takes place in the relationships between human and nonhuman agencies, resonates with Simpson's definition of radical resurgence as entailing "an extensive, rigorous, and profound reorganization of *things*."[94] But the brutal and pervasive deaths that follow the freeway travelers in *Bearheart* and *Parable of the Sower* are a reminder that recognizing the agency of nonhumans, particularly as a move to decolonization, can be a brutal, even apocalyptic, encounter. Vizenor's and Butler's characters endure an experience less like that of Lila Mae Watson in *The Intuitionist,* and more akin to Whitehead's 2011 zombie apocalypse novel, *Zone One,* in which most (perhaps all) humans are "too ill-equipped to deal with the realignment of the universe."[95] Decolonizing the human relationship to things means moving on from private property ownership and from resource extraction practices that provide human life with some very basic comforts. It also entails placing newly imagined limits on the human capacity to function as an agent of change. But this does not mean that Vizenor and Butler advocate for a posthumanist cosmos in which human and planet merge into an indistinct postagentic, postsubject morass. Instead, both novels ask if we can imagine other ways of being human that replace the models provided by the colonial-capitalist state and its sanctioned definitions—via institutional, biological, and economic modes of recognition—of what constitutes a human subject.

Learning to recognize and live with terrestrial sovereignty in Vizenor and Butler's narrative ontology turns out to be a far cry from many posthumanist and new materialist approaches to ontological change that privilege the human perceiver. Bruno Latour, for example, describes the "recruitment process of new candidates for collective life" as one in which entities are "detected, welcomed, and given shelter" by humans who recognize this life.[96] Many of the object-oriented philosophers writing at the beginning of the twenty-first century begin their treatises with this experience of recognition. These moments tend to be articulated in the familiar terms of personal revelation, "an *event* rather than a philosophical position," as Ian Bogost writes on the heels of his description of the weirdly chameleon mountain ranges of New Mexico, "a moment when the epistemological tide ebbed, revealing the iridescent shells of realism they had so long occluded."[97] Unlike the decolonial ontology in which the human subject is required to work at "renegotiation" and "reorganization," these object-oriented events occur when a human *perceives* the independence or intractability of the nonhuman. "*A rock jumps,*" writes Jeffrey Jerome Cohen, "this world coming to animal life reveals the elemental vibrancy already within green pine, arid sand, vagrant mist, and plodding hiker alike. When a toad that seemed a stone leaps into unexpected vivacity, its lively arc hints that rocks and toads share animacy."[98] Rather than taking this moment of surprise as the opening of an uncrossable ontological rift between being and appearance, the perceiver instead sees an invitation, the opening of lines of communication. The object-oriented revolution in perception is an opportunity to populate the human party with a host of delightful new guests. Latour, the benevolent patriarch of assembling collectivities, invites all entities into relation. These modes of perceptual recalibration are *recognition ontologies,* modes of thought that redefine the entities that exist in reality by perceiving differently. These ontologies are not unlike the recognition politics that Coulthard defines as misunderstanding the relationship "between recognition and freedom" in a way that is "incapable of transforming the generative material conditions that so often work to foreclose the realization of self-determination."[99] Recognition ontologies position the human subject as a liberal multicultural state that grants special concessions and ontological distinctiveness to all beings who can demonstrate their "unexpected vivacity" on the political stage.

In *Bearheart* and *Parable of the Sower,* recognizing the sovereignty of the earth is a far more violent, disruptive, and unavoidable encounter, more akin to the lightning strike that kills Vizenor's Bishop than to a rock coming to toadish life, in that it does not strike all people equally, or pleasantly, or entirely contingently. Because the ontological event of decolonization is spatial and relational in these novels, the perceptual adjustment described by contemporary materialist philosophers becomes the need to work at becoming human. In their consideration of what this work entails, Vizenor and Butler follow Sylvia Wynter in her argument that we need "a new descriptive statement" for constituting the human.[100] This statement must move beyond the privileged category or "genre of the human" developed by colonial capitalism in which white, Western, bourgeois "Man" is the only cipher that properly codes as human.[101] Vizenor and Butler agree on this need to redefine the human. However, even as their renegotiation of the human relationship to the object world does away with property rights and the property-protective function of state power, their redefinition of the human becomes a kind of new, postcapitalist currency. In the same way that object-oriented ontologists privilege the perceiving subject, the newly minted humanity defined by its capacity to successfully navigate the decolonial apocalypse comes to occupy the prime real estate of being in the novels. *Bearheart* and *Parable of the Sower* hold a unique place in this study because they are the only novels that privilege reciprocal relations among humans and nonhumans over forms of human solidarity. For other works of angry planet fiction, recognizing nonhuman agencies is a way back to the human, to more equitable and productive forms of solidarity among peoples. In these novels, conversely, privileged subjectivity becomes not only the new property but also a kind of Voight-Kampff test of humanity, based on who is able to perceive, articulate, and live on the new terms defined by the Fourth World.

For Proude, subsumption by the land—solidarity in nonhuman relations—takes priority over protecting and supporting fellow pilgrims.[102] For Lauren, followers are welcome but are never as significant as her relationship to Earthseed. When her partner, Bankole, suggests that others will attempt to "make [Earthseed] more complicated, more open to interpretation, more mystical, and more comforting," she snaps at him, "Not around me they won't!"[103] For Lauren, Earthseed is a mode of ontological recognition that cannot be modified or spiritualized and is certainly not designed to comfort through adapting to the demands of individual followers. Instead, Earthseed is something that can be possessed in a sense that aligns the possessor with a nonhuman community rather than with fellow humans. Proude's judgment of his fellow travelers is, in turn, more akin to this Earthseed relation than to the MOVE house in *Philadelphia Fire,* the freeway community in *Tropic of Orange,* or the homeless encampment in *The Tattooed Soldier.* In the possessive investment that Lauren and Proude bring to their decolonial ontologies, *Bearheart* and *Parable of the Sower* share with contemporary object-oriented philosophers an implicit sense of the exceptional subjectivity required to benefit from a realignment of the universe.[104] Antecedently, grimly, they beg the question of whether there will be gatekeeping at the threshold to decolonial futurity.

Part of what shapes Lauren's possessive investment in ontology is that the realization of Earthseed as a community becomes welded to staking out a Promised Land. At novel's end, Lauren and her band of survivors arrive at their destination, a secluded hill property near Cape Mendocino, only to find its inhabitants murdered and their buildings destroyed. The travelers decide to stay "with the bones and ashes" and build the self-sustaining community that they christen Acorn.[105] They bury the dead and plant "a grove of oak trees . . . life commemorating life."[106] *Parable of the Sower* thus concludes in a space much like that which begins *Bearheart*. As in the cedar nation, *Parable of the Sower*'s travelers will live in a community comprising humans and nonhumans, the living and the nonliving. Lauren's band hopes to disappear into the Lost Coast and build something that connects them with the emergent material conditions dictated by the resurgent Fourth World. "If we're willing to work, our chances are good here," Lauren says in a speech to the new inhabitants of Acorn.[107] However, the instability haunting these chances is present in the ruins of the last community. The "building and planting" that Acorn plans is an assertion of self-determination but also a yearning for return to the old order of things.[108] It will be a *re*building of the old community, and a *re*planting of the seeds that Lauren has carried with her from Robledo, all on a plot of land owned by Bankole, not only one of their number but Lauren's lover. The possessiveness with which the travelers approach the labor of creating their new community on their own terms returns them to the same problem of collapsing human worth into land tenure that ignited the novel's apocalyptic crisis.[109]

Parable of the Sower is untroubled by the terms of quantifying the value of human life. Lauren watches carefully to gauge whether or not fellow travelers are "worth some trouble," or contain "something worthwhile" that can be incorporated into the new community.[110] People experiencing drug addiction, thieves, or opportunists "looking for trouble, looking for victims," fall outside of the purview of this "worthwhile."[111] After confrontations in which Lauren's band kill their attackers, her diary entries pointedly record the fact that the pockets of the dead attackers contain "a packet of small, round, purple pills" or "little plastic pill boxes" that justify their "junkie" deaths.[112] Some humans—specifically those who don't respect the rights of others to their personal property—have no place in Earthseed. While this attitude follows the fairly straightforward "politics of survival" that Phillips identifies at work in the novel, it also reinforces the rights of those that have—supplies, able bodies, property, and diaries in which to record the new history unfolding—over those that have nothing.[113] Indeed, Butler's "street poor—squatters, winos, junkies, homeless people in general—are dangerous."[114] They are not the victims of colonial-capitalist order but rather its effluvia, "the poisonous rottenness outside the wall."[115] Humans must "get busy now and work out ways to survive," in order to prove that they are "worth something," or be punished by the same logic that forfeits the lives of transgressors that come over the walls of Robledo in the novel's early pages.[116] If the land has claimed sovereignty by becoming the ultimate owner of its own physical body, the humans that recognize this sovereignty in turn benefit by becoming the privileged perceivers, users, and importantly, executors of this reconfigured mode of ownership.

The sovereign planet, which is nothing if not imperious, requires social actors to cast off old modes of being human. Racist and capitalist violence is anathema to the new spatial order but so are all anthropogenic ideological structures that produce those descriptive statements that Wynter identifies as delineating who qualifies as more or less human. In *Bearheart,* Little Big Mouse, a physically healthy pilgrim, romanticizes gangs of "cripples . . . bizarre creatures" and "those suffering from various cancers" who share the road with the pilgrims.[117] She dances naked for crowds of sick and dying freeway travelers to demonstrate her unconditional love for them.[118] Transported by fantasies of the spiritual ideality of difference—"I want to touch them all and feel their energies," she exclaims—she does not recognize the crowd's cannibalistic hunger and rage until they descend on her, raping and dismembering her, carrying off her limbs as trophies.[119] Like Bishop Omax Parasimo, Little Big Mouse's death is portrayed as inevitable. The doomed pilgrims privilege their investment in articulating a particular identity politics over responsiveness to material conditions. The Bishop privileges the Catholic metaphysics of guilt over recognition of the sovereignty of the Antelope Hills. Little Big Mouse imposes her postmodernist idealization of difference on the embodied experiences of others. Both extremes of essentialist fantasy are penalized in a world unsupported by the juridical structures that place the expression of identity at the core of social belonging. To "carry the fire" here, as does the boy in McCarthy's *The Road,* is contemptibly anthropocentric. Any attempt to articulate a privileged subject position, even in terms of identities marginalized by settler-colonial forms of racial capitalist belonging, feeds into the reproduction of state-sanctioned modes of social participation. Thrown into relief against the indifference of the emergent terrain, these idealized forms of identity and belonging become monstrous.

In *Bearheart,* Proude's assessment of who is "worth some trouble" is often expressed through silence or by nonanthropogenic means of communication. When the pilgrims face off against an evil gambler in a bid for gasoline, they use a word game to choose a member of their group to play the role of the "good gambler" going up against this evil.[120] The word "game" itself is a mode of misrecognition that imposes an imagined equality among the pilgrims even though they are not all equally suited to face the evil gambler. Proude offers a gentle warning against this strategy ("We are fools with terminal creeds when we gamble with chance"), but despite being the group's de facto leader, he does not offer to step up.[121] When their chosen "good gambler," Lilith Mae Farrier, loses her life to the evil gambler, the group turns on Proude. "How come you never did it in the first place?" they ask, "Where were you old man?" Proude "did not answer the question but when he turned to face the circus pilgrims his face was burning with the rage of bears. When he roared the first time the boxers whimpered and the pilgrims retreated."[122] Meaning here is indeterminate. Is Proude's refusal to answer the question and his subsequent roar indicative of rage over the loss of Lilith Mae, or is it rage at being questioned, as the pilgrims' retreat seems to suggest? Regardless of the correct interpretation of Proude's nonverbal signification, what I emphasize in this scene is that he, in the tradition of patriarchal authority figures, does not feel any obligation to justify himself to his fellow travelers. He may be their leader, but he is already operating in a different order beyond the "word wars" of bad humanism. And like Earthseed, for those who want to follow this leader, this is not a consensus-based community.

When the surviving pilgrims arrive in the Pueblo territories of New Mexico, Proude and his favorite wingman, Inawa Biwide, begin to disappear for long periods into the mountains and desert. The two "spoored the mountain vision bears" and "followed the clown crows," in search of a transformation that will make them part of "the ancient place of vision bears."[123] The old women in the pueblo where the other pilgrims rest warn that "those two shamans . . . will never speak again from wandering too far into the mountains with the bears."[124] This warning recalls Pueblo stories of wanderers losing their human identities and integrating with bear and coyote communities, but in this case, losing language as part of disidentification with a stable identity is precisely the point. Inawa Biwide, blinded by human torturers, learns "to see with birds."[125] Proude leaves his wife Rosina a message: if she is looking for him, she must "listen to the crows and the bears ha ha haaaa."[126] Others, then, are welcome to join in the journey, but only if they too can shed now dated modes of understanding human belonging.

The shamans receive a vision that directs them to a solstice window at Pueblo Bonito, and "during the first winter solstice sunrise, Proude Cedarfair and Inawa Biwide flew with vision bears ha ha ha haaa from the window on the perfect light into the fourth world."[127] Although evocative of the cosmological traditions of the Pueblo people, Vizenor's use of the term "the fourth world" in *Bearheart*'s conclusion is likely not a direct reference to these traditions, as many of *Bearheart*'s readers suggest.[128] While the conclusion of the novel is rooted in the terrains of Pueblo mythography, the fourth world, in Pueblo creation myths, is either the current world or the world before the current, fifth world, but it is not typically the world to come. Conversely, Vizenor may intend the Fourth World in the sense proposed by Manuel, as an alternative to colonial capitalism that requires a journey away from the three-world system to achieve new modes of economic and political being. Manuel insists on the right to transformative motion as key to such a project: "The Fourth World is not, after all, a Final Solution. It is not even a destination. It is the right to travel freely, not only on our road but in our own vehicles."[129] The conclusion to *Bearheart* expresses this decolonial relationship between human bodies and land based on Vizenor's concept of transmotion and anticipating Simpson's definition of radical resurgence, in which the right to move through space, and to do so as an autonomous being that is nonetheless part of a collective, is itself the destination. Writing in 1978, Vizenor would have been well aware of the currency of Manuel's Fourth World concept and may have used it to envision Proude and Inawa's flight as a transition into the resurgent spatial order. The pilgrims' movement from the window and into the Fourth World can be read, in the terms I describe, as a crossing of the subject-object/ideational-material rift into a mode of decolonized being in which the violent distinctions between human and nonhuman, self and other, are dissolved.

In this sense, Vizenor advocates for a mode of "space travel" not unlike that suggested by Butler's Earthseed, whose destiny "is to take root among the stars."[130] This conclusion does, however, bear the markers of investment in a privileged subjectivity that inflects the rest of the novel with a sense both of Proude's unique humanity and his position as the heteropatriarchal leader of the travelers whose dependence he sheds like dead skin before his and Inawa's flight. The conclusion almost directly echoes the last lines of *The Fourth World*, which read, "I hope you join with us along the way. Please understand if we do not feel we can wait for you."[131] But while Manuel's "you" is an imagined settler reader, Proude and Inawa leave two pilgrims, Rosina and Sister Eternal Flame (a Two-Spirit pilgrim), behind, "holding each other in front of the corner winter solstice window."[132] The women are invited to "listen" and "follow"—to take action if they can.[133] And while the Fourth World is only accessible through Lauren in Butler's novel, it is accessible to all willing to engage in the labor of ontological renegotiation in *Bearheart*. Nonetheless, within the narrative space of Vizenor's novel, Rosina and Sister Eternal Flame are not counted among the special individuals who have been fully welcomed on the journey. The affect of grief evoked by "the two women . . . still holding each other" frames the pain of their abandonment as evincing what Leanne Simpson calls the "gendered nature" of resurgence work that reproduces colonial heteropatriarchal structures in privileging the roles of cisgender males in decolonization.[134] That the final separation of the pilgrims is deliberately gendered is supported by the rest of the novel in which nonheteronormative sexualities are tied to the evils of property ownership. The same disgust is extended to the evil gambler who the pilgrims leave to die in the road at the mercies of his own collection of sexual torture devices as is evinced for a polyamorous woman-run household whose survival depends on eating their pets. And it is this same narrative framing device that appears when Rosina is left waiting at the solstice window as Proude and Inawa Biwide vanish into the fourth world. Although not connected explicitly, Proude disappears permanently only after Rosina is pressed into sexual activity with Sister Eternal Flame.[135] While *Bearheart* is a novel filled with queer sexual identities and expressions, this final scene punctuates the deep-seated conservatism underlying these representations. Nonheteronormative sexualities are invariably punished in this universe, and so a sense of the rightness of the patriarch and his policing of the bodies of women and Two-Spirit folk also somehow makes the transition into the Fourth World. The strangeness of these importations is what generates the sense of identity-based possessive investment in this novel. While landed property ownership is rejected, a premium on owning the means of knowledge production and the subsequent right to judge the humanity of others remains intact, and maps unsettlingly onto colonial models of gendered power.

Proude and Inawa, and Lauren Olamina, to a lesser extent, access the potential for entry into a new kind of human community by rejecting membership in a state-sanctioned order of hierarchized being that was never, as Wynter suggests, particularly human to begin with. But by gatekeeping entry into this community, both novels reject colonial property relations only to take up identity-based modes of privileged ownership and spatial access. *Bearheart* and *Parable of the Sower* assert the right of those who have embraced grounded normativity to enter into the Fourth World, but in doing so, they leave a politics of human solidarity behind. This is dramatized by Lauren's gradual withdrawal from sympathy with her fellow survivors and by Proude and Inawa's flight from Pueblo Bonito.[136] These withdrawals suggest that to belong with the sovereign earth may be to become, like the Antelope Hill's Master Stranger, strangers to ourselves. Inawa Biwide's name means "the one who resembles a stranger."[137] And in one of the moments of narrative confluence that bring these novels together so generatively, Lauren also begins to figure as a stranger through her demand that fellow travelers "adapt to your surroundings or you get killed."[138] When Lauren issues this warning, her friends "look at me as though I were a stranger."[139] To become a stranger, in this sense, is to delink from the racializing, property-centric hierarchy of colonial-capitalist order and to resurge, simultaneously, as a new kind of human being that is radically self-determining to the degree that she is left alone with her special relationship to the earth.

By renegotiating their relationship to objects, the survivors in *Bearheart* and *Parable of the Sower* join the ranks of what Timothy Morton calls "strange strangers"—all the others and otherness populating the universe alongside the human fantasy of an "us" and drawing attention to our own self-strangeness.[140] Sara Ahmed also uses "the figure of the stranger" to describe what she defines as "an ontology of the stranger as given in and to the world," which "conceals how 'the stranger' comes into being through the marking out of inhabitable spaces, bodies and terrains of knowledge."[141] Stranger-ness, for new materialists as for decolonial thinkers, is a mode of strategic misrecognition that is both spatial and relational, a tactic of defining the self (at the level of the subject) and of defining space (at the level of the political) by clearly delineating what is excluded by these definitions. To strive to become a stranger in this narrative ontology is to reject allegiance to the state-sanctioned ideologies of subject formation and political affiliation and to reach toward an antithetical mode of belonging among strangers and within the irreducible strangeness of a sovereign planet that has decolonized its terrestrial surfaces. Such an ontological recalibration presents what Wynter calls "a new frontier to be opened onto a non-adaptive mode of human self-cognition: onto the possibility, therefore, of our fully realized autonomy of feelings, thoughts, behaviors."[142] But this fully realized autonomy may be the result of a becoming so radical that it sheds the imperative for community and solidarity that once seemed the ontological precondition for needing a category of being like "the human."

Both novels model narrative modes of ontologizing the human that are emancipatory, based in mobile, flexible subjectivities that reorganize human agentic capacities by engaging in respectful, nonexploitative relations with the angry planet and its nonhuman citizens. However, each author's final vision of a flight into another world places a kind of limit on the forms of relationality accessible between humans themselves. While *Parable of the Sower*'s Fourth World is more communitarian than *Bearheart*'s, and *Bearheart*'s is more generously available to individual seekers than *Parable of the Sower*'s, both novels explore an ontological engagement with decolonial politics while arriving at that approach's limitations: by pursuing the strangeness, the iridescence, and the vibrancy of nonhuman others, decolonial ontology implicitly relegates the human to the register of the mundane at best and at worst the irredeemably spoiled and corrupt. The apocalyptic frameworks of each novel draw out the full implication of this claim, which is that the best possible world would be one without human life hanging around to ruin it. That 1990s pessimism that so inflects angry planet fiction is ultimately doubtful that colonial-capitalist order can be transformed before the end of the world. As the decades to follow the end of the twentieth century attest, the space for such an imaginary was always slim and grows narrower as our solutions to environmental and political catastrophes grow increasingly anthropocentric. Left behind by the twenty-first century, angry planet fiction remains rooted in the struggle between the First and Third Worlds, the Fourth World that it fights to imagine, and the brutal conditions that would have to be just as brutally overturned in order for its ontological imaginaries to be realized.

CONCLUSION
THE ANGRY PLANET
IN THE ANTHROPOCENE

In a box at the Huntington Library in Los Angeles, there is a collection of dead ends and false starts, what Gerry Canavan calls a "cycle of narrative failure . . . recorded over hundreds of pages of discarded drafts."[1] This box is part of Octavia Butler's archive, and it represents attempts, made across the better part of two decades, to write the third book in the Parable series. Butler intended *Parable of the Trickster* to be the speculative exploration of a fresh start, following a group of Earthseed space travelers who attempt to fulfill Lauren Olamina's prophecy that the religion's "destiny" is "to take root among the stars."[2] Earthseed colonists travel to space on a ship called the *Christopher Columbus* (an ill omen, to be sure), and attempt to create a new society on a distant planet they name Bow. But Butler, despite her lifelong faith in the emancipatory promises of space travel, wrote draft after draft without imagining her way beyond the colonial moment. As happens with the doomed community of Acorn in *Parable of the Talents,* the effort to imagine land occupation otherwise, even on an uninhabited planet, emerges for Butler as a moment of narrative impasse; caught, like the rest of angry planet fiction, on the threshold of decolonial futurity.

The failure of one of the twentieth century's most boundary-breaking speculative authors to narratively decolonize her genre is emblematic of the fundamental limitation of angry planet fiction: it struggles, under the narrative ontologies it delineates, to move into the space-time of a decolonized future. The novels that I discuss in this project agree that decolonization requires transforming the human relationship to land; and they agree that a reorganized relationship to land, one that is dis-alienated, that rejects capitalist material conditions predicated on private property ownership, and that takes the demands and agency of the planet seriously, creates the conditions of possibility for other, more expansive and collective modes of being human than those that can seem stuck to social-spatial frameworks of belonging today. But decolonization and space travel have something in common that is described in that old joke about the worst part of going on vacation: you have to bring yourself. The problem of the human is just this type of baggage, dragged along on the journey to the Fourth World. Travel to another planet might be, as Butler imagined, the opportunity we need to transcend the boundaries of our species-being, but it could also be the proof of our limits. "We can't afford to assume that another living world with its own biota and its own eons of existence will be able to tolerate our nonsense," she writes in her draft notes, "taking, and putting back nothing—or putting back poisonous waste."[3] But the repetition of this pattern became, for Butler, what Canavan identifies as "a crisis of the imagination."[4] Her inability to write her way through a decolonial space exploration narrative suggests that even the end of the world may not be enough to transform the relationship between human beings and our physical environments.

Does this suggest that there is no such thing as a decolonial space exploration story, either in terms of science fiction or the reorganization of and journey toward transformed spatial orders? And is this, then, a genre problem? Butler was a writer obsessed, as one of her frequent notes to self illustrates, with the drive to "Tell stories Filled with Facts. Make People Touch and Taste and KNOW."[5] She was an ontological thinker, and her science fiction, however speculative, needed to be realistic. She tried out dozens of scenarios for how the members of Earthseed would inhabit a new planet without falling into the old patterns of "taking, and putting back nothing," that deadly combination of "intelligence and hierarchical behavior" that she saw as biologically ingrained in human life.[6] No scenario, it seems, met her standards for "Facts that make people KNOW." This imaginative impasse is itself suggestive in terms of angry planet fiction's fraught engagements with literary genre. All of the authors brought together by this project share Butler's commitment to ontological rigor, and in this sense, angry planet fiction is deeply engaged with realist narrative conventions. But these stories also run the genre gamut: the historical novel, satire, neo-noir detective fiction, magical realism, postmodernism, Black postmodernism, Indigenous literature and the problem of the category of Indigenous literature, postracial fiction, fantasy, science fiction, speculative fiction, apocalypse and postapocalypse, the road novel, the city novel, eco-fiction, Afrofuturism, and Indigenous futurism. Many works of angry planet fiction transition among and negotiate between generic registers from page to page, the authors seeking strategies for storying their complex ontological propositions and decolonial worlds into being. Amitav Ghosh identifies the crisis expressed by this narrative strategizing in his work on "the challenges that climate change poses for the contemporary writer," which, he argues, "derive ultimately from the grid of literary forms and conventions that came to shape the narrative imagination in precisely that period when the accumulation of carbon in the atmosphere was rewriting the destiny of the earth."[7] Following Ghosh, the "crisis of imagination" that swirls around the genre negotiation in angry planet fiction suggests that not only literary realism, but *all* genres are deeply invested in affirming and confirming colonial modernity's liberal humanist frameworks, including those of identity, the subject, and their construction against the backdrop of an inert and exploitable physical environment. The wildest apocalyptic sci-fi destroys humanity only to fiercely reassert its value, as we see in the zombie apocalypse narratives that come to such prominence in the early decades of the twenty-first century. The final scene of Danny Boyle's 2002 film, *28 Days Later,* opens with the surviving heroes busily sewing a giant hello sign, one hundred feet tall and twice as wide, which they roll out to flag down passing aircraft, desperate to be reinterpellated into human orders of meaning-making. It is hard to tell stories, even posthuman stories and speculative stories, that do not confirm the anthropocentrism defined along those lines normalized by colonial-capitalist modernity.

This does not mean that the angry planet has disappeared in the twenty-first century. Some of the most boundary-breaking work imagining decolonial futures is being done by Indigenous, Latinx and Chicanx, Asian diasporic, and Afrofuturist fiction being written across the resurgent Turtle Island. Authors such as Nalo Hopkinson, Junot Díaz,

Kiese Laymon, Daniel Heath Justice, Catherine Hernandez, and N. K. Jemisin are developing narrative work that, as theorists of the decolonial imaginary contend, break down colonial categories and hierarchies of identity.[8] And authors including Jemisin, Larissa Lai, Sesshu Foster, Rebecca Roanhorse, Cherie Dimaline, and Waubegeshig Rice are following thinkers like Vizenor and Butler in imagining the conditions of decolonization that might be generated through transformative upheavals of the angry earth.[9] Jemisin's Broken Earth trilogy and Great Cities series envision planets and universes as sentient entities that engage in contingent and complex relationships—geologic and anthropogenic, loving and violent—with the subjects inhabiting their surfaces and subsurfaces. Roanhorse's Sixth World series invokes an apocalyptic event in which the end of the world arrives in the form of what people call the Big Water. "Earth herself stepped in and drowned them all regardless of personal politics," Roanhorse writes of floods and hurricanes that reorganize life on Turtle Island around the center of the continent.[10] Dimaline's *The Marrow Thieves* presents the apocalypse in similar terms: "The earth was broken. Too much taking for too damn long, so she finally broke. But she went out like a wild horse, bucking off as much as she could before lying down."[11] These futurist thinkers share with angry planet fiction a sense of the need to listen to the demands of the planet as a guide to new ontological orders that create decolonized conditions for the work of becoming human.

Contemporary decolonial futurist writing also attempts to think through some of the basic narrative conditions that can challenge the impasses to decolonial futurity encountered by the authors of angry planet fiction. Grace Dillon's foundational introduction to Indigenous futurisms, *Walking the Clouds* (2012), identifies elements of Indigenous science fiction that contribute to shaping decolonial futurity, including narrative reconfigurations of science, technology, and space-time that disrupt colonial approaches to and constructions of history, modernity, and the worlds to come. Dillon points to authors like Silko and Stephen Graham Jones, who explore Indigenous physics rooted in "nonlinear thinking about space-time."[12] Thinking history and temporality through Indigenous knowledge creates narrative space for reimaging apocalyptic events as opportunities for the resurgence of Indigenous communities and lifeways. This is the approach taken up by Roanhorse, Dimaline, and Rice, who each story apocalyptic events produced by climate change and other compounding global crises and find on the other side spaces for asserting Indigenous ontological and technological agency. "One of the most powerful narratives offered by Indigenous Futurism," Lou Cornum asserts, "is that we Indigenous peoples are carriers of advanced technical knowledge that can be applied in ways much more profound and generative than the extractive, destructive, life-denying processes of capitalism and Western progress."[13] Cornum's is a powerful articulation of the ways in which the resurgence of Indigenous cultural traditions—and relations with the earth—are futuristic practices and technological solutions to the failures of modernity. In these terms, decolonial futurity operates beyond the linear colonial *telos* in which the past is the space of return and tradition, and the future is the space of newness and difference. Instead, contemporary authors take on the temporality of creation, upsetting clear distinctions of old and new, past and future, to imagine and build different relations between humans and this earth that draw on the intelligence of grounded normativity.

But the stellar work being done by futurist thinkers in the twenty-first century does not mean that the barriers met by angry planet fiction in approaching decolonial futurity have been overcome. In much decolonial futurism, particularly when it is written in an apocalyptic register, the fact of confronting the brutal reassertion of human divisions is the focus of the narrative tension. In *The Marrow Thieves,* the protagonists are a pan-Indigenous group whose connections emerge out of their status as "the hunted."[14] They flee north ahead of white bounty hunters who would turn them in to the authorities for their valuable bone marrow, said to cure a plague of dreamlessness that has afflicted white people. While the community they create allows the group to enter into improved relations with the land, the scenario of a fresh wave of genetic colonialism repeats colonial spatial patterns of forced displacement and bodily precarity, intimating that an environmental apocalyptic event is never an automatic solution to the violence of coloniality. Indeed, the novel instead suggests that the moment of decolonization is always at risk of renormalizing white supremacist violence. This is a crisis for anticolonial thinkers embedded in Indigenous intellectual and legal traditions. How to represent Indigenous resurgence and decolonial violence simultaneously? Diné thinkers have asked this question about Roanhorse's novels, whose protagonist, Maggie Hoskie, is an ass-kicking monster-hunter who jibes with the tradition of much apocalyptic sci-fi but less so with the values of the Diné community she represents. As Jennifer Denetdale writes of the novel, "There is a difference between resurgence, abundance and resilience, and a desecration and violence to the sovereignty of spirituality and cultural knowledge."[15] Spatially, too, in Roanhorse's novel series, Navajoland not only survives the apocalypse but rises to power when a towering wall grows out of the earth to surround the four corners of Diné territory. While the wall is a compelling vision of the continental surface aligning itself with its first nations, the resource and territory guarding that come with such infrastructural arrangements evoke the spatial violence of colonial containment and its most recent and bizarre iteration in the form of the Trump presidency's agenda to complete a border wall between the United States and Mexico. What's the worst thing about the decolonial apocalypse? You have to bring your human.

Angry Planet centers on land use as the most significant barrier to decolonial futurity both at the end of the twentieth century and today. But while the following conclusion looks more carefully at other sites of impasse identified throughout this project that act as blockages on the journey to decolonial futurity, it is necessary to stress that the persistence of colonial power is not a failure on the part of decolonial thinkers, organizers, and workers. The responsibility and culpability remain firmly in the hands of settler-colonial state power and the racial capitalist industries that thrive on and bolster this power. It is these deeply historically and infrastructurally embedded institutions that will not denaturalize (let alone reconsider) the colonial relationship to land that is destroying the planet. The following sites of impasse are not those of failure but of the impossibilities—imaginative and material—that confront decolonial workers in challenging, breaking down, and living difference in the face of these structures and systems. These impasses, then, might best be understood as those pressure points where decolonial solidarities present the most powerful challenges to colonial capitalist state power. It is, of course, at these pressure points that such challenges are met by the most terrifying expressions of state violence in all its epistemic, bodily, and infrastructural force.

If the first site of decolonial impasse has already been identified as that of narrative genre, the next is the differences that we bring to narrating the politics of decolonization, which Sylvia Wynter problematizes in terms of genres of the human. Do the radically different stories that we tell about the human relationship to land, the necessary product of our site-specific relationship with the ground beneath our feet, make it impossible to find common ground? The third site is that of the stories we tell about colonization itself. I frame these stories below in terms of the neocolonial discourse of the Anthropocene, which uses climate crisis to make demands on a global human collectivity, while simultaneously acting as the very crisis that makes such collectivity impossible. The final site of impasse discussed in this conclusion is that of the stories we tell about the relationship between infrastructural development and environmental crisis, which I approach in terms of cumulative impact. I consider both the calcifications of colonial-capitalist development that make different futures difficult to access physically and imaginatively, and the force of human and planetary decolonial movement, which I encounter a final time as a model and framework for moving forward through the threshold of the cumulative impasses gathered here, and into decolonial futurity.

Genres of the Human

Throughout *Angry Planet,* I use the blanket term "colonial-capitalist" to reference a global history of land expropriation, Indigenous genocide, and environmental destruction that is, of course, anything but a blanket. The history and effects of colonial modernity and racial capitalism are specific to place and to the relationships between the land, humans, and nonhuman beings that shape given land bases as distinct places. And from the standpoint of shattered grounded normativity, in which the relationship of humans to land is one of alienation, this distinctiveness, difference itself, is an uncomfortable relation. Differences on shattered ground produce sites of intense friction that inflect the struggle for decolonial solidarity in terms of how to tell the story of decolonization, and where that story begins. For the Latin American modernity/ coloniality/ decoloniality project [MCD], decoloniality begins with breaking down the logic of coloniality. Walter Mignolo situates this agenda in the tradition of great Caribbean decolonial thinkers: "Marcus Mosiah Garvey, Jr.['s] . . . dictums are legend and are collected in books. One of them was: 'Emancipate yourself from mental slavery, none but ourselves can free our minds.' The sentence became better known through Bob Marley's magnificent 'Redemption Song' . . . So that is the answer: escaping from mental slavery (delinking) is the way to escape coloniality."[16] For the MCD thinkers, the struggle is epistemic and cultural. This position is in almost polar opposition to that of Eve Tuck and K. Wayne Yang's land-centric agenda, which draws on Indigenous decolonial thought rooted in Turtle Island: "Until stolen land is relinquished," they write, "critical consciousness does not translate into action that disrupts settler colonialism. So, we respectfully disagree with George Clinton and Funkadelic (1970) and En Vogue (1992) when they assert that if you free your mind, 'the rest'—your ass—'will follow.'"[17] Tuck and Yang voice the perspective of many practitioners of Indigenous resurgence: if the civil rights era taught us anything, it is that culture, even mind-blowing, booty-shaking culture, is not enough. The decolonization of minds and bodies requires a land base upon which to generate healing, growth, and learning. But the question of how to acquire that land base, or if other decolonial formations are fundamentally limited without it, can itself curtail and diminish the force of revolutionary epistemes and practices unfolding within the ongoing conditions of coloniality.

The question—land or mind? Materiality or ideality? Nature or culture?—is both one of the perpetually shifting and undecidable battlegrounds of ontological inquiry and a false equivalence in terms of decolonial struggle. George Manuel calls the pressure on Indigenous communities to choose between economic development in line with state agendas and the preservation of cultural traditions a "false choice that has grown out of . . . a question that should never have been posed."[18] The terms of decolonization, in other words, cannot be based on the same bad faith choices laid out by the foundational moment of colonial expropriative violence and land alienation. Just as colonialism is the history of physical and epistemic violence—structure and event both—decolonization needs to unfold on all fronts simultaneously: through infrastructural development, environmental policy, and labor practices; education, culture, and media; diet, medicine, childcare, and sexuality.

As Hayden King writes in the Land Back Red Paper, "This is not deterministic process of one before the other, but rather as a simultaneous re-weaving ourselves back together."[19] Any emphasis on particular forms of decolonization as more or less critical risks reproducing structures of power that fall along old hierarchies of racialization, gender inequality, and the staking out of privileged sites of knowledge production.

Decolonial thinkers know this to be true, and the powerful metaphor King uses of reweaving suggests that all the threads of decolonial struggle are equally indispensable, but the metaphor itself also points to a difficulty: which thread is most critical from where I stand? For Wynter, the struggle over which thread to follow is rooted in the problem of the human itself, or what she calls "the issue of the genre of the human."[20] She argues, diverging from the purely organicist accounts to which Butler adhered, that "human being" is as constructed by narrative as it is by biology. She calls this being *homo narrans,* "a hybrid-auto-instituting-languaging-storytelling species."[21] According to Wynter's theory, this narrative component of our biological existence is what produces cultural difference. Human groups tell different stories about the world depending on their relationship to their physical environment, and being *homo narrans,* we can no more escape the ways in which "ethno-class" or culture *genres* our modes of being human than "bees can preexist their beehives."[22] This resonates with Indigenous ontologies that reject universalizing knowledge claims on these grounds. "Because the world we inhabit is a very diverse place, we ought to understand what nearly all American Indian worldviews readily acknowledge," writes Daniel Wildcat, "cultural diversity is not an issue of political correctness but is a geographic, historical, and biological reality."[23] Both Wynter and Wildcat stress that cultural differences are as immutable as biology. They are, Wynter proposes, physical laws. If the same is true for literary genres, it is possible to see why, in writing the story of decolonization, escaping generic conditions of possibility becomes so difficult. And if the same is true for decolonial praxes, then the politics of reweaving becomes all the more challenging.

Wynter suggests that we can start to fight this genre trouble by understanding how it works, so that its laws "be no longer allowed to function *outside our conscious awareness.*"[24] Ultimately, what human collectivity needs, she argues, is a descriptive statement for the human that takes into account its genre-specific way of "auto-instituting," *while simultaneously* pursuing the possibility of "a new science of the Word," following the theory of Aimé Césaire, that allows for a "nonadaptive mode of human self-cognition: onto the possibility, therefore, of our fully realized autonomy of feelings, thoughts, behaviors."[25] She is speaking from a biological rather than psychoanalytic perspective, of both the impossibility of escaping our narrative existence (a Heideggerian might call this the rift between earth and world; a Lacanian, the Symbolic Order) but also reaching toward or fighting for the necessity of doing so and accessing those real conditions of existence with which human cognition always stands in mediated relation. Instead of asserting that this is necessarily impossible, Wynter argues that the stakes—human and ecosystemic—are too high to accept the reality of the beehive: the one built by Eurowestern "man," most particularly and immediately, but beehive thinking, more broadly, as a crisis in human cognition that will always reward us for affirming our genre-specific affiliations and for expelling difference, thereby crippling the potential for a fully realized global human collectivity that can confront the planetary crises of the present.[26]

If we follow Wynter, the impulse to reaffirm the rightness of our own deeply entrenched genres of being human can be found in the genetic DNA of narrative, and so our decolonial narratives are in some sense doomed to reproduce our genre-specific affiliations. Wynter's theory of the genre of the human and the need for a new descriptive statement is in constant negotiation between the dream of a truly universal human collectivity that escapes the constraints of genre and the ontic facticity of genre as a characteristic of being human. And if we link this insight to what Indigenous intelligence based in grounded normativity teaches, then we gain the additional understanding that this characteristic of being human is generated by our relationship to land and the ways that we live and survive with and through land. When these relationships are defined by alienation, then, shattered by colonial violence, the challenge of finding common ground becomes difficult if not impossible.

As I propose in the introduction to *Angry Planet,* one of the most revolutionary aspects of Manuel's decolonial theory is his articulation of the Fourth World as a space where a shared idea of land unites human groups across the cultural and ethnic differences that emerge out of the distinctiveness of place. He calls this the expression of how "customs and practices vary as the different landscapes of the continent, but underlying this forest of legitimate differences is a common soil of social and spiritual experience."[27] Manuel's is a dream for a decolonized future in which a shared idea of land as the first principle of any human community allows for an understanding of difference based in the recognition of the material conditions—the land base—that necessarily produce differences, or "genre-specific" human groups. A shared idea of land that becomes the material basis for accounting for difference is thus one way that grounded normativity might create the conditions for, as Wynter suggests, no longer allowing our genre-specific being to "function *outside our conscious awareness*." But the paradox of coloniality is that we cannot move into this awareness without becoming dis-alienated from the relationship to land that would create the conditions for knowing the ontological priority of shared differences that emerge out of our distinctive environments. And we are simultaneously hard-pressed to arrive at a reorganized relationship to land when we are caught in social relations defined by this alienation.

The novels in this project get stuck at this very narrative point, with subjects whose alienation is intensified by their awareness of shattered human relationality: *Solar Storms* with its survivors of Indigenous apocalypse caught up in the stone corridors of the settler legal system; *Mason & Dixon* in uncomfortable encounter with what will be, under colonial modernity, a permanently embattled whiteness; *The Intuitionist* with Lila Mae Watson drawing plans for the city of the future alone in an abandoned warehouse; *Philadelphia Fire* mourning the smoldering ruins of the civil rights era; *Tropic of Orange* with the explosion of state violence that leaves the urban multicultural fabric falling apart at the seams; *Almanac of the Dead* on the eve of revolution but unable to meet its dawn; *The Tattooed Soldier* longing for the return of the L.A. riots that offered a welcome alternative to normal life under racial capitalism; *Bearheart* with a qualified exit into a Fourth World gatekept by the mystic visionaries of heteropatriarchal authority; and *Parable of the Sower* with the beginning of a fragile community already doomed by its investment in private property and possessive individualism. That box of Butler's unfinished drafts, along with the incomplete decolonial project of angry planet fiction itself, makes the grim suggestion that if we are bound to our narrative DNA, then there is no way out.

The Anthropocene

The next site of impasse to decolonial futurity identified in angry planet fiction also centers on barriers to global solidarity that return us to how we tell stories of the legacy of colonialism and its ongoing impacts. In their consideration of the "elusive if not difficult practice" of solidarity, Coulthard and Simpson ask, "In what ways can and do marginalized subjects and communities work across their micro-specificities to align more effectively against macro-structural barriers to freedom and self-determination? What is the composition of these macro-structures of exploitation and domination and what sorts of ideological attachments do they produce to blur them from view and thus block our ability to work collectively against them?"[28] These are questions about how we narrate colonial impacts and spaces of resistance. The "macro-structures of exploitation and domination" that Coulthard and Simpson evoke, for example, thrive in the twenty-first century. And if the angry planet as a narrative ontology wanes in the early years of the new century, it is for this reason. Every major disaster that the United States has confronted since 9/11 has worked to visibly dramatize (as Hurricane Katrina did) and to solidify (e.g., the federal resistance to recognizing the land rights of the Standing Rock Sioux Tribe in the development of the Dakota Access Pipeline) existing macro-structures of environmental and infrastructural violence rooted in colonial foundations. What has the planet shaken loose? In cities and suburbs, Black bodies like those of Trayvon Martin, Michael Brown, Eric Garner, and George Floyd lie dead in the street. Where is the lightning bolt to strike down their killers? In Canada, 871 Indigenous women and girls have gone missing or been murdered since 1996.[29] These women's bodies are often found frozen in ditches or along roadsides, if they are found at all. Where is the earth that Gloria Anzaldúa promises will nurture us if we "root ourselves in" its "soil and soul"?[30] In 2014, armored vehicles rampaged through the streets of Ferguson, Missouri, as they did in Los Angeles in 1992 and in Detroit in 1967, "enormous treads clanking against the asphalt," Jeffrey Eugenides writes in *Middlesex* (2002), "encountering no greater obstacle than a lost roller skate."[31] Why does the asphalt, so vulnerable to decay in *The Tattooed Soldier* and *Bearheart*, not collapse under the awful weight of these machines? In 2016 during the Backwater Bridge confrontation between

#NODAPL water protectors and the Morton Country Sheriff's Department, police fired rubber bullets and water cannons at protesters in freezing November conditions, echoing policing tactics used against MOVE activists in Philadelphia in 1985. The images of this confrontation that flooded the internet depicted heavily militarized police forces blasting protesters across a prairie expanse where razor wire, suggestive of trench warfare, cut through tall yellow grasses that sway, bent but unruffled in the late autumn wind, indifferent to a country on the verge of going to war against its own people.[32] Where are the tectonic plates that crack open to swallow Energy Transfer Partners and the government organizations that authorize its agenda of accumulation by dispossession?

This is the world that twenty-first-century scholars across disciplinary boundaries eagerly designate as the Anthropocene, a critical term that is perhaps one of the most serious "ideological attachments" that "blur . . . from view" pathways to narrating decolonial futurity today because of the ways that it imagines human collectivity. To be human in the Anthropocene, as Dipesh Chakrabarty phrases it, is to be part of a "geophysical force" with "no corresponding 'humanity' that in its oneness can act as a political agent."[33] In other words, uneven access to the privileges of global modernity does not mean uneven distribution of responsibility for its effects. We are all part of this collective human force, which achieves its impact through a conceptual apparatus that fails to distinguish, as Stacy Alaimo writes, "indigenous Amazonian peoples whose lands have been destroyed by oil companies from those who benefit from oil company revenues, or middle-class U.S. citizens driving automobiles from the citizens of Pacific islands being driven from their homes by rising sea levels."[34] Theorized by the social sciences, and confirmed by the geological record, the Anthropocene presents nothing so much as a descriptive paradigm for planetary colonialism in which human force occupies the very crust of the earth, and we are all colonialists. "The Anthropocene names an empire that is not yet at an end," Kathryn Yusoff writes, challenging this naming as a generative paradigm for making visible or calling to account our world-killing order of things.[35] Its affirmation of order is how Anthropocene thinking projects into the future the unbroken ascendance of "settler colonial formations," in Glen Sean Coulthard's terms, that appear to be *territorially acquisitive in perpetuity.*[36] "Humanity" takes on the role of geological agent through the erasure of the global unevenness of human subject agency and does so through the familiar Euro-American settler-colonial tactic of racialized partitioning effected via territorial occupation and administration. In the Anthropocene, difference is erased to strategically offload corporate and state responsibility for ecological debt onto already dispossessed populations through policy mechanisms like carbon trading and "sustainable development." This move reproduces U.S. settler-colonial assimilationist policies that offered Indigenous North Americans citizenship rights in exchange for turning tribal land over to the state to be sold off as private property. The promise of political inclusion through spatial disenfranchisement is the bad faith logic that colonial-cum-Anthropocene thinking employs to assimilate populations who have not reaped the benefits of global modernity into a geological agency that further occludes spaces of self-determination for these already-marginalized populations. Similarly, identifying the Earth's crust as the locus of evidentiary proof of an anthropogenic epoch makes the planet not the negotiable subject of mineral and crude oil extraction agendas but an impoverished, vulnerable, and therefore necessarily subordinated object in need of a firm colonial-administrative hand.

If the concept of the angry planet attempts to reimagine the human relationship to the earth as a conduit to deactivating the force of racialization, and to imagining new human communities, the Anthropocene does the opposite, displacing the power and agency of the earth onto a collective human subject forced into stewardship of the damaged planet to the degree that its own differences—human diversity's genre-specific relationships to land—are erased, and their deeply imbedded, historically specific inequalities deprioritized. It is for this reason that scholars such as Yusoff, as well as those such as Donna Haraway and Anna Tsing working with frameworks like the Plantationocene and the Capitalocene, argue for a recalibration of Anthropocene thinking that maintains the need for global human solidarity while attending to the historically specific colonial-capitalist partitioning of human life that has driven the very extractive, exploitative, and planet-transforming disasters that have produced this demand on global humanity community. What if, Tsing suggests, echoing Wynter, instead of a global human agent, we thought of the Anthropocene as referring to the planetary disaster created by that "false universal of homogeneous 'Man,' which was created with a white, Christian, heterosexual male person as the basis for the universal. Paying attention to that legacy can help us to figure out what's happening on the planet."[37] And what if, Christina Sharpe's work adds, instead of marking the Anthropocene in terms of the human impact on the stratigraphic record, we thought instead in terms of the climate produced by this false universal subject, using the tools of the climate scientist rather than the cartographer as a discursive framework for understanding the entanglements of environmental disaster and racialization produced by the last five hundred years of colonial capitalism.

Sharpe suggests this reframing in terms of encountering racial violence as the weather: "antiblackness," Sharpe writes, "is pervasive *as* climate. The weather necessitates changeability and improvisation; it is the atmospheric condition of time and place; it produces new ecologies. . . . When the only certainty is the weather that produces a pervasive climate of antiblackness, what must we know in order to move through these environments in which the push is always toward Black death?"[38] Sharpe's collapse of distinctions between human and planetary ecology prioritizes the relationship between the environment and its organisms. That this relationship in the afterlives of slavery invests the weather with the force of racialization has far-reaching implications for understanding the Anthropocene as requiring a move toward human unity through being *subject to* climate rather than being the *subject of* geological record. The weather is something that follows us everywhere, and exposes us all equally but contingently, "necessitating," as Sharpe posits, "changeability and improvisation." The terms of stratigraphic human impact are recast through climate outside of the historical partitioning of being and its "strip[ping] out" as Jodi Melamed writes, of "other (and other possible) relations to land, resources, activity, community, and other possible social wholes that have been broken up for capital."[39] Rather than the agent of anthropogenic climate change, we might instead tell the story of a universal human subject that experiences the climate of racialization and its currents of anti-Blackness, Indigenous land expropriation, genocide, war machines, xenophobia, Islamophobia, refugee crisis, border detainment, lack of documentation, labor exploitation, food insecurity, environmental toxicity, surveillance, police brutality, state violence, and premature death. To save the world *from* the Anthropocene, in this counter-scene of the weather, calls for a radical global positioning of racialized exposures that attends to the climate disasters overspilling the walls of racial partition as the prerequisite to imagining or constructing new collectivities.

Again, at this site of impasse, we are confronted with the pressure of imagining a decolonial future in the vacuum of the conditions of possibility required to do so. It would be a descriptive and interpretive error to suggest that Sharpe's theory of anti-Blackness as climate is intended to be transportable to the material conditions overdetermining the lives of all overexposed subjects. Sharpe is engaged here specifically with the ontology of anti-Blackness generated by the material legacies of the transatlantic slave trade, not with racialization in the abstract. Seeking a counter or oppositional Anthropocene that produces solidarities begs for these types of elisions, but as scholars of decolonial solidarity point out, "The possible conversations remain stymied, half-formed, guarded, and weary."[40] Commenting on the limits to alignment across specificities, Justin Leroy writes that too often, the "mutually constitutive origins [of Indigenous erasure and anti-Blackness] are lost in recent claims that indigenous dispossession or racial slavery must vie for exceptional status as the foundational violence of modernity. Such claims are a form of colonial unknowing; the refusal to see the full scope of slavery and settlement's interconnected history abets a colonial ontology."[41] That this refusal links Anthropocene discourse to critical decolonial studies evokes both the challenge and difficulty of Coulthard and Simpson's questions regarding decolonial solidarity. In *As We Have Always Done,* Simpson proposes that this time of overspilling crises calls for engagements, mindful of specific places and community, "with the theories and practices of coresistors."[42] Applying this approach to Manuel's vision of a shared understanding of land that can produce space for working with and through differences, we might ask how marginalized communities can maintain their micro-specificities while attending to the ways that global capitalism, racial violence, heteropatriarchy, and environmental exploitation pour across the boundaries of these specificities, uncontained by the partitions that are built to keep marginalized subjects—but not the harms to which they are exposed—in their place.

Many scholars of decolonial solidarity propose the value of working with the necessary contingency of coalitional work that must navigate constantly between the concerns of individual and place-specific interests, and the demands of global crises. Thinking in the context of

U.S. Third World feminisms, Chela Sandoval proposed the tactics of "oppositional consciousness" as "a model . . . by which social actors can chart the points through which differing oppositional ideologies can meet, in spite of their varying trajectories."[43] Sandoval describes this model as producing "mutant unity . . . unity mobilized in a location heretofore unrecognized . . . a mobile unity, constantly weaving and re-weaving an interaction of differences into coalition" from within which "differences are viewed as varying survival tactics constructed in response to recognizable power dynamics."[44] Sandoval's oppositional conscious-ness moves among registers of political affiliation and antioppressive practices, solidifying around specific goals and claiming the privilege of a *tactical subjectivity* free to shift when certain goals are met and new agendas appear on the horizon.[45] Oppositional consciousness sounds to me like the grounded normativity of water, rain, mud, a landslide. What if the global subject of the Anthropocene's counter-scene was not exposed to the weather but was itself changeable, even improvisational, like the weather? And this not in the sense of that swarm subjectivity proposed by Hardt and Negri's theory of the delocalized multitude but rather a basis for action welded to particular relationships held by com-munities with their land base and the earth as the ontological framework for political action. The affirmation of the right of marginalized social actors to take on this tactical, mutant political subjectivity is one pos-sible response to the question, voiced by Juliana Hu Pegues, of how we might "engage the seeming incoherence posed between diaspora and indigeneity, racial justice and sovereignty, for more capacious visions of liberation and self-determination?"[46] Sandoval suggests that refusing the pejorative assumptions undergirding incoherence may be a strategy for responding to that bad faith question posed by the settler-colonial construction of human agency, in which we are expected to choose and render coherent subject positions constructed through the terms of rec-ognition proffered by settler state power. Rather than engaging in a race to the bottom for what Leroy labels "exceptional status," we might ask how the search for tactical interconnection among different sites of struggle can produce unities that by their very "mutant[ness]" and "incoherence" challenge the basic ontological structures of colonial-capitalist power.

This is, in some ways, the mode of solidarity offered by the angry planet. These are the mutant unities of bringing the Black radical tradition into coalition with technologies designed to confirm white supremacist relations of power, as in Lila Mae Watson's alliance with *The Intuitionist*'s "elevator-citizen"; of challenging the stability of borderlands and property lines by bringing Indigenous people's movements into solidarity with landslides, as in *Almanac of the Dead,* and positing the freeway system as an agentic earth being in *Tropic of Orange;* of breaking down the boundaries of what constitutes the inhuman in the colonial construction of racial difference by tracking affinities among Black and Latinx embodiment and earth, dirt, grass, and weeds, as in *Philadelphia Fire* and *The Tattooed Soldier,* but refusing this collapse of Indigenous bodies into an idealized or threatening natural world as a reversal of the logic of conquest in *Mason & Dixon* and *Bearheart.* Of course, as the preceding chapters suggest, what all these mutant unities have in common is powerful but contingent forms of solidarity forged among humans and nonhumans. The best examples of human community in angry planet fiction—Silko's revolutionaries, Wideman's memorial to MOVE, Yamashita's homeless freeway occupation, and Vizenor and Butler's bands of travelers—are mutant in the less generative sense of limited in their capacity for reproduction. They show the price of unity as attracting the attentions of catastrophic internal divisions at best, and at worst, state terror. Again on the threshold of decolonial futurity we arrive at the strange paradox of requiring the conditions of decolonization to operate before its terms can be fully met or even explored. And yet, as the discursive persuasiveness of the Anthropocene suggests, the alternative is a forced march to state-sanctioned climate democracy that smacks of neocolonial political and spatial arrangement; survival as a planet "despite" and not by virtue of the colonial narrative.[47] Kathryn Yusoff makes a grim but perhaps necessary prediction in these terms: "The Anthropocene is a project initiated and executed through anti-Blackness and inhuman subjective modes, from 1492 to the present, and it cannot have any resolution through individuated liberal modes of subjectivity and subjugation. In short, that world must end for another relation to the earth to begin."[48] In this other relation to the earth, as *Angry Planet* contends, what are now contingent and qualified "half-formed" and "mutant" modes of solidarity under the yoke of colonial capitalism may emerge as the modes of production and sociality that allow life to flourish on a postapocalyptic but now sovereign planet.

Cumulative Impact

The final site of impasse identified by angry planet fiction at the threshold to decolonial futurity is the decolonial mandate itself, which dictates that for decolonization to be realized, the conditions of coloniality built into the surface and subsurface of the earth need to be transformed. In Tuck and Yang's terms, this "requires the abolition of land as property and upholds the sovereignty of Native land and people."[49] For the Land Back movement, decolonization means the state ceding jurisdiction to Indigenous legal and land stewardship frameworks, not only on ancestral and unceded territories but over all forms of "resource extraction, commodity production, mining and transport, and energy infrastructure."[50] As Silko suggests, in the context of Turtle Island, this does not require "that the European people themselves will disappear, only their customs."[51] Because of the racial capitalist settler state's egomaniacal adherence to its own rightness, this disappearance would be difficult to achieve without the world-ending violence that Yusoff intimates. Customs, as angry planet fiction explores, are not only beliefs and traditions; they are bridges and tunnels, flooded valleys and drained lakes, the belief in petroculture that builds pipelines through Indigenous land and in nuclear power that builds plants and mines uranium in proximity to vulnerable communities of color; custom is the legacy of conspicuous consumption that fishes oceans to species extinction, razes rainforests for cattle farming, and welds citizenship to property rights undergirded by the racial ontology of organized death.

But to fear the infrastructural and spatial violence that accompanies the destruction of these customs would also be to ignore the violence that the angry planet is currently inflicting on human life on a global scale. This violence has climate refugees drowning in the Aegean Sea; ocean acidification decimating coral reefs and fishing industries that thrived for generations; sea-level change and increasing extreme weather events costing billions of dollars annually in damage to private property and infrastructure. In the terms dictated by the shattered grounded normativity of the angry planet, another relation to the earth has already begun. The first decades of the twenty-first century have seen what environmental scientists call the cumulative impacts of climate change put the lie to the stable relationship between settler spaces and the physical environment. Land Back scholars describe cumulative impact as the compounded effects over time of ever-multiplying extraction projects: "The loss from earlier periods of land alienation and ecological destruction—from railway expropriation to dam flooding—increase the ecological instability of regions and watersheds."[52] Cumulative impact makes assessment of the environmental implications of extraction infrastructure difficult to predict and reshapes all human life through the colonial-capitalist production not of predictable working landscapes but of environmental instability. Cumulative impact is thus a colonial trajectory toward destruction. What interests me, however, is the strange generativity of the concept as a description of human-environmental relationality. How might our approach to cumulative impact change if we understood it not as a barrier to development in need of solutions but as an expression of George Manuel's Fourth World—the world that exists before and after colonial capitalism—struggling to reassert its presence and power to direct developmental agendas away from economic and political violence and toward that environmental economy that Manuel's project describes? And further, what if we followed the angry planet's response to cumulative impact—the slow rise of sea levels and air-surface temperatures—as a model for decolonization. What might the cumulative impact of many journeys to the Fourth World look like as these journeys interweave? In describing her hopes for political grassroots solidarity against racial capitalist state power, Ruth Wilson Gilmore concludes her book *Golden Gulag* with a dream of "hopeful action": "all an individual organization can do on its own is tweak Armageddon," she writes. "When the capacities resulting from purposeful action are combined towards ends greater than mission statements or other provisional limits, powerful alignments begin to shake the ground. In other words, *movement* happens."[53] Perhaps this *movement,* recalling again Sandoval's mutant unities, does not need to be combined simultaneously or even coherently on all fronts. Maybe human organizing, in and against the Anthropocene, can accumulate impact. Maybe this is already happening.

The West Coast of the North American continent is warmer and drier every year. Seasonal forest fires are destroying communities and displacing populations along coastal inlands on what is fast becoming an annual basis. Whether we understand these fires as produced by drought conditions or bioregional cycles, environmental scientists are pointing to the use of Indigenous land management practices like controlled burning, rather than wildfire suppression, as the path forward to living with the natural cycles of forest life.[54] What if every disastrous forest fire became an opportunity to return land to jurisdictional models dictated by Indigenous law? To rebuild with a different relationship to the forest, and different requirements for stewardship placed on communities living in proximity to the planet's arboreal economies. Indeed, what if we took the same approach to structure fires, accidental and created by human genre wars? How different might the planet look today if New York's World Trade Center had been rebuilt as an Indigenous healing center?

On the East Coast, rising sea levels, combined with more frequent and powerful storm surges, are wiping out infrastructure and inundating coastal communities, which receive varying degrees of protection and support from the state depending on their relative size and wealth. "A large city like, say, Norfolk, or Miami, Manhattan, they can come up with the funding necessary to protect themselves," explains David Schulte, a marine biologist with the U.S. Army Corps of Engineers, "but some of them, we're probably going to have to relocate, so it's going to be a mix of protecting some areas and abandoning some areas."[55] Shulte is referencing frameworks developed in the last decades to deal with sea-level rise that decide whether particular communities and infrastructures merit protection, accommodation, or retreat from rising oceans.[56] But overwhelmingly, instead of prioritizing accommodations—learning to live, infrastructurally, with the water's implacable force—economic considerations determine which cities will live or die. What if instead of this capitalist logic, we invested in the protection of small communities, and started to plan, like some large cities, decades and even centuries in advance for changing our relationship to coastal bioregions, bringing them more in line with long-sustained Indigenous relationships to shoreline?[57]

The brutal calculative costs of making these decisions currently fall into the hands of the same federal agencies, like the Army Corps, that have worked with individual states for decades to expropriate Indigenous land and exploit the water systems that are now showing their Fourth World difference from and indifference to settler agendas. These crises are not only coastal. Inland struggles against long histories of ecological violence enacted upon lakes and rivers are reaching breaking points, like those of the 1944 Pick-Sloane Plan's transformation of the Missouri River and its bottom lands on Oceti Sakowin territory. Nick Estes describes the plan's dam construction and the flooding of this territory as "nothing short of genocide: by destroying the land—and with it the plants, animals, and water—the dams targeted and destroyed the very nations of people who reproduced themselves upon the soil. In this way, taking land and water also took away the possibility of a viable future."[58] Estes explains that the jurisdictional power stripped from Oceti Sakowin reservations under the aegis of the Plan paved the way for the "Army Corps' discretion to plot the path of the Dakota Access Pipeline in 2014."[59] Under the Plan, water became death, but what futures could be built if biologists and engineers were instead guided by the grounded normative imperative voiced by #NoDAPL land defenders: water is life? What if we listened to the river that the Oceti Sakowin Oyate call Mni Sosi ("roiling water"—take the hint!), and to the annually flooding Red and Assiniboine Rivers just to its north, and rebuilt communities to reflect human being as a practice of being-with, rather than against, the world's water systems?

In the interior of settler-colonial British Columbia, a reversal of this history of flooding and tunneling unfolds around what was once Sumas Lake, drained between 1920 and 1925 to make room for settler farmland in the Fraser Valley. Today, the interior of the Canadian province is being ravaged—again on an increasingly annual basis—by catastrophically high rainfall, leading to flooding of the communities built on and around the former lake, as well as the destruction, in surrounding areas, of mountain highways where clear-cutting created the conditions for avalanches. This is one history of how cumulative impact puts environmental processes out of the control of settler-colonial development. Still, there is no plan on the settler-state agenda other than rebuilding on the same treacherous mountainsides and drained lakebed upon which human settlement has been devastated (and not for the first time) by the return of the Fourth World body of water. This insistent settler-state agenda—we will rebuild!—pushes forward despite the nearby Sumas First Nation, built above the high-water line of the former lake, which physically models how to live in relation to the water.

"It is something that our people never would have even thought of doing, altering nature in such a way," says Sumas Chief Dan Silver.[60] What if we were to allow these assertions of Fourth World hydrological agency to redefine the thinkable and unthinkable, along the lines of this grounded normative ontology? What if every time a part of the valley flooded, the settler state rebuilt above the high-water line? What if, more radically, the decision was made not to rebuild the destroyed mountain highways? What if we decided to live with the Rocky Mountain earth beings by making use of the knowledge that they cannot be easily traversed or infinitely exploited or let the trees regrow and be swept away by avalanches without behaving each time as though these earthly algorithms are an insult to human ontological authority?

It is the need to accumulate movement against our own human disastrousness that drives the authors of angry planet fiction to enlist the planet as a force with the power to recomprehend material histories and to alter material conditions. As I have argued, these authors are interested not only in changing the ways that we tell stories but in using narratives as argumentative vehicles for positing different material conditions that might suggest different ways of being human and building human worlds. The novels in this project imagine not redeveloping the mountain road but being human without vehicles, and by extension, without petroculture and what Stephanie LeMenager calls "the confusion of oil and life."[61] They imagine an extension of human mobility and agency counterintuitively expanded by returning rivers to their course and lakes to beds, slowing down global circuits of commodity and information exchange. They imagine communities in which smelling bad is good and kissing dirt is sweet, where mud sends a message and animals are so obviously people, too, that the topic begs the question of human-nonhuman difference. They are all written in the subjunctive, like *Mason & Dixon,* in service to "all that *may yet be true,*" but in a subjunctive that is also argumentative, prescriptive, and not so much hopeful as resonant with a furious demand for the conditions of possibility required to imagine the different futures that dance just outside of their narrative grasp.[62]

The racial violence and land exploitation that is alive and thriving in the twenty-first century American Third World can make attempts to imagine its mitigation, or to make an ontological argument for the conditions that might bring about its end, seem to be a kind of stubborn-ness. The planet might move in disruptive ways, but it does not actually strike down evil capitalists with lightning bolts. Landslides do not defeat the military-industrial complex and free the wretched of the earth. Ele-vators are not secretly our friends. But, as the authors of angry planet fiction realized in the decades following the end of the civil rights era, state-authorized social reform does not accomplish these things either, nor, it seems, do better terms of representation, better access to the privileges conferred by free-market capitalism, or a global mandate to take responsibility for the crimes of anthropocentrism. It is to refuse the limitations of these modes of social reform—those of official state recognition as well as of liberal multicultural terms of inclusion—that these authors enlist the planet's fierce movements. They seek to not only describe this motion but to make it their ally because it is not good enough to change the way we tell stories, to say that all stories are equal, or finally to cede agency over our future to the dictates of our narrative DNA. To look to a future beyond colonial-capitalist violence—in the 1990s and in our present—we need to imagine new structural conditions under which to exist as humans, conditions that do not begin with the story of colonial conquest and its dehumanizing techniques of raciali-zation, or with the current structures and infrastructures of colonial-capitalist normalcy that naturalize the narrative of conquest. In this sense, angry planet fiction is not only stubborn in its refusal to concede the metaphysics of landed property and qualified humanism. It is stubborn in its belief in what acts of narrative mediation can accomplish. It believes that telling different stories can bring different worlds into being, and not because they make us feel differently, or see differently, but because they might persuade us to build differently and interact in new and trans-formative ways with our physical environments.

　　While no one has decided to turn freeways into antiracist, anti-capitalist cooperative living spaces yet, what traces of angry planet fiction's stubbornness linger in the twenty-first century are everywhere in the persistent demands for new, decolonial imaginaries. These demands are being met by futurist thinkers and artists in a less subjunctive mood—much like those discussed in this conclusion's opening pages. But they are also being met by the political work of decolonial organizations and social justice movements like Occupy Wall Street, which was not so unlike the liberated freeway in Yamashita's *Tropic of Orange;* like Idle No More, Land Back, and Leanne Simpson's Radical Resurgence Project, which organize Indigenous resurgence practices that look a bit like Butler's Earthseed communities and are direct descendants of the megadam protesters in Thomas King's *Green Grass, Running Water,* and Linda Hogan's *Solar Storms;* like Black Lives Matter, which updates the radical activism of Wideman's *Philadelphia Fire* and Silko's *Almanac of the Dead* for our new, violent century; and like #NODAPL, which galvanized a global Indigenous community to march and row and cross-country run toward Standing Rock, North Dakota, with the relentless motion of the people's armies that appear at the borders and on the freeways of angry planet fiction. As deep into the earth and its agencies as this book travels, it is these decolonial, anticapitalist workers and the political imaginaries that they story with their bodies and energies and future-embracing minds that this book works to serve. I write stubbornly, like angry planet fiction, hoping that the walls dividing our imaginaries from our embodied political realities are not as strong or as stubborn as the earth that connects us.

ACKNOWLEDGMENTS

I am beyond lucky to be part of the communities of practice that have contributed their time and insights generously to this project. Deep gratitude for their mentorship of *Angry Planet* and of my development as a researcher and critical thinker go to Heather Houser, James H. Cox, Martin Kevorkian, and Stacy Alaimo. Phillip Barrish, Barbara Harlow, Wayne Lesser, Gretchen Murphy, and Jeffrey Severs all contributed invaluable knowledge, insight, and intellectual rigor at stages in this project when these lifelines were most needed. Erin Cotter, Yvette DeChavez, Sheila Giffen, Sam Ginsburg, Meghan Gorman-DaRif, Zach Hines, Riley Kearns, Sequoia Maner, Kirby Manià, Regina Mills, Will Mosley, Alejandro Omidsalar, Jennifer Anne Scott, Myka Tucker-Abramson, Elliott Turley, Laura Knowles Wallace, and Rae Wyse contributed their wisdom and expertise to iterations of each chapter, and their friendship to all the thinking that happens between the lines.

Thank you to my editors at the University of Minnesota Press, Leah Pennywark and Anne Carter, for their support, insight, and calm responses to my most panicked emails. And many thanks to my outside readers, John Gamber and Hsuan Hsu, both of whom identified themselves and generously supported the transition of the manuscript to its final form. I hope that you can both see your energizing influence in these pages.

Thanks also are due to the organizations and institutions whose support helped to fund the development of this manuscript, in particular the Social Sciences and Humanities Research Council of Canada and the English department of the University of Texas at Austin. At the University of British Columbia, the collegiality of fellow faculty in the Co-ordinated Arts Program played a key role in getting these pages through the home stretch.

To the group, you know who you are, and your friendship makes me who I am.

Aidan McQuay, Jack Stewart, Suzanne Stewart, Daniel Stewart, Kensie Simpson, Violet Stewart, and Marilyn Kobrinsky are the kind of loving, brilliant family that makes a mockery of a writer's attempt to feel tortured and isolated. Through every stage of this process they have supported, cheered, centered, and calmed me. And finally thanks go to Bonny Stewart for napping at my feet and making sure I stand up, go for a walk, and eat my kibble every day, whether I want to or not.

NOTES

Introduction

1. King, *Green Grass,* 454.

2. As a settler scholar who grew up on Treaty 1 territory in Winnipeg, Manitoba, I use "North America" to refer to the transformation of the continent into our current megaplex of settler-colonial states. I use "Turtle Island" to refer to the pre-invasion continent and to writing and ideas that speak for and from that uncolonized land. I take up the latter term less in the context of the specific Indigenous mythographies that employ it, and more directly in solidarity with decolonial struggle on this continent today, and the land and water protectors who make use of this term to show the continent's difference from the agendas of the settler state.

3. On the dam as a global neocolonial structure, see Nixon, "Unimagined Communities," and Roy, "The Greater Common Good."

4. King, *Green Grass,* 149.

5. See Girty, *Perilous Earth.*

6. King, *Green Grass,* 157.

7. King, 157.

8. King, 454.

9. While the broader claim in this project is that it is possible to read for planetary motion in many distinct textual situations, the angry planet also reappears in contemporary Canadian and U.S. literatures, particularly but not solely in the Indigenous and Afrofuturist fiction discussed in this project's conclusion.

10. Anzaldúa, *Borderlands,* 25.

11. On historicizing the U.S. political imaginaries of "the long nineties" in terms of their critiques of economic globalization, see Wegner, *Life between Two Deaths.*

12. Silko, *Almanac of the Dead,* 617.

13. Tobar, *The Tattooed Soldier,* 306.

14. Whitehead, *The Intuitionist,* 198.

15. In dialog with Vine Deloria Jr., Daniel Wildcat likens this awareness of and respect for change in Indigenous thought to "the relatively new concept of emergence as used in ecology and physics." Deloria and Wildcat, *Power and Place,* 15.

16. Leanne Betasamosake Simpson describes the distinctions between urban and rural environments as "an artificial colonial division. We are all related, and this is all Indigenous land." *As We Have,* 81. Understanding this division as an artifice of colonial reason helps us to track the movement of the planet across urban terrain.

17. Leopold, *Fluvial Processes,* 3–4.

18. See Althusser, *Philosophy of the Encounter,* "The Underground Current."

19. For a wonderful account of the power grid as an agentic assemblage, see Jane Bennett, *Vibrant Matter,* chapter 2.

20. Pasternak and King, "Land Back," 8.

21. As Stacy Alaimo cautions, as the "mushrooming areas [of posthuman and new materialist analysis] are disciplined one hopes that the authoritative version of those fields does not marginalize the scholarship by and about those who have not been recognized as central to the (Western, Humanist) human." *Exposed,* 11.

22. Heise, *Sense of Place,* 17, 21.

23. Manuel and Posluns, *The Fourth World,* 6.

24. Simpson, *A Short History,* 19–20.

25. Coulthard, *Red Skin,* 60.

26. Coulthard, 60.

27. Manuel describes the Fourth World as based in a necessarily anti-capitalist economic system that exists in a "highly organized" relationship with the environment (55). The Fourth World "uses all the benefits of global technology" in ways that respect its environmentally-organized economic order (254). It also allows sovereignty and autonomy ("home rule" 217) to exist without the "belief in racial supremacy" integral to the capitalist economic system (245), instead allowing an emphasis on "a diversity of languages and cultures, and a mutual respect for one another's view of the world" to flourish (216). Developing this last point, Manuel also stresses, whenever he describes the Fourth World, that it is a journey in which much of the distance traveled requires "developing

a new language in which the truth" of Indigenous "presence and humanity" can be recognized (224). Manuel's vision of the Fourth World, although based in a relationship to land, is nonetheless engaged in the necessity of cultural and spiritual transformation. Distinctions among these registers are themselves an error of colonial reason. Manuel and Posluns, *The Fourth World.*

28. Manuel and Posluns, *The Fourth World,* 7.

29. As Leanne Simpson writes, "*Red Skin, White Masks* clearly speaks to an international audience, and the scholarly community has embraced and celebrated the work in this context." *As We Have,* 64.

30. Wynter, "Novel and History," 99.

31. Wynter, 100.

32. Wynter, 99.

33. Wynter, 96.

34. Wynter, 99.

35. Wynter, 100.

36. See Kevin Bruyneel on the limitations and potential of postcoloniality as a critical and descriptive term that helps "to uncover and theorize the active cultural and political life occurring in the interstitial, in-between, neither-nor locations that we commonly refer to as boundaries." *The Third Space,* xviii. It is angry planet fiction's interest in crossing boundaries and pushing the limits of colonial space-time that prompts this project's deemphasis on postcoloniality in favor of theorizing the conditions of decolonization. The critical decolonial theory that I identify emerging in the 1970s develops in close proximity to the rise of the Native American Literary Renaissance, defined by N. Scott Momaday's *House Made of Dawn* (1968), James Welch's *Winter in the Blood* (1974), and Silko's *Ceremony* (1977).

37. Tuck and Yang, "Decolonization," 5.

38. Tuck and Yang, 19.

39. Simpson, *As We Have,* 170. This should not be taken to mean that cultural, spiritual, and embodied struggle are "issues that can wait until we have the land back," as Simpson puts it. *As We Have,* 53. Like Manuel, Simpson stresses the centrality of land without framing it as a separate issue from the interlocking network of oppressions and violence inflicted on the bodies and minds of Indigenous peoples and all of settler colonialism's others on a daily basis.

40. Simpson, *As We Have,* 197.

41. Coulthard, *Red Skin,* 60.

42. Fanon, *The Wretched,* 1.

43. Tuck and Yang, "Decolonization," 35.

44. See Asher, "Latin American Decolonial Thought."

45. Hogan, *Solar Storms,* 28.

46. Byrd, *Transit,* 189.

47. Hogan, *Solar Storms,* 344.

48. Weheliye, *Habeas Viscus,* 6.

49. Hogan, *Solar Storms,* 341.

50. Wynter, "Unsettling," 321.

51. Ferreia da Silva, "Globality," 36.

52. "Such instances were the agrarian socialist revolutions among the Indian peasants of Mexico early in this century; the coterminous social revolutions and nationalist upheavals within the Russian Empire; the revolutionary peasant movements of China and India; and in the period following the Second World War, the national liberation movements of Madagascar and Cuba and on the continents of Africa and Central and South America. The critique of the capitalist world system acquired determinant force not from movements of industrial workers in the metropoles but from those of the 'backward' peoples of the world." Robinson, *Black Marxism,* 317.

53. Melamed, *Represent and Destroy,* 26.

54. Manuel and Posluns, *The Fourth World,* 245.

55. Cook-Lynn, "The American Indian Fiction Writer," 33.

56. Coulthard, *Red Skin,* 60.

57. Cook-Lynn, "The American Indian Fiction Writer," 31.

58. Haunani-Kay Trask describes the decades of Indigenous labor that went into the development of UNDRIP "as the world's indigenous peoples ma[d]e their expensive and arduous trek to Geneva each summer when the Working Group on Indigenous Populations convene[d]." "Settlers of Color," 16. The power of Trask's evocation of this trek rests in its emphasis on the sheer amount of physical energy, emotional, and cognitive labor that went into passing UNDRIP while the world quite literally burned around community-specific claims to land title and sovereignty.

59. Pulido, *Environmentalism,* xv.

60. On issues including land theft, government weapons testing, housing discrimination, and protectionist policies where environmentalist and social justice movements do not meet eye to eye, see Moore et al., "SouthWest Organizing Project."

61. The need to make these connections was particularly salient at a moment when ecocritical thought positioned identity politics as a dematerialized discourse that took attention away from environmental crises. Cheryll Glotfelty begins her introduction to *The Ecocriticism Reader* with this turn: in "the literary profession . . . race, class, and gender were the hot topics of the late twentieth century, but you would never suspect that the earth's life support systems were under stress. Indeed, you might never know that there was an

earth at all." xvi. Similarly, Lawrence Buell's *The Future of Environmental Criticism* begins with this strange juxtaposition: "W.E.B. Du Bois predicted that the great public issue of the twentieth century would be the problem of the color line . . . But ultimately a still more pressing question may prove to be whether planetary life will remain viable for most of the earth's inhabitants without major changes in the way we live now," vi.

62. See Owens, *Other Destinies,* 20–24.

63. Alaimo, *Bodily Natures,* 62.

64. For discussions of terraforming in speculative fiction and as a future colonial frontier, see Robinson, "Terraforming Earth," Heise, "Terraforming for Urbanists," and Woods, "'Terraforming Earth.'"

65. See Sharpe, *In the Wake,* chapter 4.

66. Weheliye, *Habeas Viscus,* 50.

67. Hogan, *Solar Storms,* 224.

68. For comparisons of *Almanac of the Dead* and *Solar Storms,* see Hellegers, "From Poisson Road," and Huhndorf, "Mapping by Words."

69. Silko, *Almanac of the Dead,* 723–24.

70. Thomas King, *Green Grass,* 120.

71. Deloria and Wildcat, *Power and Place,* 6.

72. Thomas King, *Green Grass,* 455.

73. Manuel and Posluns, *The Fourth World,* 256.

74. Deloria and Wildcat, *Power and Place,* 22.

75. Karuka et al., "Introduction."

76. King, "Humans Involved," 176.

77. Manuel and Posluns, *The Fourth World,* 256.

78. Latour, *We Have Never,* 67.

79. Wynter, "The Ceremony," 20.

80. Wynter, 36; emphasis added.

81. Wynter, "Unsettling," 260.

82. Sandoval, "US Third-World Feminism," 77.

83. Wynter begins her influential essay, "Unsettling the Coloniality of Being/ Power/ Truth/ Freedom," in dialog with Quijano and Walter Mignolo.

84. Mignolo describes his direct debt to Anzaldúa's work in an interview discussing how his interests in semiology and "immigrant consciousness" coalesced: "From there came the concept of 'colonial difference' and 'border thinking' that I learned from Gloria Anzaldúa's *Borderland/La Frontera. The New Mestiza.*" "Interview."

85. Maldonado-Torres, "On the Coloniality of Being," 243.

86. Manuel and Posluns, *The Fourth World,* 158.

87. The report that Latour cowrote with medical sociologist Amina Sha-bou identified antiblack racist ideologies, rooted in colonial attitudes toward Indigenous populations, as the key barrier to indigenizing management in Ivoir-ian industry. The insight that researchers do not anthropologize white Euro-pean rationality in the same ways applied to Indigenous subjects shifted Latour's work on the construction of rationalism from the fields of philosophy and theology to sociology. See Latour and Shabou, "Les ideologies."

88. Lamy, "Sociology of a Disciplinary Bifurcation," 124.

89. Latour, *We Have Never,* 39. See Zoe Todd on "how a Euro-Western audience consumes Latour's argument (and the arguments of others writing and thinking about the climate, ontologies, our shared engagements with the world) without being aware of competing or similar discourses happening out-side of the rock-star arenas of Euro-Western thought." While Todd generously suggests that this is not "entirely Latour's fault," the formative neocolonial shock that shaped his ethnographic fieldwork suggests that too little pressure has been placed on how Indigenous contexts have influenced the ontological turn. Todd, "An Indigenous Feminist's Take," 8.

90. Latour, *We Have Never,* 8.

91. It is hard to think of this as an accident of differing intellectual gene-alogies given that in the 1980s and 1990s, "Traditional Ecological Knowledge was in its heyday in the eyes of white policy makers [and] academics." Leanne Simpson, *As We Have,* 12.

92. Coulthard, *Red Skin,* 60.

93. Simpson, *As We Have,* 79.

94. Hunt, "Ontologies of Indigeneity," 31.

95. Yusoff, *A Billion,* 31.

96. Cohen, "Introduction: Ecostitial," ix. Just a few examples of the rise of materialist and elemental ecocritical theory can be traced from Timothy Morton's *Ecology without Nature* (2007) and *The Ecological Thought* (2010); to Serenella Iovino and Serpil Oppermann's *Material Ecocriticism* collection (2014); and to the prolific output of Jeffrey Jerome Cohen and Lowell Duckert in their collections: a special issue of *postmedieval* on Ecomaterialism (2013); *Elemental Ecocriticism: Thinking with Earth, Air, Water, and Fire (2015), and Veer Ecology: A Companion for Environmental Thinking* (2017).

97. Alaimo and Hekman, "Introduction," 7.

98. Ghosh, *The Great Derangement,* 66.

99. Meillassoux, *After Finitude,* 7.

100. Key texts on infrastructuralism include Manuel DeLanda's *A New Philosophy of Society: Assemblage Theory and Social Complexity* (2006); Bruce Robbins's "The Smell of Infrastructure: Notes toward an Archive" (2007); Tony

Bennett and Patrick Joyce's *Material Powers* (2010); the special issue of *Modern Fiction Studies* on Infrastructuralism, edited by Michael Rubenstein, Bruce Robbins, and Sophia Beal (2015); and Penny Harvey and Hannah Knox's *Roads: An Anthropology of Infrastructure and Expertise* (2015).

101. Alaimo, *Bodily Natures,* 17.

102. Whitehead, *The Intuitionist,* 62.

103. Deloria and Wildcat, *Place and Power,* 27.

104. Brown, "Reification," 179.

105. Saldívar identifies contemporary multiethnic American novelists, including Whitehead and Yamashita, as working in a speculative realist narrative mode that "refuses the hegemony of postmodern metaphysics" in order to explore—not a postracial world—but a "postrace aesthetic" that invents "a new 'imaginary' for thinking about the nature of a just society and the role of race in its construction." See "Second Elevation," 5.

106. Taylor, *Universes without Us,* 11.

107. Taylor, 85, 133. It is important to note that the emancipatory moment here is that of the mortal equality of death and dissolution into the earth. "In Chesnutt's and Hurston's texts," as Taylor writes, "this radical permeability to the universe leads to self-abnegation rather than self-sovereignty.... By this account, certain African diasporic spiritualities refute racist ontologies but do not thereby liberate us as free subjects." 20.

108. Deloria and Wildcat, *Place and Power,* 23.

109. Felski, *The Limits of Critique,* 158. See also Caroline Levine's *Forms* (2015) and David Alworth's *Site Reading* (2015).

110. Tuck and Yang, "Decolonization," 3. See Brown, "Reification."

111. TallBear, "Beyond the Life/Not-Life Binary," 198.

112. Hogan, *Solar Storms,* 326.

113. Hogan, 326.

114. Hogan, 224.

115. Harman, "Well-Wrought," 188.

116. Mignolo, "Delinking," 453.

117. See Negri, "Crisis of the Crisis-State."

118. On the limitations to colonial recognition politics, see Alfred, *Peace Power Righteousness,* 46–76; Coulthard, *Red Skin,* chapter 1; Melamed, *Represent and Destroy,* chapter 4; and Karuka et. al., "Introduction."

119. Klein, *No Logo,* 317.

1. Terraforming the New World

1. On the history of Mohawk steelworkers involved in 9/11, see Montour, "The World Trade Center and 9/11."

2. On the history of Mohawk steelworkers in New York, see Schilling, "They Helped Build the Twin Towers."

3. Mitchell, "The Mohawks," 14.

4. Mitchell, 14.

5. Valois, "The Mohawks."

6. See *High Steel,* directed by Don Owen.

7. Valois, "The Mohawks."

8. Wegner, *Life between Two Deaths,* 37.

9. DeLillo, *Falling Man,* 185.

10. Like many first responders on 9/11, Mohawk ironworkers who went to the Twin Towers site have since lived with and died from the respiratory and carcinogenic afterlife of the toxins they were exposed to that day. See Montour, "The World Trade Center and 9/11." The tightening of the Canada-U.S. border post-9/11 also heightened the policing of Mohawk border crossing, "our rights were constructed, along with those of others," Simpson writes, "as a threat to national security and our forms of self-identification (and formal identification by the state) became subjected to greater scrutiny." Simpson, *Mohawk Interruptus,* 123.

11. Vizenor, *Survivance,* 15.

12. Audra Simpson makes this point when she opens *Mohawk Interruptus* by pointing out that the fame of the skywalkers tends to overshadow the material realities of Kahnawà:ke survivance and "the hard labor of hanging on to territory, defining and fighting for your rights, negotiating and maintaining governmental and gendered forms of power." *Mohawk Interruptus,* 3.

13. Simpson, 115.

14. Gass, "Why the Mohawks."

15. Manuel and Posluns, *The Fourth World,* 6.

16. Melamed, "Racial Capitalism," 78.

17. Yusoff, *A Billion,* 63.

18. Quijano, "Coloniality of Power," 216.

19. King, "Humans Involved," 175.

20. King, 175.

21. King, 175.

22. Bennett, *Vibrant,* 92.

23. Latour, *Reassembling the Social,* 66.

24. Morton, *The Ecological Thought,* 31.

25. Barad, *Meeting the Universe Halfway,* 26.

26. Indigenous scholarship frequently describes this understanding of relationality. See Leanne Simpson, *As We Have Always Done,* particularly chapters 4 and 9, and Daniel Heath Justice, *Why Indigenous Literature Matters,* chapter 1.

Thomas King's is perhaps the most widely cited: "'All my relations' is at first a reminder of who we are and of our relationship with both our family and our relatives. It also reminds us of the extended relationship we share with all human beings. But the relationships that Native people see go further, the web of kinship to animals, to the birds, to the fish, to the plants, to all the animate and inanimate forms that can be seen or imagined. More than that, 'all my relations' is an encouragement for us to accept the responsibilities we have within the universal family by living our lives in a harmonious and moral manner (a common admonishment is to say of someone that they act as if they had no relations)." "Introduction," ix.

27. Simpson, *As We Have,* 56.
28. Marx, *Capital,* 874.
29. Alfred, *Peace Power Righteousness,* 60.
30. Manuel and Posluns, *The Fourth World,* 55.
31. Wynter, "The Ceremony," 21.
32. Collado Rodríguez, "*Mason & Dixon,*" 80.
33. McHale, "Mason & Dixon in the Zone," 43.
34. Whitehead, *The Intuitionist,* 163.
35. Manuel and Posluns, *The Fourth World,* 6.
36. Wegner, *Life between Two Deaths,* 36.
37. Lazarus, "The Global Dispensation," 26.
38. Lazarus, 27.
39. See *V.* for the waterspout that injects the element of contingency into the novel's quest to uncover the global networks and agents controlling history. Pynchon, 492; and *Gravity's Rainbow* for Byron the Bulb, an immortal light bulb that interferes with capitalist commodity circulation. Pynchon, 650.
40. Pynchon, *Mason & Dixon,* 772.
41. On *Mason & Dixon* as a novel about the neoliberal 1990s, see Hinds, "Introduction," and Olster, "The Way We Were(n't)."
42. See McLaughlin, "Surveying," 184, and Seed, "Mapping the Course," 93.
43. Teskey, *Allegory and Violence,* 5.
44. McHale, "Mason & Dixon in the Zone," 59.
45. Pynchon, *The Crying,* 148.
46. Pynchon, *Mason & Dixon,* 615; 544; 666.
47. Horvath, "Introduction," 11.
48. Mignolo, "Delinking," 461.
49. Schaub, "Plot, Ideology, and Compassion," 190.
50. Pynchon, *Mason & Dixon,* 615.
51. Tuck and Yang, "Decolonization," 20.

52. On linearity "as a kind of spatial code for encoding ideological positions," see McHale, "Mason & Dixon in the Zone," 59; on coloniality as a discursive violence, see Mattessich, *Lines of Flight,* and Benea, "Spaces of Native American Ghostliness."

53. Manuel, *The Fourth World,* 7.

54. Pynchon, *Mason & Dixon,* 80. Although most closely tied to the fields of cartography and geography, Pynchon's attention to surveying as a practice of cutting into the earth's surface also ties it to the "White Geology" of extraction that, Yusoff writes, "renders matter as property, that makes a delineation between agency and inertness, which stabilizes the *cut* of property and enacts the removal of matter from its constitutive relations as both subject and mineral embedded in sociological and ecological fields." *A Billion,* 4.

55. Pynchon, *Mason & Dixon,* 478.

56. Pynchon, 499.

57. Pynchon, 615.

58. David J. Greiner describes Mason and Dixon as becoming "personifications of the Age of Reason." "Thomas Pynchon," 78.

59. Melley, *Empire of Conspiracy,* 12.

60. Yusoff, *A Billion,* 4.

61. Pynchon, *Mason & Dixon,* 599.

62. Pynchon, 701.

63. Pynchon, 9.

64. Thompson, *The Making of the English Working Class,* 217.

65. Pynchon, *Mason & Dixon,* 9.

66. See Hinds, "Animal"; Seed, "Mapping the Course"; Rozelle, *Zombiescapes;* and Lensing, "Postmodernism at Sea."

67. Lensing, 127.

68. Byrd, *Transit of Empire,* xxi.

69. Pynchon, *Mason & Dixon,* 220.

70. Pynchon, 665.

71. Pynchon, 665.

72. Pynchon, 615.

73. Pynchon, 158, 207.

74. García-Caro, "America Was the Only Place," 121.

75. Pynchon, *Mason & Dixon,* 635, 634.

76. Pynchon, 68.

77. Yusoff, *A Billion,* 69.

78. Pynchon, *Mason & Dixon,* 675.

79. Hawthorne, "Young Goodman Brown," 134.

80. See Sara Ahmed for a description of the relationship between linearity and white privilege in "the constitution of a field of unreachable objects." *Queer Phenomenology,* 15.

81. Simpson, *As We Have,* 59.

82. Pynchon, *Mason & Dixon,* 619.

83. Rozelle, *Zombiescapes,* 40.

84. Pynchon, *Mason & Dixon,* 620.

85. Brooks, *The Common Pot,* 23.

86. This is a salutary reference from Pynchon since his ancestor, John Pynchon, was instrumental in turning the beaver trade in the Northeast into an unqualified massacre. While John's father, William Pynchon, was a more ambiguous figure in colonial history, the environmental and direct violence of the beaver trade under John Pynchon, as Brooks writes, put "beaver skins on Pynchon's table, human flesh in the forests and fields." Pynchon, the trader, gained control of the spatial relations governing the land, but in this apparent triumph he inherited "the legacy of his own greed," a land restructured as the terrain of exploitation and warfare. Brooks, *The Common Pot,* 22–24. See also Madsen, "Family Legacies."

87. Simpson, *A Short History,* 15.

88. Morton, *The Ecological Thought,* 31.

89. Taylor, *Universes,* chap. 1.

90. Other late 1990s novels that explore the cathexis of white masculinist agency panic include Chuck Palahniuk's *Fight Club* (1996), David Foster Wallace's *Infinite Jest* (1996), and Jonathan Lethem's *Motherless Brooklyn* (1999).

91. Pynchon, *Mason & Dixon,* 693.

92. Mbembe, *Necropolitics,* 105.

93. Pynchon, *Mason & Dixon,* 772.

94. Schaub, "Plot, Ideology, and Compassion," 200. A concluding note also present in *Vineland* (1990) and *Bleeding Edge* (2013).

95. Tuck and Yang, "Decolonization," 9.

96. Wynter, "The Ceremony," 21.

97. Koolhaas, *Delirious New York*; italics in original, 87.

98. Lefebvre, *The Production of Space,* 98; Koolhaas, 87.

99. Petry, *The Street,* 430.

100. Ellison, *Invisible Man,* 489.

101. Melamed, "Racial Capitalism," 81.

102. There is a great deal of debate over periodizing *The Intuitionist,* which does not specifically flag the year in which it is set. Michael Bérubé writes that "the time is and is not the 1940s or 1950s." "Race and Modernity," 169; Lauren Berlant posits that "it is around 1964," the year Lyndon Johnson passed the Civil

Rights Act and the beginning of the end of de jure Jim Crow. "Intuitionists," 850; Ramón Saldívar hedges his bets by evoking "a grim mid-century American urban life." "Second Elevation," 7.

103. Kirn, "The Promise of Verticality." Reviews and articles referencing Kirn's comparison include Bérubé, "Race and Modernity"; Liggins, "Urban Gothic Vision"; Russell, "Recalibrating the Past"; Tucker, "Verticality"; Saldívar, "Second Elevation"; and Fain, *Colson Whitehead.*

104. Saldívar, "The Second Elevation," 7.

105. Berlant, *Cruel Optimism,* 74.

106. Jameson, *Postmodernism,* 42.

107. Teskey, *Allegory and Violence,* 130.

108. Whitehead, *The Intuitionist,* 80.

109. Whitehead, 79.

110. Whitehead, 79.

111. For a description of the Croton's architecture, see "Early History: Potter's Field."

112. Whitehead, *The Intuitionist,* 79.

113. As Frederick Law Olmsted pointed out in the wake of the Chicago conflagration, the city's "weakness for 'big things'" was in no way curbed by the fire. Pauly, "The Great Chicago Fire," 673.

114. Green, "The Iroquois on the Girders," 2.

115. Brown, "Black Skyscrapers," 540.

116. Brown, 547.

117. Brown, 558.

118. Whitehead, *The Intuitionist,* 11–12.

119. Whitehead, 47.

120. Whitehead, 47.

121. Whitehead, 47.

122. Teskey, *Allegory and Violence,* 131.

123. Byrd, *Transit of Empire,* xxv.

124. Whitehead, *The Intuitionist,* 62.

125. Kevorkian, *Color Monitors,* 147.

126. Simpson, *As We Have,* 80–81.

127. Petry, *The Street,* 430.

128. Vizenor, *Survivance,* 11.

129. Whitehead, *The Intuitionist,* 57.

130. Weheliye, *Habeas Viscus,* 26.

131. Whitehead, *The Intuitionist,* 239.

132. Whitehead, 238–239.

133. Whitehead, 60.

134. Whitehead, 231.
135. Deloria and Wildcat, *Power and Place,* 26.
136. Deloria and Wildcat, 144.
137. Negri, "Notes," 49.
138. Negri, 60.
139. Fouché, "Say it Loud," 640.
140. Fouché, 650.
141. Whitehead, *The Intuitionist,* 227.
142. Whitehead, 35.
143. Whitehead, 42.
144. Whitehead, 239.
145. Whitehead, 208.
146. Berlant, *Cruel Optimism,* 74.
147. Berlant, 74.
148. Whitehead, *The Intuitionist,* 227.
149. Whitehead, 227.
150. Whitehead, 229.
151. Whitehead, 227–229.
152. Hogan, *Solar Storms,* 326.
153. Whitehead, *Intuitionist,* 239.
154. Vizenor, *Manifest,* vii.
155. Whitehead, *Intuitionist,* 233, 43.
156. Whitehead, 57, 77.
157. Whitehead, 29.
158. Whitehead, 122.
159. Melamed, "Racial Capitalism," 81.
160. Whitehead, *Intuitionist,* 27.
161. Knight, "It's a New Day," 29.
162. Whitehead, *Intuitionist,* 24.
163. Simpson, *As We Have,* 79.
164. A preoccupation that also plagues modernity's infrastructural aspirations in novels like John Dos Passos's *Manhattan Transfer* (1925) and Upton Sinclair's *Oil!* (1927).
165. Whitehead, *Intuitionist,* 198–99. For a very similar reimagining of the typewriter, cf. Amiri Baraka, "Technology and Ethos."
166. Jameson, *Postmodernism,* 42.
167. Whitehead, *Intuitionist,* 199.
168. Manuel and Posluns, *The Fourth World,* 245.
169. Whitehead, *Intuitionist,* 255.
170. Whitehead, 24, 75, 100.

171. Tuck and Yang, "Decolonization," 9.
172. Vizenor, *Survivance,* 18.
173. Tuck and Yang, "Decolonization," 35.
174. Wynter, "Unparalleled Catastrophe," 73.

2. First World Problems

1. Bambara, *Bombing.*
2. Cobb's Creek historian John W. Eckfeldt records that by the early 1800s, niter mills busy with the production of gunpowder dominated the creek. See Eckfeldt, *Cobb's Creek.*
3. Adam Levine, *Philly H2O.*
4. Bambara, *Bombing.*
5. Assefa and Wahrhaftig, incarcerated MOVE women quoted in an unpublished letter, *Extremist Groups,* 11.
6. Dungy, "Introduction," xxi–xxii.
7. Young, *Soul Power*, 156.
8. Byrd, *Transit of Empire,* 189.
9. Alfred, *Peace Power Righteousness,* 88.
10. On modernity as colonial warfare, see Maldonado-Torres, "Coloniality of Being."
11. Maldonado-Torres, "Coloniality of Being," 255.
12. Harman, *Guerrilla,* 75–76.
13. Kelley, *Different Drummer;* all capitals in original, 60.
14. Alfred, *Peace Power Righteousness,* 72.
15. Melamed, *Represent,* 227.
16. Song, *Strange Future,* 29.
17. Melamed, *Represent,* 227.
18. Tuana, "Viscous Porosity," 208.
19. For a definitional account of how the groundwork for the 1990s neoliberal order is laid in the 1960s, 1970s, and 1980s, see Peck and Tickell, "Neoliberalizing Space."
20. Dubey, *Signs,* 64.
21. James Kyung-Jin Lee, *Urban Triage,* 108.
22. Wideman, *Philadelphia Fire,* 81.
23. Assefa and Wahrhaftig, incarcerated MOVE women quoted in an unpublished letter, *Extremist Groups,* 11.
24. Byrd, *Transit of Empire,* 197.
25. Byrd, 198.
26. Wald, "'Refusing to Halt,'" 87.

27. Vint, "Orange County," 408.

28. Anzaldúa, *Borderlands,* 68.

29. Wideman, *Philadelphia Fire,* 83.

30. As Jean-Pierre Richard suggests in his reading of the novel, "not only is Philadelphia burning; with present-day 'private developers' (78) the city feeds on fire, it lives on it, it expands through fire, as they choose systematic arson to clear the old slums and make room for a new Philadelphia." See "Philadelphia Fire," 606.

31. Dubey, *Signs,* 79.

32. Dubey, 61.

33. Wideman, *Philadelphia Fire,* 100.

34. Wideman, 100. The narrator echoes a sentiment repeated by those who experienced the fire: that it was out of place, that it took them away from Cobb's Creek and Philadelphia and to theaters of global conflict, to Vietnam, or, says one photographer who filmed the conflagration from a crane, "*Dresden.* The Allied firebombing in World War II. [I] felt like crying." Fagone, "Birdie Africa."

35. Wideman, 100.

36. Massiah and Bambara's documentary traces the connections between anti-Black race rioting in Philadelphia and the strategic withholding of fire department services, particularly in the 1938 fire that destroyed the newly built Philadelphia Hall, an abolitionist meeting place that stood for only three days before being destroyed by white rioters. The documentary emphasizes that "what happened with the MOVE situation is nothing new in the history of Philadelphia Blacks." Massiah, *Bombing of Osage Avenue.*

37. Yamashita, *Tropic of Orange,* 239.

38. Yamashita, 239.

39. See Radley Balko on the systematic dismantling of the Posse Comitatus Act. *Overkill,* 6. See Michelle Alexander on the era's other pivotal moment in the escalation of the militarized policing of civilian space, the Military Cooperation with Law Enforcement Act. See *The New Jim Crow,* 77.

40. Yamashita, *Tropic of Orange,* 240.

41. Yamashita, 123.

42. Wynter, "N.H.I.," 43.

43. Mbembe, *Necropolitics;* italics in original, 68.

44. Cadena, *Earth Beings,* 278.

45. Harvey and Knox, "Abstraction," 124.

46. Harvey and Knox, 140.

47. Cadena, *Earth Beings,* 168.

48. Cadena, 277.

49. Assefa and Wahrhaftig, incarcerated MOVE women quoted in an unpublished letter, *Extremist Groups,* 11.

50. Assefa and Wahrhaftig, Sharon Sims Cox quoted in an interview, 21.

51. This quote is from "a handwritten letter reportedly handed to police by MOVE." Assefa and Wahrhaftig, 27.

52. Assefa and Wahrhaftig, 4–5. Framing MOVE as an international threat was a strategy deployed in the 1970s by then-Philadelphia mayor Frank Rizzo, who characterized MOVE as international extremists. "Only in a democracy could they get away with what they're getting away with," Rizzo said at a press conference leading up to the 1976 standoff. "If they were in the countries that they represent, like some of the others that were here—the Stokely Carmichaels, the Cleavers—that all ran to Cuba, Red China, Africa, you name it—but they were very anxious to get back here because they couldn't do what they do in this country in the countries whose doctrine they represent. And that's what's wrong with this country. We're backing off too much." Osder, *Let the Fire Burn.*

53. For MOVE's current definition of Natural Law, which applies "whether you are a German Shepherd or a Supreme Court Justice," see "About MOVE."

54. "About MOVE." MOVE's call for a flat ontology, along with Africa's enthusiasm for listing disparate entities to demonstrate their contiguity, anticipates what Ian Bogost calls the new materialist "Latour litanies" of "surprisingly contrasted curiosities." See *Alien Phenomenology,* 38.

55. Assefa and Wahrhaftig, quoted from an undated, untitled MOVE document, 145.

56. Kyung-Jin Lee, *Urban Triage,* 109.

57. Wideman, *Philadelphia Fire,* 89.

58. Wideman, 164–65.

59. Dungy, "Introduction," xxvii.

60. Clifton, "*being property,*" 78.

61. Wideman, *Philadelphia Fire,* 117.

62. Wideman, 132.

63. Mbembe, *Necropolitics,* 79.

64. Avila, *Folklore of the Freeway,* 3.

65. Yamashita, *Tropic of Orange,* 33. South-Central's name change was a strategic move on the part of the city to rebrand the area after the 1992 Riots. I continue to use "South-Central" throughout *Angry Planet* to resist this act of historical erasure.

66. See Harvey, *Rebel Cities,* 15.

67. Yamashita, *Tropic of Orange,* 57.

68. Sullivan, *Materials in Use.*

69. The counterpublics that occupy the "sunless, concrete underpinnings of the freeway" in Thomas Pynchon's *The Crying of Lot 49* make a similar claim. 105.

70. Yamashita, *Tropic of Orange*, 55.

71. Yamashita, 112.

72. Bryant, *Democracy of Objects*, 114.

73. I borrow this use of the term "sincerity" from Timothy Morton, who suggests that "objects are what they are in the sense that no matter what we are aware of, or how, there they are, impossible to shake off . . . In its sincerity, reality envelopes us like a film of oil." See *Hyperobjects*, 35.

74. Yamashita, *Tropic of Orange*, 139.

75. Yamashita, 156.

76. Yamashita, 192.

77. Lefebvre, *Production of Space*, 164.

78. Sullivan, *Materials in Use.*

79. Leanne Simpson, *As We Have*, 79.

80. Song, *Strange Future*, 29.

81. Song, 204.

82. Alter, "The Other America," quoted in Tuana, "Viscous Porosity," 204.

83. Margaret's relationship to MOVE, the novel emphasizes, is a direct result of her experience of the neoracial backlash afflicting communities of color in the 1980s.

84. Wideman, 17–18.

85. Philadelphia Special Investigation Committee, 21.

86. The sticking point here is that "the destruction of important physical and medical evidence," along with negligence on the part of the pathologists who examined the bodies and "failed to discover metallic fragments, including firearms ammunition, in six of the bodies" supported the Philadelphia Police Department's contention that MOVE members had not been forced back into the house by gunfire while the house was burning. Later forensic tests carried out by the FBI and the SIC's own pathologists did uncover bullet fragments consistent with the guns used by the PPD that day. Philadelphia Special Investigation Committee, 20–21.

87. Wideman, *Philadelphia Fire*, 48.

88. Mbembe makes a similar point regarding the aftermath of civil warfare in nations struggling with histories of colonial occupation: "In the case of the Rwandan genocide—in which a number of skeletons were, when not exhumed, kept in a visible state—what is striking is the tension between, on the one hand, the petrification of the bones and their strange coolness and, on the other, their stubborn will to mean, to signify something." See *Necropolitics*, 87.

89. Dubey, "Literature," 592.
90. Wideman, *Philadelphia Fire,* 110, 18.
91. Simpson, *As We Have,* 79.
92. Otter, "Locating Matter," 38.
93. Davis, *Ecology of Fear,* 16.
94. Yamashita, *Tropic of Orange,* 41.
95. Yamashita, 42.
96. Yamashita follows this story with a joke that emphasizes its point. "I read this story where a writer and a palm tree face off," Buzzworm tells Gabriel. "Wouldn't you know it, the palm tree wins." See *Tropic of Orange,* 43.
97. Wideman, *Philadelphia Fire,* 46.
98. Wideman, 44.
99. Wideman, 188.
100. Alfred, *Peace Power Righteousness,* 72.
101. Silko, *Almanac of the Dead,* 619.
102. Wideman, *Philadelphia Fire,* 199.
103. Yamashita, *Tropic of Orange,* 268.

3. Third World Liberation

1. There are divided opinions on whether the events of April 1992 in Los Angeles should be designated as "riots," an "uprising," a "rebellion," or "civil unrest." Mike Davis suggests "rebellion" because many of those involved refer to it as "a slave rebellion." "Uprising," 142. Conversely, Min Hyoung Song uses the "derogatory" term "riots" to emphasize the event's violence and spontaneity, and to insist "on the pessimism generated by this event." *Strange Future,* 16. The following chapter uses the term "riots" to evoke, as does U.S. federal law, the emphasis on property damage that defines rioting in juxtaposition to a rebellion or an uprising. Title 18 of the United States Code defines rioting, in part, as "an act or acts of violence by one or more persons . . . which act or acts shall constitute a clear and present danger of, or shall result in, damage or injury to the property of any other person or to the person of any other individual," United States Code, Title 18, Part I. This formulation's privileging of property before persons also addresses, in my mind, the rioters' grievance with the structures and infrastructures of social-spatial order, and the antecedent emphasis on dismantling these structures. To reclaim rioting from the realm of the "derogatory" is also, I argue, following Ta-Nehisi Coates, an important acknowledgment of the reality that "property damage and looting" have been "effective tools of social progress" throughout U.S. history. "Barack Obama."
2. Davis, "Uprising," 149.

3. Maldonado-Torres, "On the Coloniality of Being," 255.

4. Wideman, "Dead Black Men," 150.

5. Wideman, 154.

6. Gilmore, *Golden Gulag,* 244.

7. Dumm, "The New Enclosures," 190–91.

8. Tobar, "South L.A. Revisited."

9. Wynter, "Novel and History," 100. On the analytical uses of the Plantationocene, and its close ties to reading terrestrial materials and reading with the angry earth, see Perry and Hopes, "The Plantationocene Series."

10. Gooding-Williams, "On Being Stuck," 3.

11. Wynter, "N.H.I.," 43.

12. Morton, *Realist Magic,* 65.

13. Los Angeles has a long history of such brutal reconsolidations of racial order, including the 1871 Chinese Massacre; the city's enthusiastic exclusion and internment of Japanese-American citizens in World War II; the 1943 attacks on Latinx youth by xenophobic U.S. military servicemen (best known as the Zoot Suit Riots); the aftermath of the 1965 Watts Riots, which Thomas Pynchon describes as "a siege of persuasion; to coax the Negro poor into taking on certain white values," "A Journey into the Mind of Watts"; and the police attack on the peaceful 1970 Chicano Moratorium March, which was closely tied to illegal federal activities undermining efforts by Chicano movement organizers to oppose the Vietnam War. See Martínez, 99–113.

14. Wynter, "N.H.I.," 70.

15. Simpson, *As We Have,* 197.

16. Silko, *Almanac of the Dead,* 431.

17. Tobar, *Soldier,* 283.

18. Coulthard, *Red Skin,* 60.

19. On the novel form's reification of capitalist bourgeois reality, see Jameson, *Political Unconscious,* chap. 3; and Moretti, "Serious Century." On the uses of catastrophism, see Ghosh, *The Great Derangement,* 19–24.

20. Mignolo, "Delinking," 455.

21. Mignolo, "Interview."

22. Klein, *The Shock Doctrine.*

23. Harvey, *Rebel Cities,* 117.

24. Gilmore, "Terror Austerity Race," 30.

25. Klein, *Shock,* 20.

26. Gilmore, "Terror Austerity Race," 34.

27. Vizenor, *Manifest Manners,* 15.

28. Mignolo, "Delinking," 461.

29. Tillett, *"Sixty Million Dead Souls,"* 23.

30. Song, *Strange Future;* italics in original, 25.

31. Silko quoted in Coltelli, *"Almanac,"* 204.

32. Sharer, "Who Were the Maya?," 16. The fragments of the ancient almanac in Silko's novel track the environmental catastrophes—"plague, earthquake, drought"—and human failures—"incest, insanity, war, and betrayal"—that converged to transform Maya empires. *Almanac,* 575. These descriptions echo Mayanist assessments of recent paleoclimate data indicating that severe droughts often developed alongside or just ahead of the political destabilization of kingdoms on the Yucatan peninsula. See Traxler, "Time Beyond Kings."

33. Maldonado-Torres, "On the Coloniality of Being," 247.

34. Silko, *Almanac of the Dead,* 617.

35. Klein, *The Shock Doctrine,* 21.

36. Silko, *Almanac of the Dead,* 723–24.

37. Silko, 618.

38. See Coulthard, *Red Skin,* "Chapter 2," and Alfred, *Peace Power Righteousness,* 1–30.

39. Silko, *Almanac of the Dead,* 618, 619, 718.

40. Silko, 618.

41. Silko, 749.

42. Houser, *Ecosickness,* 211.

43. Houser, 213.

44. Silko, *Almanac of the Dead,* 524.

45. Michaels, *The Shape,* 24.

46. Silko, "Fourth World," 125.

47. Silko, *Almanac of the Dead,* 619. See Cadena, *Earth Beings.*

48. Pasternak and King, "Land Back," 64.

49. Silko, 710.

50. Silko, 711.

51. See Traxler on how the abandonment of cities by materially deprived populations led to the end of the Classical age of Maya kings. "Time Beyond Kings," 36.

52. Silko, *Almanac of the Dead,* 513.

53. Silko, 513.

54. Silko, 418.

55. Silko, 710.

56. Irr, "Neomedievalism," 449.

57. Irr, 439.

58. On the psychic slide into nonidentity experienced by many Central American refugees, and its relationship to state formation through racialization, see Arias, "Central American-Americans."

59. Tobar, *The Tattooed Soldier*, 284.

60. Tobar, 219.

61. Tobar, 217.

62. Tobar, 225.

63. Caroline Levine, "The Strange Familiar," 588.

64. Levine, 588.

65. Tobar, *The Tattooed Soldier*, 224.

66. Tobar, 272.

67. Tobar, 283.

68. Masters, "Five Structures."

69. Petersen, "Irwindale."

70. Tobar, *The Tattooed Soldier*, 306.

71. Silko, *Almanac of the Dead*, 710.

72. Tobar, *The Tattooed Soldier*, 225.

73. See "Anatomy of the L.A. Riots."

74. Reed, "Toxic Colonialism," 37.

75. Silko, *Almanac of the Dead*, 202.

76. Silko, 201.

77. Silko, 222.

78. Manuel and Posluns, *The Fourth World*, 55.

79. Irr, "Timelines," 242.

80. Tobar, *The Tattooed Soldier*, 13.

81. Tobar, 15.

82. Tobar, 15.

83. Tobar, 54.

84. Davis, "Uprising," 149. For detailed histories of this violence see Davis, *City of Quartz*, Chapters 4 and 5, and Soja, *Seeking Spatial Justice*, chap. 4.

85. See Hamilton and Stoltz-Chinchilla, *Seeking Community*, chap. 3.

86. Arias, "Central American-Americans," 173.

87. On the expropriation of the Kizh, see "Tribal History"; on the mismanagement of treaty documents, see Miller, "The Secret Treaties."

88. For the definitive history of this period of development on Crown Hill, see Comer, *In Victorian Los Angeles*.

89. See Crown Hill Chronicles, "The Los Angeles Oil Boom."

90. Historic Resources Group, "Historic Resources Survey Report."

91. See Maese, "Crown Hill."

92. Song, *Strange Future*, 48.

93. Song, 47.

94. Tobar, *The Tattooed Soldier*, 15.

95. Dubey, *Signs*, 22.

96. Dubey, 22.

97. Tobar, *The Tattooed Soldier*, 49.

98. Tobar, 55.

99. Tobar, 229.

100. Marx, *Capital*, 163.

101. Ahmed, *Queer Phenomenology*, 43.

102. Ahmed, 49.

103. See Smith, "There's No Such Thing," and Díaz, "Apocalypse."

104. Mbembe, *Necropolitics*, 97.

105. Tobar, *The Tattooed Soldier*, 45.

106. Tobar, 47.

107. Tobar, 47.

108. On technocapitalist accidents, see Negri, "Notes"; on the accidental in risk society, see Heise, *Sense of Place,* chap. 4.

109. Tobar, *The Tattooed Soldier*, 47.

110. Lefebvre, *The Production of Space*, 164.

111. *The Tattooed Soldier* abounds with examples of immigrant and poor white laborers who have "seen or lived the randomness." 236: "The men stumbled around in the darkness, plastering walls . . . until one of them, a Salvadoran, slipped off a scaffold and broke his ankle." 50; "Darryl said he was once a steelworker by trade, until an accident ruined his life." 235. Like novels including Ana Castillo's *So Far From God* (1993) and Helena María Viramontes's *Under the Feet of Jesus* (1995), *The Tattooed Soldier* emphasizes that for undocumented workers, exposure to dangerous and toxic working conditions is not so much accidental as engineered by the racial partitioning that fuels the capitalist mode of production in the United States.

112. Vizenor, *Manifest Manners*, 15.

113. Althusser, *Philosophy of the Encounter*, 169.

114. Althusser; italics in original, 195.

115. Silko, *Almanac of the Dead*, 704.

116. On redeeming the novel's terrible characterization of humans by reading them figuratively, see Fischer-Hornung, "'Now We Know,'" and St. Clair, "Cannibal Queers."

117. Yusoff, *A Billion*, 67.

118. Yusoff, 67.

119. Silko, *Almanac of the Dead*, 120.

120. Silko, 120.

121. Silko, 261.

122. Silko, 484.

123. Silko, 503.

124. Silko, 500.
125. Silko, 328.
126. The Octagon Earthworks that were incorporated into the Mound-builders Country Club in Newark—"a contemporary captive" of colonial order, as Chadwick Allen puts it—are the most famous example of this form of colonial infrastructural violence. The Country Club can only exist by strategically ignoring the earthwork's function as "forms of Indigenous *writing*" that are vessels for knowledge, history, and technology. Allen, "Re-scripting Indigenous America," n145, 129.
127. Silko, *Almanac of the Dead,* 509.
128. Silko, 504.
129. Silko, 509.
130. Silko, "Indian Hater," 99.
131. Tobar, *The Tattooed Soldier,* 63–64.
132. Minich, "Mestizaje as National Prosthesis," 216.
133. Tobar, *The Tattooed Soldier,* 216.
134. Houser, *Ecosickness,* 169.
135. See Mr. RTD, "From Crown Hill."
136. See Yokota, "The Belmont Tunnel."
137. See Fredric Jameson and Mike Davis for an intense debate over the Bonaventure as an object of global postmodernity or localized urban warfare, particularly Davis's response to Jameson's reading of the hotel: "Urban Renaissance," and Jameson's rebuttal: *Postmodernism* n19, 421.
138. Song, *Strange Future,* 48.
139. Tobar, *The Tattooed Soldier,* 267.
140. Tobar, 267.
141. Tobar, 267.
142. Tobar, 269.
143. Tobar, 299.
144. Tobar, 300.
145. Tobar, 300.
146. Tobar, 301.
147. Tobar, 301.
148. Tobar, *The Tattooed Soldier,* 243.
149. Tobar, 222.
150. Jameson, *Postmodernism,* 42.
151. Silko, *Almanac of the Dead,* 757.
152. Tobar, *The Tattooed Soldier,* 306.
153. Silko, *Almanac of the Dead,* 747.

154. See Davis on the city's increased surveillance budget. "Uprising"; Garfield on Weed and Seed. "Landscaping Neoliberalism"; McDonald et al. on the failures of Rebuild LA. "Then & Now"; on the city's abandonment of Korean business owners, see Song, *Strange Future,* chap. 4, and Lee, *K-Town'92.*

155. Tobar, *The Tattooed Soldier,* 306.

156. Tobar, 306.

4. The Fourth World Resurgent

1. See Leon and Nadeau, "Moving with Water."

2. "History," The Forks.

3. "The Forks," Canada's Historic Places.

4. "History," The Forks.

5. See Leslie and Dangerfield, "Ripple Effect."

6. See MacPherson and Vermette, *This River.*

7. Simpson, *As We Have,* 197.

8. Mbembe, *Necropolitics,* 79.

9. Vizenor, *Bearheart,* 243.

10. Corntassel, "Re-Envisioning Resurgence," 88.

11. Simpson, *As We Have,* 48–49.

12. Simpson, 197.

13. Pasternak and King, "Land Back," 8.

14. Justice, "Go Away, Water!" 151.

15. Vizenor, *Darkness,* xiv. All other citations of *Bearheart* refer to the 1990 edition.

16. Vizenor, *Bearheart,* 146.

17. That oil supports particular plot structures is a preoccupation of Reza Negarestani's 2008 speculative realist novel, *Cyclonopedia.* "To understand the militarization of oil and the dynamism of war machines in War on Terror," Negarestani writes, "one must grasp oil as an ultimate Tellurian lubricant, or a vehicle for epic narratives. To instrumentalize oil through production, to impose any authorial line on this narrative carrier, is like feeding on the Devil's excrement or its derivatives; there is always the danger of being poisoned to death or even worse," 69.

18. Butler, "Science Fiction Writer."

19. On Vizenor's decolonizing of textual practices, see Owens, "Ecstatic Strategies," *Other Destinies;* Teuton, "Trickster Leads the Way," *Deep Waters;* and Cox, "Freedom from the Word," *Muting White Noise.* While Butler is less cited as a decolonial thinker, her antiracist reformulations of community belonging and Black identity are well-documented in the work of Madhu Dubey, "Urban

Writing," *Signs and Cities;* Agustí, "The Relationship"; and Joo, "Old and New Slavery."

20. See Rozelle, "Decentralized Visions," *Ecosublime;* Gamber, *Positive Pollutions;* Schweninger, *Listening to the Land.*

21. McCoy, "Walking the 5," 225.

22. Butler, *Parable of the Sower,* 59.

23. Vizenor, *Manifest Manners,* 7.

24. Brooks, *The Common Pot,* 3.

25. Vizenor, *Fugitive Poses,* 15. In Christopher Schedler's terms, Vizenor "sees the inherent Native rights of presence, motion, and survivance on this continent as an 'originary' form of sovereignty." "Wiindigoo Sovereignty," 36.

26. Lipsitz, *How Racism Takes Place,* 3.

27. McCoy, "Walking the 5," 228.

28. Vizenor, *Bearheart,* 7.

29. Hume, "Gerald Vizenor's Metaphysics," 585.

30. Justice, "Go Away, Water!" 162.

31. Vizenor, *Bearheart,* 26.

32. Vizenor, 26.

33. Vizenor, 25.

34. Coulthard, *Red Skin,* italics in original, 13.

35. Goeman, "Disrupting," 254.

36. Phillips, "The Intuition of the Future," 302.

37. McCoy, "Walking the 5," 227.

38. The murder of Trayvon Martin in a multiethnic gated community in Florida in 2012 threw this spatial logic into brutal relief. On the connection between racialized policing and gated communities, see Davis, "Fortress L.A.," *City of Quartz.*

39. Butler, *Parable of the Sower,* 50.

40. For a study of the middle-class American suburbanite's sense of victimization, see Jurca, *White Diaspora.*

41. Butler, *Parable of the Sower,* 121.

42. Butler, 127.

43. See McCoy, "Walking the 5," 224.

44. See Marlene Allen, "Octavia Butler's Parable Novels," 1357.

45. The same developmentalist logic links these spatial forms to the slave plantation, a spatial form integral to this conversation but beyond the scope of my primary texts. Toni Morrison's *Beloved* (1987) is a key intertext here in its attention to the ways in which the plantation's boundaries pursue former slaves and scar the psychic landscape of the nation.

46. Houser, *Ecosickness,* 169.

47. Vizenor, *Bearheart*, 23.

48. This distinction recalls that made by M. King Hubbert's Peak Oil theory in 1956. Hubbert's peak theory does not measure the moment when the earth's oil supplies run out but rather the moment when production peaks and goes into decline. Wikipedia, "Peak Oil."

49. Vizenor, *Bearheart*, 98.

50. Butler, *Parable of the Sower*, 83.

51. Butler, 118.

52. Butler, 118–19.

53. Ghosh, *The Great Derangement*, 37.

54. Ghosh, 37.

55. Butler, *Parable of the Sower*, 119.

56. Ghosh, *The Great Derangement*, 36.

57. Menne, "'I Live in This World,'" 722.

58. On the occupation's solidarity with Third World struggle, see Estes, *Our History*, 179.

59. Vizenor, *Bearheart*, 26.

60. Vizenor, 26.

61. Hume, "Gerald Vizenor's Metaphysics," 602.

62. Justice, "Go Away, Water!" 151.

63. Alfred, *Peace Power Righteousness*, 54, 60.

64. Vizenor, *Bearheart*, 28.

65. I follow other critics who read Earthseed as "a political disposition [cast] in religious terms." Menne, "'I Live in This World,'" 724.

66. Butler, *Parable of the Sower*, 219.

67. Butler, 221.

68. For a summary of objections to the language problem, see Meillassoux, *After Finitude*, and Bryant, *Democracy of Objects*; for theorists who see objects as themselves generative of narrative and aesthetic meanings, see Iovino and Oppermann, *Material Ecocriticism*, Cohen and Duckert, *Elemental Ecocriticism*, and Morton, *Realist Magic*. For the significance of this question to poststructuralist debates, see Judith Butler, *Bodies that Matter*, particularly chapter 7.

69. Butler, *Parable of the Sower*, 79.

70. Butler's third, unfinished novel in the Earthseed trilogy is entitled *Parable of the Trickster*, suggesting that the depth of her engagement with the ontology of change led to investigations of the trickster figure that is a polymorphic force of change in many Indigenous traditions of mythic reason, including that of the Anishinaabe and the Yoruba from which Lauren gets her surname, Olamina.

71. Vizenor, *Bearheart*, 212.

72. Vizenor, 210.
73. Vizenor, 214.
74. Vizenor, 213–14.
75. Borrows, *Drawing Out Law,* xiii.
76. See Bercovitch, *The American Jeremiad,* xiv.
77. Vizenor, *Bearheart,* 214.
78. Vizenor, 215.
79. Butler, *Parable of the Sower,* 227.
80. Butler, 228.
81. Butler, 234; Berlant, "Intuitionists," 858.
82. Butler, *Parable of the Sower,* 228.
83. Butler, 178.
84. Butler, 176–77.
85. In this sense, my reading of Butler's narrative ontology is consonant with Matthew Taylor's analysis of the African diasporic cosmology present in the work of Charles Chesnutt and Zora Neale Hurston, which, he writes "refute racist ontologies but do not thereby liberate us as free subjects." *Universes Without Us,* 20.
86. Vizenor, *Bearheart,* 51.
87. Vizenor, 161–62.
88. Vizenor, 161.
89. Butler, *Parable of the Sower,* 77–78.
90. Manuel and Posluns, *The Fourth World,* 55.
91. Coulthard, *Red Skin,* 48.
92. Coulthard, *Red Skin*; italics in original, 13.
93. Whitehead, *The Intuitionist,* 62.
94. Simpson, *As We Have;* emphasis added, 48–49.
95. Whitehead, *Zone One,* 25.
96. Latour, *Reassembling the Social,* 259.
97. Bogost, *Alien Phenomenology,* 5.
98. Cohen, *Stone,* ix.
99. Coulthard, *Red Skin,* 19.
100. Wynter, "Unsettling," 330.
101. Wynter, 313.
102. Elizabeth Cook-Lynn asserts that Vizenor represents a postmodernist intellectual trend in Native writing that privileges "an Indian identity which focuses on individualism rather than First Nation ideology." See "American Indian Intellectualism," 67.
103. Butler, *Parable of the Sower,* 262.

104. This speaks to concerns voiced by Indigenous scholars over the use of "ontology" as a decolonial term. How can a concept of knowledge rooted in policing the terms of being-in-the-world be transported into other knowledge traditions without reproducing a privileged relationship to knowledge production? See Hunt, "Ontologies of Indigeneity," and Todd, "An Indigenous Feminist's Take."

105. Butler, *Parable of the Sower*, 316.

106. Butler, 326.

107. Butler, 321.

108. Butler, 321.

109. The struggle, and indeed, impossibility of bringing the possessiveness that accompanies this labor into sync with the Earthseed ontology is the focus of the next book in the series, *Parable of the Talents*.

110. Butler, *Parable of the Sower*, 193, 311.

111. Butler, 184.

112. Butler, 190, 236.

113. Phillips, "The Intuition of the Future," 308.

114. Butler, *Parable of the Sower*, 10.

115. Butler, 26.

116. Butler, 56.

117. Vizenor, *Bearheart*, 145.

118. Vizenor, 150.

119. Vizenor, 147.

120. Vizenor, 111.

121. Vizenor, 112.

122. Vizenor, 121.

123. Vizenor, 241.

124. Vizenor, 239.

125. Vizenor, 242. Leslie Marmon Silko references stories of "those who go to the bears" and coyotes in *Ceremony*, 118–121.

126. Vizenor, *Bearheart*, 240.

127. Vizenor, 243.

128. Zubeda Jalalzai refers to it as the "mythic fourth world" and "the fourth world, beyond good and evil." "Tricksters, Captives, and Conjurers," 29–30; for Elizabeth Blair it is the "visionary fourth world." "Text as Trickster," 79; Maureen Keady, Christopher Schedler, and Louis Owens seem to take Vizenor's use of the term as self-evident. "Afterword," *Other Destinies*. Lee Rozelle connects Vizenor's usage to Manuel's definition as evoking the shared struggle of a global pan-Indigenous community. See *Ecosublime*, 82.

129. Manuel and Posluns, *The Fourth World*, 217.

130. Butler, *Parable of the Sower*, 222.

131. Manuel and Posluns, *The Fourth World*, 266.

132. Vizenor, *Bearheart*, 245.

133. Vizenor, 240.

134. Simpson, *As We Have*, 53.

135. Vizenor, *Bearheart*, 239–40.

136. Lauren's disidentification with humans is even more pronounced in *Parable of the Talents*, in which her daughter chronicles the development of Earthseed alongside her own distance from her mother. Butler's choice to move away from the access to Lauren's subjectivity offered by her first-person narration in *Parable of the Sower* further dramatizes this distancing.

137. Vizenor, *Bearheart*, 75.

138. Butler, *Parable of the Sower*, 182.

139. Butler, 182.

140. Morton, *The Ecological Thought*, 41.

141. Ahmed, *Strange Encounters*, 79.

142. Wynter, "Unsettling," 331.

Conclusion

1. Canavan, *Octavia E. Butler*, 179.

2. Butler, *Parable of the Sower*, 222.

3. Canavan, *Octavia E. Butler*, 161.

4. Canavan, 161.

5. Butler, "Tell Stories."

6. Butler, *Parable of the Sower*, 338

7. Ghosh, *The Great Derangement*, 7.

8. See Hanna, Vargas, and Saldívar, *Junot Díaz*.

9. This is not including the many decolonial futurists writing around the globe and in U.S.-occupied territories, including Rita Indiana, Giannina Braschi, Pedro Cabiya, Dilman Dila, Oghenechovwe Donald Ekpeki, and Nnedi Okorafor, to name just a few.

10. Roanhorse, *Trail of Lightning*, 54.

11. Dimaline, *The Marrow Thieves*, 87.

12. Dillon, *Walking the Clouds*, 3.

13. Cornum, "The Creation Story."

14. Dimaline, *The Marrow Thieves*, 47.

15. Denetdale, "Guest Column."

16. Mignolo, "Interview."

17. Tuck and Yang, "Decolonization is Not a Metaphor," 19.

18. Manuel and Posluns, *The Fourth World*, 166.
19. Pasternak and King, "Land Back," 6.
20. Wynter, "Coloniality," 288.
21. Wynter, "Unparalleled Catastrophe," 25.
22. Wynter, 72.
23. Deloria and Wildcat, *Power and Place*, 37.
24. Wynter, 29.
25. Wynter, "Coloniality," 331.
26. There is some debate among scholars of Wynter's work in terms of her position on genre as something that should be accepted or struggled against. This tension is fully developed by Wynter's own questions in this passage: "So how do we deal with the new reality of the now emergent empirically ecumenically human *referent-we* 'in the horizon of humanity'? And how do we grapple with this in relation to the cognitive contradiction that our law-likely correlated genre-specific mode of mind/minding/conscious-ness, that is necessarily opiate rewarded, in the terms of its genre-specific sociogenic code of symbolic life/death, must law-likely undermine a *species perspective* in favor of a *genre-specific perspective* that honors those of us who are interpellated as 'normal subjects' and who thereby constitute the middle-class *referent-we*? How, then, as Thomas Nagel proposes, can we be enabled and empowered 'to climb out of our present order of conscious-ness?'" "Unparalleled Catastrophe," 45. I take these questions to mean that if global crisis generates an "empirically ecumenically human *referent-we*," then the need for a way out of our *genre-specific perspective* is paramount.
27. Manuel and Posluns, *The Fourth World*, 7.
28. Coulthard and Simpson, "Grounded Normativity," 250–51.
29. See Pearce, *An Awkward Silence*.
30. Anzaldúa, *Borderlands*, 68.
31. Eugenides, *Middlesex*, 242.
32. Taylor, "Water Cannons."
33. Chakrabarty, "Postcolonial Studies," 14.
34. Alaimo, *Exposed*, 155.
35. Yusoff, *A Billion*, 25.
36. Coulthard, *Red Skin*; italics in original, 125.
37. Mittman, "Reflections on the Plantationocene."
38. Sharpe, *In the Wake*, 106.
39. Melamed, "Racial Capitalism," 81.
40. Byrd, "Weather with You," 207.
41. Leroy, "Black History."
42. Simpson, *As We Have*, 67.

43. Sandoval, "US Third-World Feminism," 76.
44. Sandoval, 92–93n3.
45. Sandoval, 89.
46. Pegues, "Empire, Race."
47. Yusoff, *A Billion,* 63.
48. Yusoff, 63.
49. Tuck and Yang, "Decolonization is Not a Metaphor," 26.
50. Pasternak and King, "Land Back," 65.
51. Silko, "Fourth World," 125.
52. Pasternak and King, "Land Back," 30.
53. Gilmore, *Golden Gulag,* 248.
54. See Kimmerer and Lake, "The Role of Indigenous Burning."
55. Testa, *The Human Element.*
56. See Tyler and Moench. "A Framework for Urban Climate Resilience."
57. See City of Vancouver, "Sea Level Rise."
58. Estes, *Our History is the Future,* 135.
59. Estes, 135.
60. Gomez, "Sumas First Nation."
61. LeMenager, *Living Oil,* 7.
62. Pynchon, *Mason & Dixon,* 345.

.

BIBLIOGRAPHY

Agustí, Clara E. "The Relationship between Community and Subjectivity in Octavia E. Butler's Parable of the Sower." *Extrapolation,* 46, no. 3 (2005): 351–83.

Ahmed, Sara. *Queer Phenomenology.* Durham, N.C.: Duke University Press, 2006.

Ahmed, Sara. *Strange Encounters: Embodied Others in Post-Coloniality.* London: Routledge, 2000.

Alaimo, Stacy. *Bodily Natures: Science, Environment, and the Material Self.* Bloomington: Indiana University Press, 2010.

Alaimo, Stacy. *Exposed: Environmental Politics and Pleasures in Posthuman Times.* Minneapolis: University of Minnesota Press, 2016.

Alaimo, Stacy, and Susan Hekman. "Introduction: Emerging Models of Materiality in Feminist Theory," in Alaimo and Hekman, 1–19.

Alaimo, Stacy, and Susan Hekman. eds. *Material Feminisms.* Bloomington: Indiana University Press, 2008.

Alexander, Michelle. *The New Jim Crow.* New York: New Press, 2012.

Alfred, Taiaiake. *Peace Power Righteousness: An Indigenous Manifesto,* Oxford: Oxford University Press, 1999.

Allen, Chadwick. "Re-scripting Indigenous America: Earthworks in Native Art, Literature, Community." In *Twenty-First Century Perspectives on Indigenous Studies: Native North America in (Trans)Motion,* edited by Karsten Fitz Dawes and Sabine N. Meyer, 127–47. London: Routledge, 2015.

Allen, Marlene D. "Octavia Butler's Parable Novels and the 'Boomerang' of African American History." *Callaloo* 32, no. 4 (2009): 1353–65.

Alter, Jonathan. "The Other America." *Newsweek,* September 19, 2005.

Althusser, Louis. *Philosophy of the Encounter: Later Writings, 1978–1987.* Brooklyn, N.Y.: Verso, 2006.

Alworth, David J. *Site Reading: Fiction, Art, Social Form.* Princeton, N.J.: Princeton University Press, 2015.

"Anatomy of the L.A. Riots." ABC News, May 28, 1992. YouTube, www.youtube.com/watch?v=JJyarJc5QPU.

Anzaldúa, Gloria. *Borderlands: The New Mestiza / La Frontera.* San Francisco: Aunt Lute, 2012.

Arias, Arturo. "Central American-Americans: Invisibility, Power and Representation in the US Latino World." *Latino Studies* 1, no. 1 (2003): 168–87.

Asher, Kiran. "Latin American Decolonial Thought, or Making the Subaltern Speak." *Geography Compass* 7, no. 12 (2013): 832–42.

Assefa, Hizkias, and Paul Wahrhaftig. *The MOVE Crisis in Philadelphia.* Pittsburgh: University of Pittsburgh Press, 1990.

Avila, Eric. *Folklore of the Freeway: Race and Revolt in the Modernist City.* Minneapolis: University of Minnesota Press, 2014.

Balko, Radley. *Overkill: The Rise of Paramilitary Police Raids in America.* Washington, D.C.: Cato Institute, 2006.

Barad, Karen. *Meeting the Universe Halfway.* Durham, N.C.: Duke University Press, 2007.

Baraka, Amiri. "Technology & Ethos." In *Raise, Race, Rays, Raze: Essays Since 1965,* by Amiri Baraka, 155–57. New York: Random House, 1971.

Barnett, Louise K., and James L. Thorson, eds. *Leslie Marmon Silko: A Collection of Critical Essays.* Albuquerque: University of New Mexico, 1999.

Benea, Diana. "Spaces of Native American Ghostliness in Thomas Pynchon's *Mason & Dixon.*" In *Placing America: American Culture and Its Spaces,* edited by Michael Fuchs and Maria-Theresia Houlb. Wetzlar: Transcript, 2013.

Bennett, Jane. *Vibrant Matter: A Political Ecology of Things.* Durham, N.C.: Duke University Press, 2010.

Bennett, Tony, and Patrick Joyce, eds. *Material Powers.* London: Routledge, 2010.

Bercovitch, Sacvan. *The American Jeremiad.* Madison: University of Wisconsin Press, 2012.

Berlant, Lauren. *Cruel Optimism.* Durham, N.C.: Duke University Press, 2011.

Berlant, Lauren. "Intuitionists: History and the Affective Event." *American Literary History* 20, no. 4 (2008): 845–60.

Bérubé, Michael. "Race and Modernity in Colson Whitehead's *The Intuitionist.*" *The Holodeck in the Garden: Science and Technology in Contemporary*

American Fiction, edited by Peter Freese and Charles B. Harris, 163–78. Dublin: Dalkey Archive, 2004,

Blair, Elizabeth. "Text as Trickster: Postmodern Language Games in Gerald Vizenor's Bearheart." *MELUS* 20, no. 4 (1995): 75–90.

Bogost, Ian. *Alien Phenomenology, Or, What it's Like to Be a Thing.* Minneapolis: University of Minnesota Press, 2012.

Borrows, John. *Drawing Out Law: A Spirit's Guide.* Toronto: University of Toronto Press, 2010.

Brooks, Lisa. *The Common Pot: The Recovery of Native Space in the Northeast.* Minneapolis: University of Minnesota Press, 2008.

Brown, Adrienne. "Black Skyscrapers." *American Literature* 85, no. 3 (2013): 531–61.

Brown, Bill. *A Sense of Things.* Chicago: University of Chicago Press, 2003.

Brown, Bill. "Reification, Reanimation, and the American Uncanny." *Critical Inquiry* 32, no. 2 (2006): 175–207.

Bruyneel, Kevin. *The Third Space of Sovereignty: The Postcolonial Politics of U.S.-Indigenous Relations.* Minneapolis: University of Minnesota Press, 2007.

Bryant, Levi. *The Democracy of Objects.* Ann Arbor: Open Humanities, 2011.

Buell, Lawrence. *The Future of Environmental Criticism: Environmental Crisis and Literary Imagination.* Malden, Mass.: Blackwell, 2005.

Butler, Judith. *Bodies That Matter: On the Discursive Limits of Sex.* London: Routledge, 1993.

Butler, Octavia. "The Octavia E. Butler Plants an Earthseed." Amazon.com, interview by Therese Littleton and Bonnie Bouman, October 6, 1999. web.archive.org/web/20061205030424/http://cyberhaven.com/books/sciencefiction/butler.html.

Butler, Octavia. "One of the Few African-American Women Writing in the Male-Dominated Science Fiction Genre." *In Motion Magazine,* interview by Joshunda Sanders, NPC Productions, February 24, 2004.

Butler, Octavia. *Parable of the Sower.* New York: Grand Central, 1993.

Butler, Octavia. *Parable of the Talents.* New York: Grand Central, 1998.

Butler, Octavia. "Science Fiction Writer Octavia Butler on Race, Global Warming and Religion." *Democracy Now!* November 11, 2005, www.democracynow.org/2005/11/11/science_fiction_writer_octavia_butler_on.

Butler, Octavia. "Tell Stories Filled with Facts." Notes on Writing, 1970–1995. *Huntington Library,* www.huntington.org/sites/default/files/styles/press_image_slideshow/public/press-room/images/butler_tell-stories_400.jpg?itok=gj2Zo9kc.

Byrd, Jodi A. *Transit of Empire: Indigenous Critiques of Colonialism.* Minneapolis: University of Minnesota Press, 2011.

Byrd, Jodi A. "Weather with You: Settler Colonialism, Antiblackness, and the Grounded Relationalities of Resistance." *Critical Ethnic Studies* 5, no. 1–2 (2019): 207–214.

Cadena, Marisol de la. *Earth Beings: Ecologies of Practice Across Andean Worlds.* Durham, N.C.: Duke University Press, 2015.

Canavan, Gerry. *Octavia E. Butler.* Champaign: University of Illinois Press, 2016.

Castells, Manuel. *End of Millennium: The Information Age: Economy, Society, and Culture.* Vol. 3. 2nd ed. Malden, Mass.: Wiley Blackwell, 2010.

Chakrabarty, Dipesh. "Postcolonial Studies and the Challenge of Climate Change." *New Literary History* 43, no. 1 (2012): 1–18.

City of Vancouver. "Sea Level Rise" (accessed December 11, 2021) https://vancouver.ca/green-vancouver/sea-level-rise.aspx.

Clark, D. Anthony Tyeeme, and Malea Powell. "Resisting Exile in the 'Land of the Free': Indigenous Groundwork at Colonial Intersections." *American Indian Quarterly* 32, no. 1 (2008): 1–15.

Clifton, Lucille. "Being Property Once Myself." In *The Collected Poems of Lucille Clifton 1965–2010,* edited by Kevin Young and Michael S. Glaser, 78. Rochester, N.Y.: BOA, 2012.

Coates, Ta-Nehisi. "Barack Obama, Ferguson, and the Evidence of Things Unsaid." *Atlantic,* November 26, 2014. www.theatlantic.com/politics/archive/2014/11/barack-obama-ferguson-and-the-evidence-of-things-unsaid/383212/.

Cohen, Jeffrey Jerome. "Introduction: Ecostitial." *Inhuman Nature,* edited by Jeffrey Jerome Cohen. Washington, D.C.: Oliphaunt, 2014.

Cohen, Jeffrey Jerome. *Stone: An Ecology of the Inhuman.* Minneapolis: University of Minnesota Press, 2015.

Cohen, Jeffrey Jerome, and Lowell Duckert, eds. *Elemental Ecocriticism: Thinking with Earth, Air, Water, and Fire.* Minneapolis: University of Minnesota Press, 2015.

Collado Rodríguez, Francisco. "*Mason & Dixon,* Historiographic Metafiction and the Unstable Reconciliation of Opposites," in Copestake, 71–82.

Coltelli, Laura. "*Almanac:* Reading Its Story Maps after Twenty Years: An Interview with Leslie Marmon Silko," in Tillett, 195–216.

Comer, Virginia Linden. *In Victorian Los Angeles: The Witmers of Crown Hill.* Los Angeles: Talbot, 1988.

Cook-Lynn, Elizabeth. "The American Indian Fiction Writer: 'Cosmopolitanism, Nationalism, the Third World, and First Nation Sovereignty.'" *Wicazo Sa Review* 9, no. 2 (1993): 26–36.

Cook-Lynn, Elizabeth. "American Indian Intellectualism and the New Indian Story." *American Indian Quarterly* 20, no.1 (1996): 57–76.

Copestake, Ian D., ed. *American Postmodernity: Essays on the Recent Fiction of Thomas Pynchon.* Lausanne, Switzerland: Peter Lang, 2003.

Corntassel, Jeff. "Re-Envisioning Resurgence: Indigenous Pathways to Decolonization and Sustainable Self-Determination." *Decolonization: Indigeneity, Education & Society* 1, no. 1 (2012): 86–101.

Cornum, Lou. "The Creation Story is a Spaceship." *Voz-à-Voz,* http://www.vozavoz.ca/feature/lindsay-catherine-cornum.

Coulthard, Glen Sean. *Red Skin, White Masks: Rejecting the Colonial Politics of Recognition.* Minneapolis: University of Minnesota Press, 2014.

Coulthard, Glen, and Leanne Betasamosake Simpson. "Grounded Normativity / Place-Based Solidarity." *American Quarterly* 68 no. 2 (2016): 249–55.

Cox, James H. *Muting White Noise: Native American and European American Novel Traditions.* Norman: University of Oklahoma Press, 2006.

Crawford, Chiyo. "From Desert Dust to City Soot: Environmental Justice and Japanese American Internment in Karen Tei Yamashita's *Tropic of Orange.*" *MELUS* 38, no. 3 (2013): 86–106.

Crown Hill Chronicles. "The Los Angeles Oil Boom." *Crown Hill Chronicles,* November 9, 2009, crownhillchronicles.blogspot.com/2009/11/great-los-angeles-oil-strike.html.

Davis, Mike. *City of Quartz.* New York: Verso, 1990.

Davis, Mike. *Ecology of Fear: Los Angeles and the Imagination of Disaster.* New York: Vintage, 1999.

Davis, Mike. "Uprising and Repression in L.A. An Interview with Mike Davis by the *CovertAction* Information Bulletin," Gooding-Williams, 142–55.

Davis, Mike. "Urban Renaissance and the Spirit of Postmodernism." *New Left Review,* no. 151 (1985): 106–113.

DeLillo, Don. *Falling Man.* New York: Scribner, 2007.

Deloria, Vine, and Daniel Wildcat. *Power and Place: Indian Education in America.* Golden, Colo.: American Indian Graduate Center, 2001.

Denetdale, Jennifer Rose. "Guest Column: New Novel Twists Diné Teachings, Spirituality." *Navajo Times,* November 21, 2018, https://navajotimes.com/opinion/essay/guest-column-new-novel-twists-dineteachings-spirituality/.

Díaz, Junot. "Apocalypse: What Disasters Reveal." *Boston Review,* May 1, 2011, bostonreview.net/junot-diaz-apocalypse-haiti-earthquake.

Dillon, Grace L. *Walking the Clouds: An Anthology of Indigenous Science Fiction.* Tucson: University of Arizona Press, 2012.

Dimaline, Cherie. *The Marrow Thieves.* Toronto: Dancing Cat, 2017.

Dubey, Madhu. "Literature and Urban Crisis: John Edgar Wideman's Philadelphia Fire." *African American Review* 32, no. 4 (1998): 579–95.

Dubey, Madhu. *Signs and Cities: Black Literary Postmodernism.* Chicago: University of Chicago Press, 2003.

Dumm, Thomas L. "The New Enclosures: Racism in the Normalized Community," in Gooding-Williams, 178–195.

Dungy, Camille. "Introduction: the Nature of African American Poetry." In *Black Nature: Four Centuries of African American Nature Poetry*, xix–xxxv. Athens: University of Georgia Press, 2009.

"Early History: Potter's Field." BryantPark.org. www.bryantpark.org/about-us/history.html.

Eckfeldt, John W. *Cobb's Creek in the Days of the Old Powder Mill. Philly H2O.* Philadelphia Water Department, November 15, 2010. www.phillyh2o.org/backpages/cobbs_eckfeldtbook.htm.

Ellison, Ralph. *Invisible Man.* New York: Random House, 1952.

Estes, Nick. *Our History is the Future: Standing Rock Versus the Dakota Access Pipeline, and the Long Tradition of Indigenous Resistance.* Brooklyn, N.Y.: Verso, 2019.

Eugenides, Jeffrey. *Middlesex.* New York: Farrar, Straus and Giroux, 2002.

Fagone, Jason. "Birdie Africa: The Lost Boy." Philadelphia.com, February 27, 2014, www.phillymag.com/articles/birdie-africa-lost-boy/.

Fanon, Frantz. *The Wretched of the Earth.* Translated by Richard Philcox, New York: Grove, 2004.

Fain, Kimberly. *Colson Whitehead: The Postracial Voice in Contemporary Literature.* Lanham, MD: Rowman & Littlefield, 2015.

Felski, Rita. *The Limits of Critique.* Chicago: University of Chicago Press, 2015.

Ferreira da Silva, Denise. "Globality." *Critical Ethnic Studies* 1, no. 1 (2015): 33–38.

Fischer-Hornung, Dorothea. "'Now We Know that Gay Men Are Just Men After All': Abject Sexualities in Silko's *Almanac*," in Tillett, 71–90.

"The Forks National Historical Site of Canada." *Canada's Historic Places,* www.historicplaces.ca/en/rep-reg/place-lieu.aspx?id=4488&pid=0.

Fouché, Rayvon. "Say it Loud, I'm Black and I'm Proud: African Americans, American Artifactual Culture, and Black Vernacular Technological Creativity." *American Quarterly* 58, no. 3 (2006): 639–61.

Gamber, John B. *Positive Pollutions and Cultural Toxins: Waste and Contamination in Contemporary U.S. Ethnic Literatures.* Lincoln: University of Nebraska Press, 2012.

García-Caro, Pedro. "'America Was the Only Place . . .': American Exceptionalism and the Geographic Politics of Pynchon's *Mason & Dixon*," in Hinds, 101–124.

Garfield, Julie. "Landscaping Neoliberalism: The Weed and Seed Strategy." *Advocates' Forum*, 2010, 50–59.

Gass, Henry. "Why the Mohawks Are No Longer Walking the High Steel." *Globe and Mail*, August 23, 2013. www.theglobeandmail.com/news/national/why-the-mohawks-are-no-longer-walking-the-high-steel/article 13941326/.

Ghosh, Amitav. *The Great Derangement*. Chicago: University of Chicago Press, 2016.

Gilmore, Ruth Wilson. *Golden Gulag: Prisons, Surplus, Crisis, and Opposition in Globalizing California*. Berkeley: University of California Press, 2007.

Gilmore, Ruth Wilson. "Terror Austerity Race Gender Excess Theater," in Gooding-Williams, 23–37.

Girty, G. H. *Perilous Earth: Understanding Processes Behind Natural Disasters*. San Diego: San Diego State University, 2009.

Glotfelty, Cheryll, and Harold Fromm, eds. *The Ecocriticism Reader: Landmarks in Literary Ecology*. Athens: University of Georgia Press, 1996.

Goeman, Mishuana R. "Disrupting a Settler-Colonial Grammar of Place: The Visual Memoir of Hulleah Tsinhnahjinnie," in Simpson and Smith, 235–65.

Gomez, Michelle. "Sumas First Nation Built on Higher Ground, Unaffected by Flooding in Former Lake Bed, Says Chief." *CBC News*, November 19, 2021, www.cbc.ca/news/canada/british-columbia/sumas-lake-history-1.6 255693.

Gooding-Williams, Robert. "On Being Stuck," in Gooding-Williams, 1–12.

Gooding-Williams, Robert, ed. *Reading Rodney King/Reading Urban Uprising*. London: Routledge, 1993.

Green, Fiona. "'The Iroquois on the Girders': Poetry, Modernity, and the Indian Ironworker." *Critical Quarterly* 55, no. 2 (2013): 2–25.

Greiner, David J. "Thomas Pynchon and the Fault Lines of America," in Hovarth and Malin, 73–83.

Hamilton, Nora, and Norma Stoltz-Chinchilla. *Seeking Community in a Global City: Guatemalans and Salvadorans in Los Angeles*. Philadelphia: Temple University Press, 2001.

Hanna, Monica, Jennifer Harford Vargas, and José D. Saldívar. *Junot Díaz and the Decolonial Imagination*. Durham, N.C.: Duke University Press, 2016.

Haraway, Donna J. *Simians, Cyborgs, and Women: The Reinvention of Nature.* London: Routledge, 1991.

Harman, Graham. "The Well-Wrought Broken Hammer: Object-Oriented Literary Criticism." *New Literary History* 43, no. 2 (2012): 183–203.

Harman, Graham. "The Road to Objects." *Continent* 1, no. 3 (2011): 171–79.

Harman, Graham. *Guerrilla Metaphysics: Phenomenology and the Carpentry of Things.* Chicago: Open Court, 2005.

Harvey, David. *Rebel Cities: From the Right to the City to the Urban Revolution.* Brooklyn, N.Y.: Verso, 2012.

Harvey, Penny, and Hannah Knox. "Abstraction, Materiality and the 'Science of the Concrete' in Engineering Practice," in Bennet and Joyce, 124–41.

Hawthorne, Nathaniel. "Young Goodman Brown." In *Selected Tales and Sketches,* 133–48. New York: Penguin, 1987.

Hedge Coke, Allison Adele. *Blood Run.* Cambridge: Salt, 2006.

Heise, Ursula. *Sense of Place and Sense of Planet: The Environmental Imagination of the Global.* Oxford: Oxford University Press, 2008.

Heise, Ursula. "Terraforming for Urbanists." *Novel: A Forum on Fiction* 49, no. 1 (2016): 10–25.

Hellegers, Desiree. "From Poisson Road to Poison Road: Mapping the Toxic Trail of Windigo Capital in Linda Hogan's Solar Storms." *Studies in American Indian Literatures* 27, no. 2 (2015): 1–28.

Hinds, Elizabeth Jane Wall. "Animal, Vegetable, Mineral: The Play of Species in Pynchon's *Mason & Dixon.*" *Humans and Other Animals in Eighteenth-Century British Culture: Representation, Hybridity, Ethics,* edited by Frank Palmeri, 179–99. Burlington: Ashgate, 2006.

Hinds, Elizabeth Jane Wall. "Introduction: The Times of *Mason & Dixon.*" In Hinds, 3–24.

Hinds, Elizabeth Jane Wall, ed. *The Multiple Worlds of Pynchon's Mason & Dixon.* New York: Camden House, 2005.

Historic Resources Group. "Historic Resources Survey Report: Westlake Community Plan Area." Survey LA, 2014. preservation.lacity.org/sites/default/files/Westlake%20Report_0.pdf.

"History." *The Forks,* www.theforks.com/about/history.

Hogan, Linda. *Solar Storms.* New York: Simon and Schuster, 1995.

Horvath, Brooke. "Introduction," in Horvath and Malin, 11–26.

Horvath, Brooke, and Irving Malin, eds. *Pynchon and Mason & Dixon.* Wilmington: University of Delaware Press, 2000.

Houser, Heather. *Ecosickness in Contemporary U.S. Fiction.* New York: Columbia University Press, 2014.

Howe, LeAnne. "Embodied Tribalography: Mound Building, Ball Games, and Native Endurance in the Southeast." *Studies in American Indian Literatures* 26, no. 2 (2014): 75–93.

Huhndorf, Shari. "'Mapping by Words': The Politics of Land in Native American Literature." In *The Cambridge Companion to Literature and the Environment*, edited by Louise Westling, 45–58. Cambridge: Cambridge University Press, 2014.

Hume, Kathryn. "Gerald Vizenor's Metaphysics." *Contemporary Literature* 48, no. 4 (2007): 580–612.

Hunt, Sarah. "Ontologies of Indigeneity: The Politics of Embodying a Concept." *Cultural Geographies* 21, no. 1 (2014): 27–32.

Iovino, Serenella, and Serpil Oppermann. *Material Ecocriticism*. Bloomington: Indiana University Press, 2014.

Irr, Caren. "Neomedievalism in Three Contemporary City Novels: Tobar, Adichie, Lee." *Canadian Review of Contemporary Literature* 42, no. 4 (2015): 439–53.

Irr, Caren. "The Timelines of *Almanac of the Dead,* or a Postmodern Rewriting of Radical Fiction," in Barnett and Thorson, 223–44.

Jalalzai, Zubeda. "Tricksters, Captives, and Conjurers: The 'Roots' of Liminality and Gerald Vizenor's 'Bearheart.'" *American Indian Quarterly* 23, no. 1 (1999): 25–44.

Jameson, Fredric. *The Political Unconscious: Narrative as a Socially Symbolic Act.* Ithaca, N.Y.: Cornell University Press, 1981.

Jameson, Fredric. *Postmodernism, or, The Cultural Logic of Late Capitalism.* Durham, N.C.: Duke University Press, 1991.

Joo, Hee-Jung S. "Old and New Slavery, Old and New Racisms: Strategies of Science Fiction in Octavia Butler's Parables Series." *Extrapolation* 52, no. 3 (2011): 279–99.

Jurca, Catherine. *White Diaspora: The Suburb and the Twentieth-Century American Novel.* Princeton, N.J.: Princeton University Press, 2001.

Justice, Daniel Heath. "Go Away, Water! Kinship Criticism and the Decolonization Imperative." *Reasoning Together: The Native Critics Collective,* edited by Craig S. Womack, Daniel Heath Justice, and Christopher B. Teuton, 147–168. Norman: University of Oklahoma Press, 2008.

Justice, Daniel Heath. *Why Indigenous Literatures Matter.* Waterloo: Wilfrid Laurier University Press, 2018.

Karuka, Manu, Juliana H. Pegues, and Aloysha Goldstein. "Introduction on Colonial Unknowing." *Theory & Event* 19, no. 4 (2016).

Keady, Maureen. "Walking Backwards into the Fourth World: Survival of the Fittest in 'Bearheart.'" *American Indian Quarterly* 9, no. 1 (1985): 61–65.

Kelley, William Melvin. *A Different Drummer.* New York: Doubleday, 1989.

Kevorkian, Martin. *Color Monitors: The Black Face of Technology in America.* Ithaca, N.Y.: Cornell University Press, 2006.

Kimmerer, R. W., and F. K. Lake. "The Role of Indigenous Burning in Land Management." *Journal of Forestry* 99, no. 11 (2001): 36–41.

King, Thomas. *Green Grass, Running Water.* New York: Houghton Mifflin, 1993.

King, Thomas. Introduction to *All My Relations: An Anthology of Contemporary Canadian Native Prose,* edited by Thomas King, ix–xvi. Toronto: McClelland & Stewart, 1990.

King, Tiffany L. "Humans Involved: Lurking in the Lines of Posthumanist Flight." *Critical Ethnic Studies* 3, no. 1 (2017): 162–85.

Kirn, Walter. "The Promise of Verticality." *Time,* January 25, 1999.

Klein, Naomi. *No Logo: Taking Aim at the Brand Bullies.* London: Flamingo, 2000.

Klein, Naomi. *The Shock Doctrine.* New York: Random House, 2007.

Knight, Nadine M. "'It's a New Day': *The Intuitionist, The Wire,* and Prophetic Tradition." *MELUS* 40, no. 4 (2015): 28–47.

Kolodny, Annette. "Unearthing Herstory: An Introduction," in Glotfelty and Fromm, 170–81.

Koolhaas, Rem. *Delirious New York: A Retroactive Manifesto for Manhattan.* 1977. New York: Monacelli, 1994.

Lamy, Jérôme. "Sociology of a Disciplinary Bifurcation: Bruno Latour and His Move from Philosophy/Theology to Sociology in the Early 1970s." *Social Science Information* 60, no. 1 (2021): 107–30.

Land, Nick. *Fanged Noumena: Collected Writings 1987–2007,* edited by Ray Brassier and Robin Mackay. Cambridge: Urbanomic, 2011.

Larsen, Nella. *Passing.* 1929. Garden City, N.Y.: Dover, 2004.

Latour, Bruno. *Reassembling the Social: An Introduction to Actor-Network Theory.* Oxford: Oxford University Press, 2005.

Latour, Bruno. *We Have Never Been Modern.* 1991. Translated by Catherine Porter. Cambridge, Mass.: Harvard University Press, 1993.

Latour, Bruno, and d'Amina Shabou. "Les idéologies de la compétence en milieu industriel à Abidjan." ORSTOM, *Sciences Humaines,* no. 3, 1974, www.bruno-latour.fr/sites/default/files/02-IDEOLOGIES-DE-COM PETENCE-FR.pdf. Accessed December 12, 2021.

Lazarus, Neil. "The Global Dispensation Since 1945." *The Cambridge Companion to Postcolonial Literary Studies,* edited by Neil Lazarus, 19–40. Cambridge: Cambridge University Press, 2004.

Lee, Grace. *K-Town'92.* San Francisco: Center for Asian American Media, 2017. ktown92.com/.

Lee, James Kyung-Jin. *Urban Triage: Race and the Fictions of Multiculturalism.* Minneapolis: University of Minnesota Press, 2004.

Lefebvre, Henri. *The Production of Space.* 1974. Translated by Donald Nicholson-Smith. Oxford: Blackwell, 1991.

LeMenager, Stephanie. *Living Oil: Petroleum Culture in the American Century.* Oxford: Oxford University Press, 2014.

Lensing, Dennis M. "Postmodernism at Sea: The Quest for Longitude in Thomas Pynchon's *Mason & Dixon* and Umberto Eco's *The Island of the Day Before,*" in Hinds, 125–43.

Leon, Alannah Young, and Denise Marie Nadeau. "Moving with Water: Relations and Responsibilities." *Downstream: Reimagining Water,* edited by Dorothy Christian and Rita Wong, 117–38. Waterloo: Wilfrid Laurier University Press, 2016,

Leopold, Luna B. *Fluvial Processes in Geomorphology. New York:* W. H. Freeman, 1964.

Leroy, Justin. "Black History in Occupied Territory: On the Entanglements of Slavery and Settler Colonialism." *Theory & Event* 19 no. 4 (2016).

Leslie, Sean, and Katie Dangerfield. "Ripple Effect: No Easy Fix for Winnipeg's Flood-Prone Riverwalk." *Global News,* October 5, 2016, globalnews .ca/news/2984435/ripple-effect-no-easy-fix-for-winnipegs-flood-prone -riverwalk/.

Levine, Adam. *Philly H2O.* Philadelphia: Philadelphia Water Department. April 25, 2015. www.phillyh2o.org/creek.htm.

Levine, Caroline. "'The Strange Familiar': Structure, Infrastructure, and Adichie's *Americanah.*" *Modern Fiction Studies* 61, no. 4 (2015): 587–605.

Liggins, Saundra. "The Urban Gothic Vision of Colson Whitehead's *The Intuitionist.*" *African American Review* 40 (2006): 359–69.

Lipsitz, George. *How Racism Takes Place.* Philadelphia: Temple University Press, 2011.

MacPherson, Erika, and Katherena Vermette. *This River.* Montreal: National Film Board of Canada, 2016.

Madsen, Deborah L. "Family Legacies: Identifying the Traces of William Pynchon in *Gravity's Rainbow.*" *Pynchon Notes,* no. 42–43 (1998): 29–48.

Maese, Kathryn. "Crown Hill Gets the Royal Treatment." *Los Angeles Downtown News,* May 17, 2004. www.ladowntownnews.com/news/crown-hill-gets -the-royal-treatment/article_b3c556e9-33d7-53d1-82df-d0afc23f4689 .html.

Maldonado-Torres, Nelson. "On the Coloniality of Being: Contributions to the Development of a Concept." *Cultural Studies* 21, nos. 2–3 (2007): 240–70.

Manuel, George, and Michael Posluns. *The Fourth World: An Indian Reality.* New York: Free Press, 1974.

Martínez, Sara E. *The Chicano Movement: A Historical Exploration of Literature.* Santa Barbara, Calif.: Greenwood, 2017.

Marx, Karl. *Capital Volume 1.* New York: Penguin, 1976.

Massiah, Louis, dir. *Bombing of Osage Avenue,* WHYY-TV 12, 1986.

Masters, Nathan. "Five Structures That Defined L.A.'s Age of Concrete." *Lost L.A.,* KCETLink Media Group, May 2, 2017. www.kcet.org/shows/lost-la/five-structures-that-defined-las-age-of-concrete.

Mattessich, Stefan. *Lines of Flight: Discursive Time and Countercultural Desire in the Work of Thomas Pynchon.* Durham, N.C.: Duke University Press, 2002.

Mazel, David. "American Literary Environmentalism as Domestic Orientalism," in Glotfelty and Fromm, 137–48.

Mbembe, Achille. *Necropolitics.* Durham, N.C.: Duke University Press, 2019.

McCarthy, Cormac. *The Road.* New York: Knopf, 2006.

McCoy, Beth A. "Walking the 5: Octavia Butler's *Parable of the Sower.*" *The Sonia Sanchez Literary Review* 9, no. 1 (2003): 223–34.

McDonald, Patrick Range, and Ted Soqui. "Then & Now: Images from the Same Spot as the L.A. Riots, 20 Years Later." *LA Weekly, April 26, 2012.* https://web.archive.org/web/20160530001205/http://www.laweekly.com/microsites/la-riots/.

McHale, Brian. "Mason & Dixon in the Zone, or, A Brief Poetics of Pynchon-Space," in Horvath and Malin, 43–62.

McLaughlin, Robert L. "Surveying, Mapmaking and Representation in *Mason & Dixon,*" in Copestake, 173–91.

Meillassoux, Quentin. *After Finitude: An Essay on the Necessity of Contingency.* Translated by Ray Brassier. New York: Continuum, 2008.

Melamed, Jodi. "Racial Capitalism." *Critical Ethnic Studies* 1, no. 1 (2015): 76–85.

Melamed, Jodi. *Represent and Destroy: Rationalizing Violence in the New Racial Capitalism.* Minneapolis: University of Minnesota Press, 2011.

Melley, Timothy. *Empire of Conspiracy: The Culture of Paranoia in Postwar America.* Ithaca, N.Y.: Cornell University Press, 2000.

Menne, Jeff. "'I Live in This World, Too': Octavia Butler and the State of Realism." *Modern Fiction Studies* 57, no. 4 (2011): 715–37.

Michaels, Walter Benn. *The Shape of the Signifier.* Princeton, N.J.: Princeton University Press, 2004.

Mignolo, Walter D. "Delinking: The Rhetoric of Modernity, the Logic of Coloniality and the Grammar of De-coloniality." *Cultural Studies* 21, nos. 2–3 (2007): 449–514.

Mignolo, Walter D. "Interview: Walter Mignolo." Interview by Alvina Hoffman. *E-International Relations,* January 17, 2017. https://www.e-ir.info/2017/01/17/interview-walter-mignolopart-1-activism-and-trajectory/.

Mignolo, Walter D. "Introduction: Coloniality of Power and De-Colonial Thinking." *Cultural Studies* 21, nos. 2–3 (2007): 155–67.

Miller, Larisa K. "The Secret Treaties with California's Indians." *Prologue,* Fall/Winter 2013, 38–45.

Minich, Julie Avril. "Mestizaje as National Prosthesis: Corporeal Metaphors in Héctor Tobar's *The Tattooed Soldier.*" *Arizona Journal of Hispanic Cultural Studies* 17 (2013): 211–25.

Mitchell, Joseph. "The Mohawks in High Steel." In *Apologies to the Iroquois* by Edmund Wilson, 3–38. Syracuse, N.Y.: Syracuse University Press, 1959.

Mittman, Greg. "Reflections on the Plantationocene: A Conversation with Donna Haraway and Anna Tsing." *Edge Effects,* Madison: University of Wisconsin-Madison, 2019. edgeeffects.net/haraway-tsing-plantationocene/.

Moore, Richard, and Jeanne Gauna. SouthWest Organizing Project, SouthWest Community Resources, Inc. "SouthWest Organizing Project Letter Sample Copy." March 16, 1990. www.ejnet.org/ej/swop.pdf.

Moretti, Franco. "Serious Century." In *The Novel,* edited by Franco Moretti, 364–400. Princeton, N.J.: Princeton University Press, 2006.

Morrison, Toni. *Beloved.* New York: Knopf, 1987.

Morton, Timothy. *The Ecological Thought.* Cambridge, Mass.: Harvard University Press, 2010.

Morton, Timothy. *Hyperobjects: Philosophy and Ecology after the End of the World.* Minneapolis: University of Minnesota Press, 2013.

Morton, Timothy. *Realist Magic: Objects, Ontology, Causality.* Ann Arbor: Open Humanities Press, 2013.

Montour, Courtney. "The World Trade Center and 9/11." *Mohawk Ironworkers.* Montreal: Mushkeg Media, 2016.

MOVE. "About MOVE." *On A Move: Website of the MOVE Organization.* onamove.com/about/.

Mr. RTD. "From Crown Hill to the Belmont Tunnel." *50mm Los Angeles,* May 21, 2005. www.50mmlosangeles.com/viewStory.php?storyId=16.

Negarestani, Reza. *Cyclonopedia: Complicity with Anonymous Materials.* Melbourne: Re.press, 2008.

Negri, Antonio. "Crisis of the Crisis-State." In *Revolution Retrieved: Selected Writings on Marx, Keynes, Capitalist Crisis and New Social Subjects, 1967–1983.* London: Red Notes, 1988.

Negri, Antonio. "Notes on the Evolution of the Thought of the Later Althusser." Translated by Olga Vasile. *Postmodern Materialism and the Future of Marxist*

Theory, edited by Antonio Callari and David F. Ruccio, 51–69. Hanover: Wesleyan University Press, 1996.

Nixon, Rob. "Unimagined Communities: Developmental Refugees, Megadams and Monumental Modernity." *New Formations* 69, no. 3 (2010): 62–80.

Olster, Stacey. "The Way We Were(n't): Origins and Empire in Thomas Pynchon's *Mason & Dixon.*" *American Fiction of the 1990s,* edited by Jay Prosser, 107–199. London: Routledge, 2008.

Osder, Jason, dir. *Let the Fire Burn.* New York: Zeitgeist, 2013.

Otter, Chris. "Locating Matter: The Place of Materiality in Urban History," in Bennet and Joyce, 36–56.

Owen, Don, dir. *High Steel.* Narrated by Don Francks. Montreal: National Film Board of Canada, 1965.

Owens, Louis. "Afterword," in *Bearheart,* 247–54.

Owens, Louis. *Other Destinies.* Norman: University of Oklahoma Press, 1992.

Pasternak, Shiri, and Hayden King. "Land Back: A Yellowhead Institute Red Paper." Yellowhead Institute, 2019. https://redpaper.yellowheadinstitute .org/.

Pauly, John J. "The Great Chicago Fire as a National Event." *American Quarterly* 36, no. 5 (1984): 668–83.

Pearce, Maryanne. "An Awkward Silence: Missing and Murdered Vulnerable Women and the Canadian Justice System." Ph.D. diss., University of Ottawa, 2013. www.collectionscanada.gc.ca/obj/thesescanada/vol2/OOU /TC-OOU-26299.pdf.

Pearsall, Susan M. "'Narratives of Self' and the Abdication of Authority in Wideman's 'Philadelphia Fire.'" *MELUS* 26, no. 2 (2001): 15–46.

Peck, Jamie, and Adam Tickell. "Neoliberalizing Space: The Free Economy and the Penal State." *Spaces of Neoliberalism: Urban Restructuring in North America and Western Europe,* edited by Neil Brenner and Nik Theodore, 475-499. Malden, Mass.: Blackwell, 2002.

Pegues, Juliana Hu. "Empire, Race, and Settler Colonialism: BDS and Contingent Solidarities." *Theory & Event* 19, no. 4 (2016).

Perry, Laura, and Addie Hopes, eds. "The Plantationocene Series: Plantation Worlds, Past and Present." *Edge Effects.* Madison: University of Wisconsin–Madison, 2019. https://edgeeffects.net/plantationocene-series-plantation -worlds/.

Petersen, Robert. "Irwindale: Mining the Building Blocks of Los Angeles." *Lost L.A.,* KCETLink Media Group, August 2, 2016. www.kcet.org/shows/ lost-la/irwindale-mining-the-building-blocks-of-los-angeles.

Petry, Ann. *The Street.* New York: Houghton Mifflin, 1946.

Philadelphia Special Investigation Committee. "The Findings, Conclusions, and Recommendations." Philadelphia: City of Philadelphia, 1986.

Phillips, Jerry. "The Intuition of the Future: Utopia and Catastrophe in Octavia Butler's 'Parable of the Sower.'" *NOVEL: A Forum on Fiction* 35, nos. 2/3 (2002): 299–311.

Pulido, Laura. *Environmentalism and Economic Justice: Two Chicano Struggles in the Southwest.* Tucson: University of Arizona Press, 1996.

Pynchon, Thomas. *The Crying of Lot 49.* New York: HarperCollins, 1999.

Pynchon, Thomas. *Gravity's Rainbow.* New York: Penguin, 2006.

Pynchon, Thomas. "A Journey into the Mind of Watts." *New York Times,* June 12, 1966. https://archive.nytimes.com/www.nytimes.com/books/97/05/18/reviews/pynchon-watts.html.

Pynchon, Thomas. *Mason & Dixon.* New York: Penguin, 1997.

Pynchon, Thomas. *V.* New York: 1963. HarperCollins, 1989.

Pynchon, Thomas. *Vineland.* Boston: Little, Brown and Co., 1990.

Quijano, Aníbal. "Coloniality of Power and Eurocentrism in Latin America." *International Sociology* 15, no. 2 (2000): 215–32.

Reed, T.V. "Toxic Colonialism, Environmental Justice, and Native Resistance in Silko's *Almanac of the Dead.*" *MELUS* 34, no. 2 (2009): 25–42.

Richard, Jean-Pierre. "'Philadelphia Fire,' or the Shape of a City." *Callaloo* 22, no. 3 (1999): 603–13.

Roanhorse, Rebecca. *Storm of Locusts.* New York: Saga, 2019.

Roanhorse, Rebecca. *Trail of Lightning.* New York: Saga, 2018.

Robinson, Cedric J. *Black Marxism: The Making of the Black Radical Tradition.* Chapel Hill: University of North Carolina Press, 2000.

Robinson, Kim Stanley, "Terraforming Earth." *Slate,* December 4, 2012. slate.com/technology/2012/12/geoengineering-science-fiction-and-fact-kim-stanley-robinson-on-how-we-are-already-terraformingearth.html.

Rody, Caroline. "The Transnational Imagination: Karen Tei Yamashita's *Tropic of Orange.*" *Asian North American Identities: Beyond the Hyphen.* Edited by Eleanor Rose Ty and Donald C. Goellnicht, 130–48. Bloomington: Indiana University Press, 2004.

Roy, Arundhati. "The Greater Common Good." *Outlook,* May 24, 1999. www.outlookindia.com/magazine/story/the-greater-common-good/207509. Accessed 26 July 2017.

Rozelle, Lee. *Ecosublime: Environmental Awe and Terror from New World to Oddworld.* Tuscaloosa: University of Alabama Press, 2006.

Rozelle, Lee. *Zombiescapes and Phantom Zones: Ecocriticism and the Liminal from Invisible Man to The Walking Dead.* Tuscaloosa: University of Alabama Press, 2016.

Russell, Alison. "Recalibrating the Past: Colson Whitehead's *The Intuitionist.*" *Critique: Studies in Contemporary Fiction,* no. 49 (2007): 46–60.

Saldívar, Ramón. "Historical Fantasy, Speculative Realism, and Postrace Aesthetics in Contemporary American Fiction." *American Literary History* 23, no. 3 (2011): 574–99.

Saldívar, Ramón. "The Second Elevation of the Novel: Race, Form, and the Postrace Aesthetic in Contemporary Narrative." *Narrative* 21, no. 1 (2013): 1–18.

Saltzman, Arthur. "'Cranks of Ev'ry Radius': Romancing the Line in *Mason & Dixon*," in Horvath and Malin, 63–72.

Sandoval, Chela. "US Third-World Feminism: The Theory and Method of Oppositional Consciousness in the Postmodern World." In *Feminist Postcolonial Theory: A Reader,* edited by Reina Lewis and Sara Mills, 75–99. Edinburgh: Edinburgh University Press, 2003.

Schaub, Thomas H. "Plot, Ideology, and Compassion in *Mason & Dixon*," in Horvath and Malin, 189–202.

Schedler, Christopher. "Wiindigoo Sovereignty and Native Transmotion in Gerald Vizenor's Bearheart." *Studies in American Indian Literatures* 23, no. 3 (2011): 34–68.

Schilling, Vincent. "They Helped Build the Twin Towers—Mohawk Ironworkers Series on APTN." *Indian Country Today,* Indian Country Media. September 2016. indiancountrymedianetwork.com/culture/arts-entertainment/they-helped-build-the-twin-towers-mohawk-ironworkers-series-on-aptn/.

Schweninger, Lee. *Listening to the Land: Native American Literary Responses to the Landscape.* Athens: University of Georgia Press, 2008.

Seed, David. "Mapping the Course of Empire in the New World," in Horvath and Malin, 84–99.

Sharer, Robert. "Who Were the Maya?" *Expedition* 54, no. 1 (2012): 12–16.

Sharpe, Christina E. *In the Wake: On Blackness and Being.* Durham, N.C.: Duke University Press, 2016.

Silko, Leslie Marmon. *Almanac of the Dead.* New York: Penguin, 1991.

Silko, Leslie Marmon. *Ceremony,* New York: Penguin, 1977.

Silko, Leslie Marmon. "The Fourth World." *ARTFORUM* 27, no. 10 (1989): 12–126.

Silko, Leslie Marmon. "Indian Hater, Indian Fighter, Indian Killer: Melville's Indictment of the 'New Nation' and the 'New World'" *Leviathan* 14, no. 1 (2012): 94–99.

Simpson, Audra. *Mohawk Interruptus: Political Life Across the Borders of Settler States.* Durham, N.C.: Duke University Press, 2014.

Simpson, Audra, and Andrea Smith. *Theorizing Native Studies.* Durham, N.C.: Duke University Press, 2014.

Simpson, Leanne Betasamosake. *As We Have Always Done: Indigenous Freedom through Radical Resistance.* Minneapolis: University of Minnesota Press, 2017.

Simpson, Leanne Betasamosake. A *Short History of the Blockade: Giant Beavers, Diplomacy, and Regeneration in Nishnaabewin.* Edmonton: University of Alberta Press, 2021.

Smith, Neil. "There's No Such Thing as a Natural Disaster." *Understanding Katrina: Perspectives From the Social Sciences,* June 11, 2006. understand ingkatrina.ssrc.org/Smith/.

Soja, Edward. *Seeking Spatial Justice.* Minneapolis: University of Minnesota Press, 2010.

Song, Min Hyoung. *Strange Future: Pessimism and the 1992 Los Angeles Riots.* Durham, N.C.: Duke University Press, 2005.

St. Clair, Janet. "Cannibal Queers: The Problematics of Metaphor in Almanac of the Dead," in Barnett and Thorson, 207–221.

Sullivan, Daniel E. U.S. Department of the Interior, U.S. Geological Survey. *Materials in Use in U.S. Interstate Highways.* Denver: Denver Federal Center, February 2, 2006. pubs.usgs.gov/fs/2006/3127/.

Sze, Julie. "'Not By Politics Alone': Gender and Environmental Justice in Karen Tei Yamashita's *Tropic of Orange.*" *Bucknell Review* 44, no.1 (2000): 29–42.

TallBear, Kim. "Beyond the Life/Not-Life Binary: A Feminist-Indigenous Reading of Cryopreservation, Interspecies Thinking, and the New Materialisms." *Cryopolitics: Frozen Life in a Melting World,* edited by Joanna Radin and Emma Kowal, 179–202. Cambridge, Mass.: MIT Press, 2017.

Taylor, Alan. "Water Cannons and Tear Gas Used against Dakota Access Pipeline Protesters." *Atlantic,* November 21, 2016. www.theatlantic.com/photo/ 2016/11/water-cannons-and-tear-gas-used-against-dakota-access-pipe line-protesters/508370/.

Taylor, Matthew A. *Universes without Us: Posthuman Cosmologies in American Literature.* Minneapolis: University of Minnesota Press, 2013.

Teskey, Gordon. *Allegory and Violence.* Ithaca, N.Y.: Cornell University Press, 1996.

Testa, Matthew, dir. *The Human Element.* Boulder, Colo.: Earth Vision Film, 2018.

Teuton, Christopher B. *Deep Waters: The Textual Continuum in American Indian Literature.* Lincoln: University of Nebraska Press, 2010.

Thompson, E. P. *The Making of the English Working Class.* New York: Vintage, 1966.

Tillett, Rebecca. "Almanac Contextualized," in Tillett, 5–13.

Tillett, Rebecca. "'*Sixty Million Dead Souls Howl for Justice in the Americas!*' *Almanac* as Political Activism and Environmental and Social Justice," in Tillett, 14–25.

Tillett, Rebecca, ed. *Howling for Justice: New Perspectives on Leslie Marmon Silko's Almanac of the Dead.* Tucson: University of Arizona Press, 2014.

Tobar, Héctor. "South L.A. Revisited, 25 Years After the Rodney King Riots." *New York Times,* April 28, 2017. https://www.nytimes.com/2017/04/28/opinion/south-la-revisited-25-years-after-the-rodney-king-riots.html?_r=0.

Tobar, Héctor. *The Tattooed Soldier.* New York: Penguin, 1998.

Todd, Zoe. "An Indigenous Feminist's Take on the Ontological Turn: 'Ontology' Is Just Another Word for Colonialism." *Journal of Historical Sociology* 29, no. 1 (2016): 4–22.

Trask, Haunani-Kay. "Settlers of Color and 'Immigrant' Hegemony: 'Locals' in Hawai'i." *Amerasia Journal* 26, no. 2 (2000): 1–26.

Traxler, Loa. "Time Beyond Kings." *Expedition* 54, no. 1 (2012): 36–43.

"Tribal History." Gabrielino-Tongva Tribe. www.gabrielinotribe.org/historical -sites-1/.

Tuana, Nancy. "Viscous Porosity: Witnessing Katrina," in Alaimo and Hekman, 188–213.

Tuck, Eve, and K. Wayne Yang. "Decolonization is Not a Metaphor." *Decolonization: Indigeneity, Education & Society* 1, no. 1 (2012): 1–40.

Tucker, Jeffrey Allen. "'Verticality is Such a Risky Enterprise': The Literary and Paraliterary Antecedents of Colson Whitehead's *The Intuitionist.*" *Novel* 43 (2010): 148–56.

Turner, Frederick. "Cultivating the American Garden," in Glotfelty and Fromm, 40–51.

Tyler, Stephen, and Marcus Moench. "A Framework for Urban Climate Resilience." *Climate and Development* 4, no. 4 (2012): 311–26.

United States Code, Title 18, Part I, Chapter 102, § 2102. www.law.cornell .edu/uscode/text/18/2102.

Valois, Renée. "The Mohawks Who Built Manhattan." *The History Channel Club.* portal.thehistorychannelclub.com/articles/articletype/articleview/ar ticleid/296/the-mohawks-who-built-manhattan.

Vint, Sherryl. "Orange County: Global Networks in *Tropic of Orange.*" *Science Fiction Studies* 39 (2012): 401–414.

Vizenor, Gerald. *Bearheart.* 1978. Minneapolis: University of Minnesota Press, 1990.

Vizenor, Gerald. *Darkness in St. Louis Bearheart.* St. Paul, Minn.: Truck, 1978.

Vizenor, Gerald. *Fugitive Poses: Native American Indian Scenes of Absence and Presence.* Lincoln: University of Nebraska Press, 1998.

Vizenor, Gerald. *Manifest Manners: Postindian Warriors of Survivance.* Hanover, N.H.: University Press of New England, 1994.

Vizenor, Gerald. *Survivance: Narratives of Native Presence.* Lincoln: University of Nebraska Press, 2008.

Wald, Sarah D. "'Refusing to Halt': Mobility and the Quest for Spatial Justice in Helena María Viramontes's *Their Dogs Came with Them* and Karen Tei Yamashita's *Tropic of Orange.*" *Western American Literature* 48, nos. 1/2 (2012): 70–89.

Wegner, Phillip. *Life Between Two Deaths, 1989–2001: U.S. Culture in the Long Nineties.* Durham, N.C.: Duke University Press, 2009.

Weheliye, Alexander G. *Habeas Viscus: Racializing Assemblages, Biopolitics, and Black Feminist Theories of the Human.* Durham, N.C.: Duke University Press, 2014.

Whitehead, Colson. *The Intuitionist.* New York: Anchor, 2000.

Whitehead, Colson. *Zone One.* New York: Anchor, 2011.

Wideman, John Edgar. "Dead Black Men and Other Fallout from the American Dream." *Esquire,* September 1992, 149–56.

Wideman, John Edgar. *Philadelphia Fire.* New York: Houghton Mifflin, 1990.

Wikipedia contributors. "Peak Oil." *Wikipedia, The Free Encyclopedia.* Wikipedia, the Free Encyclopedia, August 28, 2016.

Woods, Derek. "'Terraforming Earth': Climate and Recursivity." *Diacritics* 47, no. 3 (2019): 6–29.

Wynter, Sylvia. "The Ceremony Must Be Found: After Humanism." *boundary 2,* 12/13, no. 3 (1984): 19–70.

Wynter, Sylvia. "No Humans Involved: An Open Letter to My Colleagues." *Forum N.H.I.: Knowledge for the 21st Century* 1, no. 1 (1994): 42–73.

Wynter, Sylvia. "Novel and History, Plot and Plantation." *Savacou* 5 (1971): 95–102.

Wynter, Sylvia. "Unsettling the Coloniality of Being/Power/Truth/Freedom." *CR: The New Centennial Review* 3, no. 3 (2003): 257–337.

Yamashita, Karen Tei. *Tropic of Orange.* Minneapolis: Coffee House Press, 1997.

Yokota, Ryan Maasaki. "The Belmont Tunnel." YouTube, July 8, 2014. www.youtube.com/watch?v=vx3pi39Ck5E.

Yusoff, Kathryn. *A Billion Black Anthropocenes or None.* Minneapolis: University of Minnesota Press, 2018.

INDEX

Earthseed community, 156, 165–66,
168, 171, 199, 228n70, 230n109,
231n136; space travel by, 169,
175, 176. *See also* Butler, Octavia

Eckfeldt, John W., 216n2

ecocriticism, 206n61, 206n95,
228n68

ecologies, 2, 24, 26, 53, 146, 189,
194, 204nn15–16; violence of,
153–54, 196. *See also* earth; environment; physical environment

economies, 84, 123, 138, 155;
anticapitalism/capitalist, 1, 63,
204n27; environmental, 40–41,
142, 161–62; failing, 153–54,
159; neoliberal, 32, 110, 111,
113, 151; political, 161–62

elevators, 4, 42, 55, 57–59, 61,
63–71, 86, 93, 95, 132, 137, 162,
192, 198. *See also* Whitehead,
Colson, *The Intuitionist*

Ellison, Ralph, *Invisible Man,* 42, 56,
58

emancipation, 62, 209n107. *See also*
freedom

emergence, concept of, 5, 204n15

Empiricism/Empiricists, 22, 63–64.
See also Whitehead, Colson, *The
Intuitionist*

enclosure. *See* borders/boundaries;
gated communities; property,
lines of

Enlightenment, 19–20, 22, 25, 48

entanglements, 28–29, 49, 78, 87,
131, 137; colonial, 29–31, 40, 44,
46, 59, 63, 79–80, 94, 143–44,
149, 155–56, 189; grounded normativity and, 40, 52; material-
semiotic, 26, 46, 48, 52, 58, 67,
108, 132; new materialist theories

of, 28, 29, 39–40, 41–42; ontologies of, 20, 38; political, 39–40;
race-space, 36, 73; racial, 29,
37–38, 39, 41, 70, 78, 92, 146;
violent, 37–38, 53, 56, 63, 76, 78

environment, 89, 91, 99, 146,
204n16; activism for, 13, 14–16;
capital excesses regarding, 112;
crises in, 3, 181, 189, 222n32;
destruction of, 5–6, 13; economy
as reflection of, 40–41, 142,
161–62; exploitation of, 22, 80,
95, 146, 156; humans' relationship to, 10, 29, 76, 183, 194;
violence in, 107, 138, 186. *See
also* climate change; earth; nature;
physical environment

environmental justice, 14, 138. *See
also* racial justice

Epicurus, 22, 129–30

erosion, 4, 109, 118–22, 124, 126,
141. *See also* landslides

Escobar, Arturo, 21

Estes, Nick, 196

ethnicity, 22, 38, 51, 151. *See also*
race; solidarity: interethnic

Eugenides, Jeffrey, *Middlesex,* 186

exceptionalism, 26, 81–82, 113,
165, 190, 191

exclusion, 72, 128

exploitation, 15, 76, 186; capitalist,
13–14, 77, 114–15, 153; environmental, 22, 80, 95, 146, 156; of
labor, 26, 112; of land, 75, 77,
197–98, 213n86; racial, 9, 144; of
resources, 16, 153; violence of, 72,
75, 80

expropriation, 38, 125, 144; of land,
1, 16, 26, 37, 112; violence of,
107, 182

25–26, 45, 73, 94–95, 105–6, 113, 141, 177, 181, 185; colonial-capitalist, 3, 5, 6, 15–16, 26–27, 63, 82, 109, 128, 134; as colonial warfare, 29, 78, 109, 136; detritus of, 120, 121; failures of, 124, 179; global, 78–79, 106, 113, 187, 188; illusion of, 136–37; Latour's critique of, 21–22; narratives of, 111, 124; normalcy of, 28, 106–7; racialized, 64, 106–7, 154; rationality and, 21, 99, 100; twentieth-century, 29, 57; urban, 37, 38, 63, 78–79, 95, 118; violence of, 98–99, 190

modernity/coloniality/decoloniality (MCD) project, 21, 30–31, 110, 181–82

Mohawk ironworkers/skywalkers, 35–38, 47, 54, 60, 210n10, 210n12

Morrison, Toni, 82; *Beloved,* 227n45; *The Bluest Eye,* 58

Morton, Timothy, 24, 39, 53, 108, 171, 219n73

MOVE organization, 13, 75–76, 77, 81, 165, 218n52, 218n54, 219n83; bombing of headquarters, 78, 83–85, 88–91, 96–98, 100–101, 102, 106, 187, 217n36, 219n86. *See also* policing

multiculturalism, 80, 83, 96, 185, 198; neoliberal, 30, 81–82, 90. *See also* communities of color; culture

Nagel, Thomas, 232n26

narrative ontologies, 23, 73, 128–29, 130; of angry planet, 32, 36, 143, 186; in angry planet fiction, 15,

16–27, 55–56, 154, 172, 173, 175–81

narratives, 4, 37, 62, 101, 113, 161–62, 197, 209n105; colonial, 73, 192; of decolonization, 31, 100, 181–82, 183; defiant, 27–33; DNA of, 184, 185, 198; of modernity, 111, 124; of victimry, 55, 73

Native American Literary Renaissance, 205n36

natural resources. *See* resources

nature, 38, 40, 91, 111, 127, 138. *See also* environment; physical environment

nature-culture hybridity, 87–88, 91–92, 99. *See also* culture

necropolitics, 86, 127–28. *See also* politics

Negarestani, Reza, 146; *Cyclonopedia,* 226n17

Negri, Antonio, 31, 65, 191

neocolonialism, 5, 91–92, 101, 192. *See also* colonialism

neoliberalism, 44, 103; capitalist, 110, 132; economies of, 32, 110, 111, 113, 151; globalization and, 5, 32, 82, 92, 96; multiculturalism and, 30, 81–82, 90

new materialism, 5, 156, 163, 204n21, 218n54; entanglement theories of, 28, 29, 39–40, 41–42; race theories of, 22, 25–27; stranger-ness concept, 171–72. *See also* materialism

New York City, 3, 41, 56, 57, 135. *See also* Mohawk ironworkers/skywalkers; September 11, 2001, attacks; Whitehead, Colson, *The Intuitionist*; World's Fair of 1853

Cobb's Creek neighborhood, 75–76, 83, 88, 99, 216n2, 217n34. *See also* MOVE organization; Wideman, John Edgar, *Philadelphia Fire*

Phillips, Jerry, 150, 166

physical environment, 24, 36–37, 127, 133, 134, 159; delinking from, 120–21, 122, 127–28; dominance over, 56, 116; humans' relationship to, 29, 176, 183; instrumentalized, 142–43; personality of, 64–65; settlers' relationship to, 193–94. *See also* angry planet; colonial terraforming; earth; environment; nature; terraforming; weather

Pick-Sloane Plan (Missouri River), 196

planetary motion, 2–6, 129, 134, 154, 204n16; disasters caused by, 114, 115; ontologies of, 19, 111–12, 143; resurgence of, 144–45; tectonic, 16–17, 91, 114, 118, 121–22, 158; transformative, 147–48, 157, 178. *See also* angry planet: movement of; hydrological cycle

Plantationocene, 27, 188

plantation-plot dichotomy, 8, 20–21. *See also* slavery: plantation

Poe, Edgar Allan, 53

policing, 39, 107, 137, 170, 187, 210n10, 227n38. *See also* L.A. riots; MOVE organization, bombing of headquarters

politics: agency of, 39–40, 67–68, 117–18, 119, 187; angry planet, 103, 120, 138; of belonging, 100, 113, 117, 124, 138; coalition, 10;

community, 94, 161–62; of culture, 144–45; of decolonization, 77, 82, 102, 172, 181; economic, 160–62; of entanglements, 39–40; environmental, 146; identity, 90, 115, 167, 206n61; of imaginaries, 36, 73, 162, 199; Indigenous, 31; neocolonial, 192; North American, 144–45; ontologies of, 17, 40, 82, 86, 116, 155, 172; property, 149–50; recognition, 12, 14, 78, 164; representational, 33, 110, 149; of resurgence, 31, 144–45; revolutionary, 72; of reweaving, 183; of social order, 222n32; of solidarity, 171, 194; spatial, 58–59; state, 155; of survival, 166; terrestrial, 31, 115, 116, 117–18, 123, 136, 143; Third World, 102. *See also* biopolitics; necropolitics

Posluns, Michael. *See* Manuel, George and Michael Posluns

postcolonialism, 8, 12, 19, 21, 30–31, 123. *See also* colonialism

posthumanism, 24–25, 53, 163, 204n21. *See also* humanism

postmodernism, 19, 58, 167, 229n102. *See also* modernity

poststructuralism, 19, 21

power, 54, 79, 155, 171; agentic, 43; capitalist, 114, 130, 180; colonial, 20–21, 26–27, 46, 48, 63, 77, 110, 143, 144, 171, 180; colonial-capitalist, 7, 19, 83, 88, 91–92, 94–95, 109, 111–12, 150, 191; earth's, 87, 188; fascist, 42; First World, 78, 101; of linearity, 72; racial-capitalist, 20, 192, 194; structures of, 14, 45, 110, 183;

171, 189; dehumanization caused by, 15–16, 29, 43, 130, 198; destabilization caused by, 144; differential, 29, 81; dispossession caused by, 5–6, 10; of Indigenous peoples, 37, 38, 119; infrastructures of, 17, 42; of labor, 39, 48, 70; logic of, 24, 55, 67; marginalization caused by, 70, 81–82, 167; of modernity, 64, 106–7, 154; of others, 13–14, 72, 78, 125, 128, 160; partitioning by, 43, 148, 188; spatial, 29, 36, 151. *See also* bodies: racialized; communities: racialized; racial capitalism

racial justice, 32, 191. *See also* environmental justice

racial uplift, 57–58, 61, 62, 67, 81

racial violence, 5, 9–10, 37, 58, 80, 108, 160, 162, 179; against communities of color, 85–86, 106–7, 219n83, 221n13; history of, 76, 152; of terraforming, 54, 112. *See also* anti-Blackness; violence; white supremacy

racism: environmental, 14–16; in land use practices, 147–48; structural, 97; urban, 63, 66–67; violence of, 110, 167, 197–98. *See also* anti-Blackness; segregation; white supremacy

radicalism, 108, 172. *See also* Black radicalism; civil rights era; MOVE organization; Silko, Leslie Marmon, *Almanac of the Dead*; Wideman, John Edgar, *Philadelphia Fire*

rationalism/rationality, 24–25, 51, 67, 91, 208n87; Enlightenment,

19–20, 22, 48; modernity and, 21, 64, 154

Reagan, Ronald, 90

realism, 3, 30, 163; speculative, 25, 175, 209n105

rebellions, 5, 83–84, 95, 118–22. *See also* L.A. riots; revolution; Third World: revolutionary struggles in

recognition, 138, 163; ontological, 164, 165; politics of, 12, 14, 78, 164; state, 31, 191, 198

Red and Assiniboine Rivers, confluence of, 141–43, 196. *See also* Winnipeg

Reed, T. V., 123

refugees, 111, 112. *See also* immigrants

relationality, 22, 30, 40, 52, 54, 72, 149, 210n26

relationships, 7, 149–50, 155–58, 171

reparations, 10, 61

resistance, 4, 8, 63, 101, 103, 107, 126, 154, 186. *See also* L.A. riots; rebellions; revolution

resources, 57, 122, 130, 154; control of, 14, 38; exploitation of, 16, 153; extraction of, 15, 23, 145, 152, 163, 188

resurgence, 28–29, 157, 170; in angry planet fiction, 73, 144–45; decolonial, 31, 144–45, 147; Fourth World, 28, 148–54, 166; politics of, 31, 144–45; racial, 71–72, 171; radical, 162, 169, 170, 199; terrestrial, 144–45. *See also* Butler, Octavia, *Parable of the Sower*: resurgence in; Indigenous peoples: resurgence of; Vizenor, Gerald, *Bearheart*: resurgence in

slavery, 25, 50, 62, 79, 118, 182;
legacy of, 68, 107, 151, 189, 190;
plantation, 8, 10, 15–16, 112,
227n45
Smith, Adam, 53
Smith, Linda Tuhiwai, 38
social order, 39, 66, 68, 109; alternative, 138; colonial-capitalist, 14,
37, 154–55, 166–67; delinking
from, 135; destabilization of, 111;
dominant structures of, 120–21;
Fourth World systems of, 145;
infrastructural foundations of,
113–14, 117, 220n1; racializing,
63
social uprisings. See L.A. riots; rebellions; revolution; Third World:
revolutionary struggles in
society, 3, 38, 39, 41; settler, 5, 7,
36. See also communities; communities of color
solidarity, 12, 112, 139, 150; with
the angry planet, 122, 192; decolonial, 181, 190–91; global, 7–8,
10, 29, 186; human, 165, 172,
188; interethnic, 14–15, 30, 32;
politics of, 171, 194. See also
stability
Song, Min Hyoung, 80, 112, 113,
125, 220n1
Sonoran Desert, 122–24, 126–27
Southwest Organizing Project, 14
sovereignty, 77–78, 86, 102, 149,
204n27, 227n25; land, 157, 167;
state, 78, 147, 155; terrestrial, 31,
143, 146–47, 154–62, 163, 167,
172. See also Indigenous peoples:
sovereignty of
space(s), 56, 64, 90, 102, 126, 136,
138–39, 169, 172, 186; of

belonging, 31, 60, 144, 157,
158; domination of, 95, 129;
negative, 125, 135; organization
of, 4, 152–53; production of, 148,
154–55, 157, 158, 161; racialized,
29, 36, 151; urban, 24, 30, 65,
68, 86, 119. See also colonial capitalism: spaces of; environment;
logic: spatial; nature; physical
environment
space-time, 175, 178, 205n36
stability, 4, 18, 67, 87, 129, 154. See
also solidarity
Standing Rock Sioux Tribe, 186–87
state, 78, 86, 127, 139, 144, 152,
155; crumbling of, 143–44; infrastructures of, 110, 145; property
of, 62, 148; racial-capitalist, 193,
194, 198; racializing, 119, 160;
settler, 9, 18, 31, 37, 79, 101,
160, 193; sovereignty of, 78, 147,
155. See also colonial-capitalist
state
state power, 10, 25, 62, 80, 86, 98,
107, 114, 121, 124, 127–28, 138,
147, 156, 164; settler state, 102,
180, 191. See also power
stuckness, 65, 102, 122, 125–28,
176, 185; in the normal, 107–9,
113, 131
subjectivity, 64, 118, 191–92; privileged, 165, 169–70. See also white
subjectivity
subject-object binary, 52, 64, 71–72,
91
subjects, 21, 73, 172, 190; agency of,
71, 94–95; human, 110, 163–64,
188; racialized, 25, 132; white
male, 50–55, 131
Sullivan, Daniel E., 92

Sumas First Nation (British Columbia), 196–97
surveying, 45, 48–50, 51–52, 212n54. *See also* borders/boundaries; Mason-Dixon Line; property: lines of; Pynchon, Thomas, *Mason & Dixon*
survival, 42, 99, 126, 146, 158, 166; tactics of, 191, 192
survivance, 36–37, 43, 68–69, 210n12. *See also* Black survivance; Indigenous peoples: survivance of

TallBear, Kim, 26–27
Taylor, Matthew A., 25–26, 53, 209n107, 229n85
technology, 47, 178, 204n27; violence of, 59, 133, 152, 192. *See also* agency: technological; elevators; skyscrapers
temporality, 112, 123–24, 126, 178–79
terraforming, 26, 42, 78; and anti-racist infrastructures, 62–68; and colonial allegory, 43–46; materializing colonial infrastructures, 46–50; and racial allegory, 55–62; and revolutionary agency, 68–73; use of term, 16; and white male victimry, 50–55. *See also* colonial terraforming; earth; Pynchon, Thomas, *Mason & Dixon*; Whitehead, Colson, *The Intuitionist*
Teskey, Gordon, 44, 58, 59, 61
Third World, 29, 83, 94; delinking in, 137–39; deserts and detritus in, 122–28; earthquakes in, 113–18; feminism in, 21, 191; First World struggles with, 173; hot zones, 78, 82, 84, 90–91;

imaginaries of, 102, 161, 162; moving between Fourth World and, 10–17, 144–45; partitioning cities in, 43, 100; revolutionary struggles in, 7, 14, 69–70, 85, 86, 90, 108, 112–13; riots in, 113–18; social movements within, 112, 154; use of term, 11–13; violence against, 85–86. *See also* American Third World; freeways; homeless communities; Silko, Leslie Marmon, *Almanac of the Dead*; Tobar, Héctor
Thurman, Wallace, 60
Tillett, Rebecca, 111
Tobar, Héctor, *The Tattooed Soldier*, 3, 224n111; acts of rebellion in, 110, 111, 113–22; angry planet in, 30–31, 108–13, 133–37, 192; delinking in, 131, 135, 137–39; narrative ontology in, 109, 111–12, 113, 122–28, 137–39. *See also* freeways; homeless communities; Los Angeles; L.A. riots
Todd, Zoe, 208n89, 230n104
transmotion, 147, 150, 161, 169–70
transnationalism, 123, 125
Trask, Haunani-Kay, 206n58
Treuer, David, *The Hiawatha,* 36–37
Tsing, Anna, 188
Tuana, Nancy, 80, 99
Tuck, Eve, 9, 10, 73, 182, 193; settler moves to innocence, 54
Turtle Island, 43, 147; colonial occupation of, 7, 29, 38, 39; first nations of, 48, 182; Heart of, 141, 143; resurgent, 144, 177–78, 193; use of term, 203n2. *See also* Indigenous peoples; North America

Anne Stewart is a lecturer in the College of Liberal Arts at the University of British Columbia.